FEMINISM
UNFINISHED

FEMINISM
UNFINISHED

A SHORT, SURPRISING HISTORY OF AMERICAN WOMEN'S MOVEMENTS

Dorothy Sue Cobble,
Linda Gordon, and Astrid Henry

LIVERIGHT PUBLISHING CORPORATION

A Division of W. W. Norton & Company

New York • London

"Poppa" lyrics by Virginia Blaisdell and Naomi Weisstein. Reprinted by permission.

For information about permission to reproduce selections from
this book, write to Permissions, W. W. Norton & Company, Inc.,
500 Fifth Avenue, New York, NY 10110

For information about special discounts for bulk purchases,
please contact W. W. Norton Special Sales at
specialsales@wwnorton.com or 800-233-4830

Manufacturing by Courier Westford
Book design by Chris Welch
Production manager: Julia Druskin

Library of Congress Cataloging-in-Publication Data

Cobble, Dorothy Sue.
Feminism unfinished : a short, surprising history
of American women's movements / Dorothy Sue Cobble,
Linda Gordon, and Astrid Henry. — First edition.
        pages cm
Includes bibliographical references and index.
ISBN 978-0-87140-676-7 (hardcover)
1. Feminism—United States—History—20th century. 2. Feminism—United
States—History—21st century. 3. Women's rights—United States—History.
I. Gordon, Linda. II. Henry, Astrid, 1966– III. Title.
HQ1421.C625 2014
305.420973—dc23
                                                    2014021871

W. W. Norton & Company, Inc.
500 Fifth Avenue, New York, N.Y. 10110
www.wwnorton.com

W. W. Norton & Company Ltd.
Castle House, 75/76 Wells Street, London W1T 3QT

1 2 3 4 5 6 7 8 9 0

To the feminists of the future

Contents

2

THE WOMEN'S LIBERATION MOMENT

3

FROM A MINDSET TO A MOVEMENT: FEMINISM SINCE 1990

PREFACE

Feminism Unfinished provides the first history of the American women's movement over the approximately one hundred years since the women's suffrage amendment passed in 1920. Equally important, it challenges many popular understandings of the women's movement. Much of what is in this book will come as a surprise to many readers. But it is time to set the record straight.

This book is divided into three chapters and moves chronologically across a near-century of American women's activism. Since the intention of *Feminism Unfinished* is to be concise, none of the three chapters is comprehensive. To keep this book brief and as useful as possible, in each chapter we have chosen to focus on a few illustrative individuals, projects, and episodes in order to demonstrate the richness of the ferment and to illuminate major themes. Were the individuals we discuss all placed in a room together, they might well disagree, possibly sharply, but that is part of why feminism has flourished. We frequently use the plural word "feminisms" to emphasize that there have always been a variety of approaches to advancing women's well-being. This is true whether we are discussing the women's movements within a particular era or comparing feminisms across time.

All three chapters situate feminist movements in the larger politics, economics, and culture of the time: the Great Depression of the 1930s, Franklin Roosevelt's New Deal presidency, World War II, 1960s prosperity, the Vietnam War, the rise of the Religious Right in the late 1970s, the introduction of the Internet, the 2008 economic crash—all influenced the women's movement. All three chapters discuss continuities with earlier periods, but also the unfortunate ways that new generations have been ignorant, even disdainful, of earlier activism. Furthermore, much as we admire what feminist activists have done and are still doing, we are by no means uncritical of these movements. We believe we do feminist movements of the past greater honor by looking squarely at their limitations. We also believe that by thinking critically about the past, we can strengthen future feminisms.

PROLOGUE

The history of feminism is important not just to feminists and not just to women. The women's movement we trace in this book has transformed the world we all live in, transformed it utterly. As individuals we have all changed, men as much as women. Institutions have changed—educational, medical, religious—as have the professions, child-rearing practices, and the armed forces. Government has changed. So has the culture, from pop music, TV, and film to literature and the fine arts. The very nature of knowledge, whether in medicine, science, history, literature, or philosophy, has changed. One cannot understand the world we live in without an understanding of the women's movement and its influence. Feminism was integral to larger progressive changes, with the result that it has sometimes blended so entirely into larger movements that historians have not noticed it. This book aims to remedy that omission.

Chapter 1 highlights labor and "social justice" feminists, from the 1920s through the 1960s, because they forged the dominant women's movement in that era. These feminists sought women's rights as part of a broad agenda concerned with economic fairness and civil rights. Chapter 2 focuses on activists involved in the myriad streams of the women's liberation movement that emerged in the late 1960s and extended into the 1980s—a shorter time because this was the period of most intense and widespread activism on behalf of women's equality and freedom. These feminists, often raised in relative prosperity and with greater access to higher education and birth control, created a feminism that emphasized sexual and reproductive freedom, economic opportunity, and challenging gender altogether. Chapter 3 describes the feminism developed by generations who grew up taking for granted the opportunities newly opened for women. In the 1990s, new technologies spawned a decentralized and wired feminism that often promoted individual responses to the persistence of gender inequality. But in the twenty-first century, these feminists increasingly came to respond collectively to America's widening economic inequality and to the feminism led by women from poorer countries.

Our century-long view allows us to sketch a new and different picture of American feminism. By providing a long and continuous rather than an episodic history, we offer a fuller and more inclusive perspective that changes how the history of feminism is understood. Much writing about the women's rights movement conceives of it as coming to a halt after women won the right to vote in 1920, then reawakening fifty years later in the 1970s and evaporating again in the 1980s. Our book challenges this conventional view. We thus decenter the movement of the late 1960s and 1970s, which is frequently taken to be the main expression of twentieth-century feminism. We show the existence of a continuous women's movement. In our view, there was no period in the last century when women were not campaigning for greater equality and freedom. Feminism has been not a series of disconnected upsurges but a continuous flow. Of course the movement was larger at some times, smaller at others, but in every period women were coming together to press collectively for more respect, more freedom, and less discrimination.

Our century-long view also challenges how feminism itself has been understood. Within its continuity, we show, feminism was constantly changing, as all social movements do. No one would have expected the civil rights movement of the 1950s and 1960s to look like that of the 1890s, or the struggles of northern big-city African Americans to look like those of southern sharecroppers. So too the feminism of the 1920s is not identical with that of the 1970s or the 2000s. Our narrative uses a historicized definition of feminism, which must be a capacious one, allowing for historical change and for social diversity. As the world has changed, so have the needs and aspirations of women. In the 1920s, as this book reveals, feminists could not have imagined the aspirations of women in the 1970s, for example. And in a diverse country like the United States, we cannot expect different groups of women to have identical agendas. We cannot expect poor women feeding their families on food stamps to have the same priorities as female lawyers hoping to become partners in law firms. We cannot expect working-class women concerned with getting sick leave to have the same priorities as college professors. We cannot expect women who face both sex and race discrimination to develop the same priorities as women who face only sex discrimination. This diversity shows, for example, that it is a mistake to characterize feminism as a movement of career women. Some feminists prioritized women's right to take employment on an equal basis with men, while others asked for greater respect and support for women's unpaid domestic labor—not to mention the majority of feminists who wanted both. There has never been a single, unified feminist agenda.

We see feminism as an outlook that is ever being reinvented by new groups of women. Feminism necessarily changes as the world women inhabit changes.

There is a historical upward spiral here in aspirations: as new generations of women have lived with the greater opportunities won by the campaigns of older generations, these younger women have dared to ask for more—for equality in more spheres, for respect

and better treatment by both governmental and private institutions. At times one set of gains has revealed problems previously
unnoticed. Once women gained control over their own property,
for example, they came to ask why they needed their husbands'
approval to make a large purchase or get a credit card.

Still, despite these intrafeminist changes and differences, there
has typically been a bottom line, a common denominator of "what
women wanted." Most feminists sought educational opportunity,
economic opportunity, equal rights to political participation, an
end to violence against women, an end to the sexual double standard, respect for women's work in the home, and jobs that allowed
them to fulfill family responsibilities. The majority of feminists
also worked to make these rights and freedoms a reality for all
women, through guaranteeing the economic and social security
necessary to enjoy them.

In campaigning for these rights, most feminists grasped the
need for women to work collectively. When these campaigns won,
women of course gained opportunities as individuals. That women
can now be physicians, lawyers, and college professors in large numbers, as well as CEOs and political leaders in smaller numbers—
this is the achievement of feminist collective struggles. One of the
accomplishments of women's movements has been more recognition of individual women of great achievement—elected officials,
religious leaders, artists, businesswomen, and reformers. But just
as tax cuts for the 1 percent did not produce a higher standard of
living for the 99 percent, so the increased number of women at the
top did not always produce gains for women at the bottom. There
is no trickle-down effect. Individual "leaning in" is not enough; the
vast majority of American women have always leaned in, working
as hard as they could to support themselves and their families.

Feminism Unfinished is about a century of feminism as a *social
movement*. The book demonstrates something about how social
movements operate: we examine not just feminism's accomplish-

ments but *how* these accomplishments were won. Because we focus on the processes of change, readers looking for the most famous or individually powerful women may not find them here. Leaders have sometimes made a difference through their intelligence, charisma, and dedication, but to see how major historical change occurs, one has to look at the activism of larger numbers of people. The feminist leaders most often met in the mass media, for example, were often not the most influential in making large-scale improvements for women. Besides, we want to use this book to introduce readers to some less familiar individuals. These are the women who most resemble the rest of us: often women who were at first timid, reserved, even apolitical, who transformed themselves into confident, resourceful leaders and who then joined with others to change society.

Today many disavow the term "feminist," but often what is being rejected is a narrow and distorted version of feminism that bears little resemblance to the rich and varied feminist philosophies of the past. Many who do not use and even reject the term "feminism" have nevertheless been feminists—that is, they have been part of the long struggle for women's rights.

People often assume that women's rights somehow accrued gradually through an inevitable process of modernization. These rights are now part of the air we all breathe. Everyone benefits from these changes—women and men, feminists and anti-feminists. The fact that people today take these feminist gains for granted is something feminists can be proud of. But to assume that these gains just "happened" is problematic. Inattention to this history—to the range of discriminations women faced and to their collective efforts to transform the world around them—has consequences. It leads not only to minimizing how crucial past social movements were in shaping today's world, and not only to dishonoring the many activists who sacrificed much for our benefit, but also to obscuring how necessary feminism and feminist movements remain for confronting the injustices and discriminations of the present day. That is why we hope to inspire readers to learn about and to honor those who constructed the new opportunities. That is why we wrote this book.

THE CHALLENGES THIS book offers are directed in particular to several popular assumptions about U.S. women's movements, assumptions that in our view are more myth than reality. One, already mentioned, is the myth that feminism was and is a predominantly upper-middle-class white women's concern. In this book, readers will see the activism of all categories of women, and as a result encounter a different understanding of feminism.

Closely related is another myth that must be discarded: the idea that one can generalize about women, as if women are all the same. Women are as diverse as men and, like men, have individual needs and priorities. Yet no individual is only a woman; each of us has many identities and allegiances. Every individual might be not only male or female but also a member of a family, a nation, a social class, a racial or ethnic group, a sexual orientation, or many other groups or communities we could name. Identity is a complex construct, created by all the social groups we are part of. So no one can have only gendered interests, and no one can have allegiance only to gendered interests. Today in many college courses this recognition of the complexity of identity is called "intersectionality," a new name for what many think is a new concept. But it has been recognized and acted upon by feminists for over a century. That many consider it a new principle is a result of the historical amnesia that we hope to correct.

Feminists have been just as diverse as are women in general. Some were Democrats, some were Republicans; some were religious, some were adamantly anti-religious; some pushed for civil rights, others did not; some endorsed marriage, others rejected it; some concentrated on creating equal opportunity for mothers' employment, others on creating the conditions that allow mothers to devote themselves full-time to children. Some feminists tended toward androgynous values (that is, toward eradicating gender difference), while others celebrated women's differences from men. Trying to reconcile women's differing needs and to form movement priorities has been a persistent problem for women's movements. Most troubling, women from groups that are in other ways privileged—for example, white elite women—have at times been unwilling to recognize the concerns of other less privileged women as feminist and have defined feminism narrowly, with their own needs predominant.

Yet another myth is that women's progress has been steadily upward. On the contrary, there have been periods of substantial losses for women and moments in which gains once thought secure were reversed. For example, women gained the right to control their reproduction in one historical period—when birth control and abortion were legalized in the 1960s and '70s—only to see those same rights attacked and curtailed in the years that followed. Furthermore, not all aspects of women's rights rise and fall at the same time: for example, even as women were losing the legal right to birth control, they were gaining rights to education and employment.

It is also a myth that feminism is only for women. It is a movement for everyone, including men and children. In every historical period there were women activists who believed they needed to work with men to achieve their goals, and in every era men identified as feminists and sought, alongside women, cultural and social changes that would realize a new gender order. In the late 1960s and early 1970s, many feminists believed they needed small, women-only groups in which to discuss their problems, and they organized an independent women's movement largely autonomous from men. But not all women agreed. NOW, the largest organization active in this period, called itself the National Organization *for* Women, not *of* Women, and always had proud male members.

Indeed, the majority of American men today would have been considered feminists sixty years ago, because they accept women's equality in education, women's right to employment, and women's right to birth control, to offer just a few examples. In fact, there is a smaller gender gap in attitudes on so-called women's issues, such as abortion, than on concerns such as global warming or homeland security.[1] All women, gay or straight, have beloved men in their lives: husbands, fathers, brothers, sons, lovers, and friends. This fact calls into question whether there actually are any "women's issues." For example, most men want to limit their fertility as much as women do; and when women earn higher wages only because male wages are falling, the result is not a gain for women.

Just as important, feminists have always led campaigns for children. Historically, pressure for compulsory education, for children's health, and for children's rights came primarily from feminists. The campaign for birth control was a campaign for family well-being and children's welfare. And when contraception fails and women must resort to abortion, the majority of them already have children and want to control their family size in order to provide for those children.

Still another myth is that every time individual women move into leadership, wealth, or power, it is a victory for feminism. Their successes are achievements that we can celebrate, but they are only a small part of the feminist agenda.

The renewed strength of neo-liberalism in the twenty-first century—that is, the faith that "free," unregulated markets can effectively produce a strong and fair economy—has spun as a by-product a neo-liberal version of feminism, a perspective that simply urges individual women to compete harder to reach the economic top. The reverse—praise for mothers who choose to leave employment, even as the vast majority of mothers cannot afford to do that—also reflects that neo-liberal myth. The media has increasingly equated individual women's choices with feminism, when historically feminism has been about changing the social conditions for all women. Most feminists aimed to raise the status of women as a whole, to open real opportunities for all women regardless of race, economic circumstance, family status, or sexual orientation. Feminism is for all women, not just the privileged.

The final myth we challenge is the tired stereotype of the feminist as a humorless, sexless reformer. Most feminists, like women in general, had gratifying romantic and sexual relationships, and, equally important, the pleasures of close friendship. Even when women came together to gripe about indignities or to rage and weep about abuse, their coming together was often riotous with laughter. Feminists flirted, dressed up, enjoyed love and sex, and joked about themselves as much as anyone. Despite sharp and sometimes painful disagreements, the process of joining with others to pursue a vision of greater equality and freedom—of a better society—has usually been deeply satisfying. This aspect of women's movements has been widely ignored and deserves emphasis. We are social animals, and the camaraderie and friendships formed in collective effort meet many needs, emotional and intellectual. Many considered the rest of their lives better for having participated in movements for social change, and many looked back on those years as among the richest and most fulfilling in their lives.

Feminism is neither a marginal cause nor a movement seeking benefits for a minority. It is a cause for everyone. It has taken many forms, always responding to changing historical circumstances, and will be reinvented by future generations. As *Feminism Unfinished* reveals, what it means to be a feminist is constantly under construction.

1. See, for example, http://www.gallup.com/poll/127559/education-trumps-gender-predicting-support-abortion.aspx, accessed May 14, 2013; Pew Research Center, release of May 4, 2010, at http://www.people-press.org/files/legacy-pdf/610.pdf, accessed May 6, 2013.

Detroit Woolworth waitresses and retail clerks occupy their store in February 1937.

MORE THAN SEX EQUALITY

FEMINISM AFTER SUFFRAGE

Dorothy Sue Cobble

Twenty-three-year-old labor organizer Myra Wolfgang pushed her way through the throngs of Detroit shoppers enjoying a sale at Woolworth's five-and-dime, a low-cost retail giant with hundreds of stores nationwide. Woolworth's sales-girls, cashiers, and lunch counter waitresses awaited her signal. Wolfgang blew the strike whistle, and, as planned, they moved away from their counters, politely escorted the customers to the door, and barricaded themselves inside. A hundred and ten workers, all young women, were already occupying the main downtown Woolworth's, and the union was threatening to escalate the strike to all forty Detroit branches. The 1937 Woolworth's sit-down strike was under way.

Aided by gifts of food, mattresses, blankets, dance records, cigarettes, and other supplies from friends and sympathizers, Woolworth strikers stayed inside the main store for six nights and seven days. Like the millions of other workers who sat down that spring in workplaces across the country, they struck for fair wages and a voice in decisions at work. In addition, their long list of grievances included abusive and disrespectful supervisors, unpredictable hours, and expensive uniforms. Dubbed the "girl strikers" by the national press who camped outside the store, they appeared on radio, in movie theater newsreels, and in major newspapers and magazines. At one point, they penned their desires on the brown wrapping paper covering the store's large front windows. "All we want is a living wage," one striker scrawled in bright red crayon letters. The occupation ended after F. W. Woolworth Company executives in New York capitulated and promised wage increases of 20 to 25 percent, union recognition, and more worker say over scheduling and job retention. Within months, following the path blazed by Myra Wolfgang and the "girl strikers," retail workers in New York, St. Louis, San Francisco, Seattle, and St. Paul struck and won similar gains.[1]

The Woolworth victory in the spring of 1937 was just one of many campaigns Wolfgang led and won. In 1932, she dropped out of art school when her family's finances collapsed in the midst of the Depression. Soon she was giving her share of soapbox speeches for radical causes and organizing for the Hotel Employees and Restaurant Employees Union (HERE). A natural orator with a wicked wit, she signed up thousands of Detroit service and retail workers and helped raise standards in a sector of the economy renowned for low pay, disrespect, and insecurity. In 1953, she became an international vice president of HERE, which represented a quarter of U.S. hospitality workers nationwide. A lifetime member of the National Association for the Advancement of Colored People (NAACP), she devised strategies to end racial segregation and open up better-paying jobs for African Americans and other minorities in hotels and restaurants. At the same time, she never lost sight of the particular problems of women in a low-wage industry where female sexuality and sociability generated hefty profit.

In the 1960s, she led a sleep-in at the Michigan statehouse to persuade legislators to raise the minimum wage and launched a successful campaign to unionize Playboy Club waitresses, or "Playboy Bunnies." With a union backing them, Wolfgang announced to the delight of scribbling reporters, the Bunnies would "bite back"

Yvonne Tiffany, dressed in a "bunny suit" and other HERE women picket Detroit's Playboy Club in October 1963 protesting the no-wage policy. Photograph © AFL-CIO, used with permission.

and challenge Hugh Hefner's Playboy philosophy that "women should be obscene and not heard." After a six-year campaign, Playboy Clubs International agreed to a national contract promising to pay *wages* to Bunnies (previously the women relied solely on tips) and allow Bunnies more discretion over uniform design, customer interactions, and company appearance standards.[2]

Wolfgang stands out as a talented organizer and, by all accounts, an unusually charismatic figure. Yet many other women like her chose an activist path in the 1930s labor movement, and in the decades following, a surprising number moved into influential positions in labor unions. Equally important, many of these same women took on leadership roles in the women's movement. Indeed, from the 1930s to the 1960s, during the heyday of New Deal reform, feminists like Wolfgang led the dominant wing of the American women's movement. This chapter tells their story.

I call these women "social justice feminists," a label that captures core aspects of their politics. They believed women faced disadvantages as a sex—a perspective not widely shared at the time—and they organized with other women and with men to end those disadvantages. At the same time, in their view, most women needed *more* than sex equality. Achieving equality with disadvantaged male counterparts was not enough for low-income women and women of color. The struggle for women's rights should be joined with efforts to advance racial and economic justice. Only by confronting multiple and intertwined injustices, they insisted, could the problems of the majority, men as well as women, be solved.

Social justice feminists like Wolfgang looked to the largest social movements of their day, the labor and the civil rights movements, as the best vehicles to achieve their vision of women's rights in a more inclusive and egalitarian society. By the end of the 1930s, most aligned themselves politically with the Democratic Party, and their efforts rose and fell in tandem with the fortunes of New Deal reform and U.S. social democratic politics. Although their dreams outpaced their achievements, by the 1960s they had changed public opinion, workplace institutions, law, and public policy in profound and lasting ways.

Putting Myra Wolfgang and other labor women like her at the center of American feminism is not the usual way the history of women's movements in this era is recounted. All too often chroniclers of women's reform define feminist activism narrowly and assume that all-female organizations dedicated only to sex equality are the prime bearers of the feminist impulse. From this perspective, the fifty years following women's suffrage in 1920 appear as a retreat for women's rights, with a dwindling band of white middle-class feminists making minimal headway in a society largely dismissive of women's issues. Expanding the definition of feminism and of women's movements to include working-class and minority feminists rewrites this standard story. Instead of decline, we see a robust and diverse group of feminists in mixed-sex organizations making considerable progress. Feminism and feminist activism did not diminish in the decades after suffrage: rather, from the 1930s to the 1960s, the struggle for the rights of low-income women and women of color surged forward as the labor and civil rights movements gained ground.

American women joined a dizzying array of social reform organizations in this era, and many of these women brought a decidedly feminist perspective to their work. African American women in the NAACP, the National Council of Negro Women, the National Urban League, or the Southern Christian Leadership Conference, to name just a few of the civil rights organizations of the day, sought black women's full rights as women and as citizens, repeatedly insisting that women's rights to good schools, jobs, and protection from physical and sexual assault were essential planks in the black freedom struggle. Mexican American and other minority women created a parallel yet overlapping civil rights movement to combat discriminatory practices, common especially in communities across the Southwest and West, barring "nonwhites" from housing, schooling, and jobs. Feminists in church, peace, internationalist, and consumer

groups as well as in welfare rights and other poor people's movements also agitated for women's rights and social reform.

This chapter is not a comprehensive history of these struggles or
of feminism in this period. It foregrounds labor-oriented social justice feminists or those who worked primarily with the labor movement. I focus on this group because they led the social justice wing
of the women's movement in this era and because their vision of
feminist reform has much to offer a twenty-first-century world facing economic and social problems not unlike those they sought to
address.

They were a diverse group in terms of race, class, and culture.
Wolfgang was raised in a Jewish immigrant family that had pros-
pered in the 1920s, but most had Protestant and Catholic backgrounds, and the majority came from poor or working-class
households. Many were African American. The life histories of Caroline Dawson Davis and Addie Wyatt, two working-class feminists
who held leadership positions in powerful and progressive labor
organizations in this era reveal the forces propelling working-class
and minority women into activism.

Caroline Dawson Davis, the head of the Women's Department of
the United Auto Workers (UAW) from 1948 to 1973, was a leading
voice for the rights of women and minorities within the auto union
and nationally. She grew up in a poor white Kentucky mining family steeped in unionism and Protestant religion. In 1934, she got a
job as a drill press operator in the same Indiana auto parts plant
that hired her father and where she met her husband. Davis had
a strong anti-authoritarian streak and a habit of standing up for
anyone she thought was being mistreated. Both these traits pushed
her toward union activity. "The worst thing about a job to me was
authority," Davis once disclosed matter-of-factly. "I loved people,"
she continued, and "I believed in people. I never saw the difference
between someone who had a title and a lot of money, and Joe Doe

and Jane Doe who swept floors and dug ditches. Unions give the people a voice for themselves—to help them not be robots that the boss can boss around."[3]

Thirty-year-old Davis helped organize her plant in 1941 and was elected vice president of Auto Workers Local 764 in 1943. When the union president was drafted soon after, she "moved upstairs" into the top slot and stayed there, prompting a 1947 feature story in *Life* magazine, with a four-page photo spread, on the new "strikingly attractive lady labor leader." In one photo, Davis lounges at home reading Freud, a thinker whose ideas, she told the interviewer, proved indispensable to running her local union. "If I hadn't been a union leader," Davis added, "I would have been a psychiatrist."[4]

In 1948, UAW president Walter Reuther tapped her to head the union's Women's Department. The department, formed in 1944 by a large, energetic group of wartime women workers, pushed hard for the needs of women and minorities to be more fully integrated into the union's reform agenda. Lillian Hatcher, the first black woman on the UAW's national staff, became Davis's close ally and friend. An Alabama-born mother of three, Hatcher had been a wartime aircraft riveter before taking the UAW job in 1944. Assigned to the UAW's Fair Practices and Anti-Discrimination Department, established in 1946, as well as to the Women's Department, she worked at the UAW until her retirement in 1980. Davis and Hatcher went everywhere together, responding to complaints of discrimination from women and minority men across the country and speaking to local after local about race and gender equity. These experiences, Davis later recalled, made her realize the pervasiveness of sex discrimination faced by women. In addition, she learned from Hatcher and other African American women about the interconnectedness of sex and race discrimination.

Addie Wyatt, an African American, found a receptive home in the left-led United Packinghouse Workers of America (UPWA),

Addie Wyatt and other UPWA delegates to the 1957 NAACP convention pose with
Herbert Hill, NAACP labor liaison, and Philip Weightman, AFL-CIO. Courtesy of the
Wisconsin Historical Society.

an industrial union in which multi-racial social justice feminism
flourished. A Mississippi-born daughter of a tailor and a teacher,
seventeen-year-old Wyatt took her first job at Chicago's Armour
meatpacking plant in 1941 after a frustrating search for a typist
position. The first union meeting she attended left a deep impres-
sion. "I saw a picture that I have never been able to forget," she later
explained. "It was a room full of black and white workers, Hispanic
workers, young and old, middle-aged workers, male and female.
They were all talking about the problems of decent wages and working conditions. And they were talking about the struggle of black
people, Hispanic people, and women. I wanted to be a part of it."

By 1952, her co-workers, mostly white men, had elected her vice
president of the local union, quite an unusual arrangement for the

time. A year later she stepped into the presidency and then ran successfully for the UPWA's national executive board on a platform emphasizing women's rights and the advancement of minorities. In 1954, she was appointed to the UPWA staff as the first black woman national representative, a position she held for the next thirty years. Her religious faith and the close-knit egalitarian community she discovered in the Church of God sustained her long career as a feminist labor and civil rights advocate. She saw no opposition in being a Christian and a unionist, she often explained: both sought to go beyond selfish individualism, and both wanted a more humane world.[5]

The Legacies of the 1920s

Before looking at the workplace and policy changes labor-oriented social justice feminists sought and won from the 1930s to the 1960s, it is important to understand the world of the 1920s in which many grew up and the bitter debates that divided women reformers in this decade. The tensions that erupted among feminists after 1920 would persist for the next fifty years, separating the women's movement into two hostile camps.

With the ratification of the Nineteenth Amendment in 1920 and suffrage affirmed, at least for the majority of women, National Woman's Party (NWP) founder Alice Paul and other leaders from the militant suffrage wing began to mobilize with a new goal in mind. They proposed a second, but quite different, constitutional amendment, the Equal Rights Amendment (ERA), which they believed would secure full legal equality of rights for women. Some longtime suffragists protested this shift in emphasis, given the continuing disenfranchisement of women of color, including African American women in the South and Mexican American, American Indian, and Asian American women in the West. NWP leadership, however, insisted that any problems related to these women's continued lack of voting rights were matters of race, not sex. Other women reformers, like prominent Progressive Era Hull House founder and peace activist Jane Addams and National Consumers' League secretary Florence Kelley, objected to the wording of the proposed amendment. They met repeatedly with NWP leaders in 1921 and 1922, hoping to persuade them to add language to the ERA exempting maternity leave and other legislation deemed advantageous to women. They too failed to convince the NWP to change course.

Alice Paul, who drafted the ERA and was the driving force behind its passage, epitomized the ardent individualism and single-issue focus of the NWP. Like the majority of other NWP members, she came from a relatively privileged background. Raised in a wealthy Quaker family with a father who was a successful businessman and president of the Burlington County Trust Company in New Jersey, Paul had earned a PhD from the University of Pennsylvania and three law degrees by the end of the 1920s. Like many of the women grouped around her, she believed deeply in removing barriers to women's individual achievement and allowing women the same freedoms as men. Raising the living standards of workers and ending race-based indignities were not her principal concerns. Rather, she maintained an unwavering, resolute focus on winning women's legal equality with men.

Animosity between NWP activists, often called "equal rights feminists," and social justice feminists worsened in 1923 after the Supreme Court overturned Washington, D.C.'s minimum wage law for women. Women, like men, now enjoyed voting rights, the Court proclaimed, and as political equals they should be subject to the same unregulated free market as men. The NWP applauded the decision. Social justice feminists were appalled. Mary Anderson, a Swedish immigrant shoemaker appointed by President

Woodrow Wilson in 1920 as the first director of the U.S. Women's Bureau, lashed out at the Court ruling as well as the reasoning of NWP feminists. The NWP, she declared, was celebrating a false freedom. The right of women to work for starvation wages was no right at all. The 1923 Court ruling, in her view, merely gave employers the power to exploit the most vulnerable without over-sight or restraint.

After 1923, social justice feminists formed a "counter-lobby" to the ERA, which included such women's organizations as the National Women's Trade Union League, the largest U.S. labor wom-en's organization of the day, the National Consumers' League, the Young Women's Christian Association (YWCA), and others. Class animosities underlay and reinforced political disagreements. In the view of feminists like Mary Anderson, who had washed dishes in a lumber camp and held a succession of low-paying jobs as a domestic before finding steady work in a boot factory and a route to union office and government affairs, the NWP's approach to wom-en's rights, particularly its single-minded pursuit of the ERA and of formal legal equality with men, was far too narrow. It promised "doctrinaire equality" without any "social justice," she explained to the readers of *Good Housekeeping* in 1925. The "woman question" was interrelated with "other great social questions," she added, and "to insist only upon women's legal rights no matter what happened to other rights could result in *greater* inequality."[6]

Passing the ERA, social justice feminists feared, would make it easier for the Supreme Court to overturn not just Washington, D.C.'s minimum wage law but all woman-specific laws and policies. Secured initially in the early twentieth century, state and munici-pal laws across the country regulated the working conditions of millions of women in low-paid service, industrial, and agricultural jobs; social justice feminists judged these laws as crucial in keep-ing women's wages above poverty level, reducing long hours, and offering women protection from dangerous and unhealthy work. Counted by some social justice feminists as among their proudest reform achievements, these laws needed to be retained, broadened, and extended to all workers, men as well as women.

As the battle over the ERA heated up after 1923, the NWP further alienated social justice feminists by forming political ties with business groups such as the U.S. Chamber of Commerce and the National Association of Manufacturers and befriending conservative politicians in both the Republican and Democratic parties. These were the very groups who had opposed labor rights, government regulation, and social welfare programs throughout the Progressive Era and who would continue to do so into the 1960s and beyond. The NWP's willingness to cooperate with such allies only confirmed the beliefs of social justice feminists that the NWP cared little about the problems of low-income women or the economic and social inequities of laissez-faire capitalism and the so-called free market.

Neither the ERA nor the social justice feminist agenda made much headway in the 1920s, a decade of disappointment for feminists. Some legislative advances occurred in maternal health and infant care, but women's lobbying power diminished over the course of the 1920s as the much-anticipated women's voting bloc failed to materialize.

Conservative women from the Daughters of the American Revolution and the American Legion Auxiliary added to the growing political discord among women by attacking progressive women's peace and internationalist ventures as un-American. In particular, they directed their ire toward prominent social justice feminists in the Women's Trade Union League (WTUL), accusing Margaret Dreier Robins, the group's national president, and Mary Anderson, who had been an organizer and officer of the league before becoming the Women's Bureau chief, of belonging to a subversive orga-

nization and of aiding insurrectionist labor and socialist groups at
home and abroad.

The WTUL was hardly a subversive or an insurrectionist organization. Most influential in the Progressive Era and the interwar
years, it brought together working-class and elite women committed to advancing the needs of wage-earning women through
democratic trade unionism and legislative reform. Firm believers
in international law and human rights, in 1919 Robins, Anderson,
and other U.S. WTUL women had helped found the International
Federation of Working Women to raise global labor standards and
ensure women's full participation in the new international organizations encouraged by the Versailles Treaty. They were stunned by
the viciousness of the personal attacks on them and on their pursuit of labor reform, women's rights, and international economic
cooperation.

Popular interest in organized feminism and women's causes
continued to dwindle as the decade wore on. The myth arose and
stuck that women's political and economic rights had been won
and that the only frontiers left for women were sexual freedom and
personal autonomy. To some, the feminism of previous decades
appeared unfashionably self-denying and sexually tame, and its
concern for broader societal transformation a quaint, unnecessary
pastime. Many older women reformers decried a younger generation seemingly turned inward, preoccupied with sexual pleasure
and individual fulfillment.

The more public, expressive sexuality of the 1920s, however, did
not necessarily mean women enjoyed greater sexual satisfaction or
personal happiness. Heterosexual activity was now deemed a central component of a healthy self. This new ideal, based in part on
the cultural diffusion of Freudian psychology, increased the possi-
bility of erotic pleasure for many. Yet it heightened expectations of
sexual performance and created behavioral norms that could limit

as well as liberate. Being sexually inactive was stigmatized, making the choice of remaining single or celibate difficult, and those who found heterosexual eroticism unfulfilling were often judged as abnormal or incomplete.

Still, the culture changed slowly, and not everyone embraced the new sexual ideals of the 1920s. Many women remained single, living alone or with their families of origin. Older patterns of homosocial and homosexual bonding persisted, bolstered in part by gay and lesbian subcultures and by the new emphasis on sexual experimentation, especially for women. Pauline Newman and Frieda Miller, for example, two social justice feminists of the 1920s who remained active into the 1950s, chose unconventional intimate lives and family arrangements. Newman and Miller served as significant intellectual mentors to younger social justice feminists in the 1930s and 1940s, and when Frieda Miller replaced Mary Anderson as director of the U.S. Women's Bureau in 1944, she would use the agency to create a national network of women labor leaders and advance the reform agenda of social justice feminism in the postwar era.

A Jewish Lithuanian immigrant, Newman worked as a child in the garment sweatshops of New York's East Side and thrilled to the 1909 citywide garment uprising, when some twenty thousand Italian and Jewish immigrants, nearly all young girls in their teens and early twenties, struck for better pay, safer workplaces, and an end to the cutthroat competition of the "sweating system," which debased everyone involved, contractors, sellers, and producers. In 1918, on assignment as a labor organizer for the WTUL in Philadelphia, she met Miller, a University of Chicago–trained economics professor at Bryn Mawr and a league ally who shared her passions for women's trade unionism, suffrage, and social reform. Both were rooming at the College Club, and when Miller fell gravely ill during the rampaging flu epidemic, Newman nursed her back to health. Except for a brief falling-out in the early 1960s, she and Miller remained committed partners for the next fifty years, raising a daughter together after 1923.[7]

In choosing a "Boston marriage," where women lived together as committed partners in arrangements that may or may not have involved sexual passion, Newman and Miller continued a practice common among earlier feminists. Although neither felt comfortable speaking publicly about their intimate lives and neither left a record of the distresses or joys their rejection of heterosexual marriage engendered, each clearly found great solace and pleasure in the other's company. Their partnership flourished, nestled within a larger reform community of close female friends, some married, some not. Still, they lived together in an era in which heterosexual eroticism and marriage were the new ideals and women whose greatest passions appeared to be social service and political reform were no longer celebrated by the culture as models of female achievement.

The 1920s shift toward a more gender-integrated heterosexual world and away from female separatism continued into the 1950s, affecting the personal and organizational choices feminist activists would make, even as other aspects of society changed dramatically. In the wake of the stock market crash of 1929, unemployment, homelessness, and industrial conflict soared. The fear of social collapse redirected the nation's attention: social and economic issues once deemed irrelevant now became of utmost urgency. Women, like men, turned to politics and labor organizing in large numbers, with the majority forming mixed-sex organizations. A new era of activism had begun.

For some, of course, especially African Americans, the economic hardships of the 1930s were not new: they were long-standing realities. In the early twentieth century, millions of African Americans had fled the South, seeking escape from a wearying grind of tenant farming, sharecropping, and low-wage work, escalating white vigilante violence and a state-sanctioned Jim Crow system of strict racial segregation. They arrived in midwestern and northern cities in the 1920s and 1930s with high hopes, many having fought in World War I. All too often, they found segregated housing and schooling, white hostility, and intense competition for a limited number of jobs.

Such racial animosity among workers was fueled in part by economic inequality. In the 1920s, the vast bulk of wealth generated by productivity gains and rising consumption ended up in the wallets and bank accounts of a small percentage of the population, creating vast economic disparity. In 1929, before the stock market collapse, the wealthiest 1 percent of Americans held some 44 percent of the nation's wealth; their worth had quadrupled after World War I while the rest of the nation saw modest gains at best.[8]

Depression and New Deal

When Franklin Delano Roosevelt took office in 1933, the uneven distribution of wealth was not his most pressing concern. His administration acted first to stave off a banking panic, end the home and farm foreclosure epidemic, and put the unemployed—by 1933 one-fourth of the nation—back to work. But pressure to address economic injustice grew, spearheaded by organized labor and others, including women reformers such as Roosevelt's secretary of labor, Frances Perkins, the first female cabinet member. A longtime ally of the New York branch of the WTUL, Perkins had championed social welfare and labor legislation in New York State since before World War I. In response, Congress eventually enacted an unprecedented and ambitious set of programs that changed the balance of power between labor and capital and helped create a new American middle class. Many of the specific policies were ones social justice feminists had advocated for decades: social security and income support for the elderly, disabled, and poor; legislation prohibiting child labor and setting a national minimum wage and other fair working conditions for men and women; and the Wagner Act guaranteeing workers freedom of speech and assembly and the right to independent trade union representation.

While an older group of women reformers like Frances Perkins and Mary Anderson, who remained head of the U.S. Women's Bureau until 1944, generated pressure for change inside the new Democratic administration, a new generation of social justice feminists pushed for reform from below. The sit-down strikes of 1937 led by Myra Wolfgang and countless others were the culmination of years of labor protests, including citywide general strikes in San Francisco and Minneapolis and nationwide walkouts in textile and other industries. Prompted to act by their own thwarted dreams and the frustration and misery around them, young activists, men and women, were drawn too by the excitement of being part of a new and creative movement they believed could remake the world. For the young women labor activists who would come to lead the American women's movement of the 1940s, both the turmoil and the exhilaration of Depression-era economic and social justice struggles left their mark.

For some, the personal and political transformations of the 1930s were profound. Esther Peterson, for example, left her conservative Mormon Republican roots far behind after she moved from Utah to New York City and threw herself into the whirlwind of 1930s labor and reform politics. In 1961, she would become the highest-ranking woman in the Kennedy administration and the leading national advocate for legislative reform on behalf of women, but in 1927, as a senior at Brigham Young University, she faced an excruciating choice: her fiancé offered her security and love in the Mormon family-centered world she knew well, but, as she remembered it, his view of the world left little room for her independence or self-expression. "The man I thought I was in love with," she recounted later, saw life as "a pocket watch, with God as the main-spring" and himself as "one of the bigger wheels." He put "sweet little me somewhere down in the parts you can't see with the rest of the women." She broke off the engagement and took a job teaching dance and physical education at Branch Agricultural College in Cedar City, Utah. After being reprimanded by the college administration for an "immoral" Isadora Duncan–style modern dance performance she organized on the college lawn, she finished her year but decided to "go East" and study at Columbia University Teachers College thousands of miles away. "I wasn't sure exactly what I was looking for," she confessed in her memoirs, "but I thought I might find it in New York."[9]

Once in New York, she attended classes, finishing her master's degree at Columbia in 1930, and frequented the many political gatherings of the day. At one, a lecture at the local YMCA sponsored by the Fellowship of Reconciliation, an interfaith peace and social justice organization, she met her husband-to-be, Oliver Peterson, a young working-class University of North Dakota graduate studying sociology at Columbia and working at the Y. Soon they were part of an energetic group of young social activists. In 1932, they married and moved to Boston, where Esther got a job at the Winsor School, an elite private school for girls, and at night volunteered to teach "working girls" through the YWCA's industrial program. When some of the young immigrant garment workers in her class struck to protest pay cuts and work speed-up, she joined the picket line and helped the women organize their own union.

A revived and powerful labor movement, Peterson now believed, was crucial for achieving economic fairness for women. She quit her Winsor School job and for the next few years traveled across New England organizing for the teachers and garment workers union. She also spent many of her summers teaching drama, popular economics, and dance at the Bryn Mawr Summer School for Women Workers, a residential leadership program for wage-earning women staffed by university social scientists, labor organizers, and progressive educators that operated for seventeen summers, from 1921 to 1938. In 1939, she joined the Education Department of the Amalgamated Clothing Workers of America (ACWA), a key union in the Congress of Industrial Organizations (CIO), the dynamic labor federation founded in 1937, which would organize millions of workers over the next decade.

Like many other young activists in the 1930s, Esther and Oliver Peterson found socialism's emphasis on a more cooperative, egalitarian society appealing, and in 1932, Oliver Peterson campaigned for Norman Thomas, the Presbyterian minister running for president on the Socialist Party ticket. Soon, however, they threw in their lot with the Democratic Party, as did the vast majority of the country. By 1936, they backed Roosevelt and saw themselves as part of a broad New Deal coalition whose primary aims were preservation of democratic governance, opposition to the rise of fascism in Europe, and reform of the capitalist system. They had found their life's political course and they stuck with it. Firm gender egalitarians and deeply in love, they also struggled with how to help each other develop as individuals and reform leaders while sustaining their relationship and caring for their growing family. The challenges were formidable: their first child arrived in 1938; three more followed over the next eight years. What social justice feminists called the "double day" would remain a central and abiding concern for Peterson and many other activists of her generation.

Peterson and most other social justice feminists worked in organizations and reform coalitions that included Communists as well as a heterodox mix of other reformers, secular and religious. A legitimate political party in the 1930s with some seventy-five thousand members at its peak in 1938, the Communist Party (CP) attracted well-known artists, writers, and reformers from all walks of life by its embrace of economic and social justice.

Tillie Lerner Olsen, who would later achieve fame as the author of *Tell Me a Riddle* (1961) and other critically acclaimed novels and short stories, was one of them. Born on a tenant farm in Nebraska to Russian-Jewish socialists, Olsen joined the Young Communist League, the CP youth organization, in 1930 after dropping out of high school and leaving home in search of a job. The CP's bold advocacy of labor and civil rights impressed her as she crisscrossed the country in the early 1930s, agitating alongside packinghouse workers in Kansas City and striking longshoremen in San Francisco. Like other labor feminists close to the Communist Party, such as United Electrical Workers leader Ruth Young or Luisa Moreno, who organized Mexican pecan shellers in Texas before becoming a national officer in the Food, Tobacco, Agricultural and Allied Workers, Olsen made her most public contributions to the movement before Cold War hostilities erupted in full force in the late 1940s.

Panamanian-born garment leader Maida Springer took a different route to labor activism than either Esther Peterson or Tillie Olsen. Inspired by a mother who identified as a follower of Marcus Garvey, the Jamaican black nationalist leader who attracted millions of black Americans to his cause in the 1920s, Springer saw herself as a Pan-Africanist as well as a feminist. Like Packinghouse leader Addie Wyatt, she also straddled the two worlds of labor and civil rights. Refused a job as a New York City telephone operator in the early 1930s—because, as the AT&T interviewer explained, "What white mother do you think would want you to sit beside her daughter?"—Springer finally found work as a seamstress. Distressed by the grueling work pace and arbitrary management practices in the garment shops, she convinced her co-workers to sign up with the International Ladies' Garment Workers' Union. On the local union's executive board by 1938, Springer became its education director in 1943 and its first black woman business manager a few years later, responsible for settling pay and other disputes for workers of all races in sixty New York shops.[10]

The 1930s activism of these young feminists shaped them in lasting ways. Many forged enduring personal and political ties with an older generation of women reformers whose social justice politics they absorbed. Esther Peterson met Pauline Newman and Frieda Miller—all aligned with the WTUL and all staunch opponents of the ERA—through the garment workers union and the Bryn Mawr Summer School. First Lady Eleanor Roosevelt, an ally of the New York branch of the WTUL since 1923, was associated with this circle of women reformers as well. She had chaired the New York league's finance and education committee in the 1920s when her husband was governor and maintained close ties with league leaders after her move to the White House. Friendships across the generations solidified as the women cooperated on organizing and legislative campaigns and, for a couple of weeks each summer, lived together on the Bryn Mawr campus. In 1938, when Bryn Mawr College severed its ties with the program—piqued that, among other headaches for the elite college, the working-class summer school students had encouraged maids at the college to organize—the gatherings shifted to Bryn Mawr dean Hilda Smith's fifty-acre family estate in upstate New York.

The older women's networks that attracted young feminists in the 1930s crossed racial as well as class and ethnic lines. The Bryn Mawr Summer School, for example, honored its declared 1926 policy of admitting students "without distinction of race, creed, or color."[11] It admitted an African American student in 1926, the first black woman to attend Bryn Mawr College, and typical summer classes in the years that followed included women of all races, religions, and cultural backgrounds. Maida Springer, just beginning

her career in the Ladies' Garment Workers' Union as one of its pioneering black leaders, participated in the 1930s summer schools,
and like Peterson she looked to the female elders in the garment
unions and the WTUL for intellectual guidance. On occasion,
Springer and her close friend Pauli Murray—who would later gain
renown as a civil rights lawyer, feminist legal theorist and popular memoirist and was one of the first African American women
ordained as an Episcopal priest—also frequented the celebrated
weekend retreats of New Dealers hosted by historian and social welfare expert Caroline Ware and her husband, institutional economist
Gardiner Means, on "the Farm," their Northern Virginia home.

Working in a coed labor movement shaped this generation of
young feminists just as deeply as did their alliances with older
women reformers. On the one hand, women active in the labor
movement recognized the many injustices men and women shared,
and they valued men's support and the power of worker solidarity.
At the same time, as they confronted the difficulties of creating sol-
idarities between men and women, their feminism as well as their
commitment to combating sex discrimination deepened. In the
1930s, the men leading the labor movement held a range of views
on women's "proper role." Some recognized the right of women,
like men, to jobs and job security. The Amalgamated Clothing
Workers, for example, opposed the widespread efforts in the 1930s
to fire married women as a solution to the economic crisis. Others
sought (in vain) to preserve an older gender order in which wom-
en's first and only priority was caring for their families.

Yet despite its sexism and ambivalence about women's rights, the
labor movement's commitment to economic and social equality, as
well as its consciousness of worker rights, inspired women to organize and, in the end, to seek their *own* rights as women. Indeed,
the labor movement spurred feminism in ways not dissimilar from
the stirrings of women in the 1960s New Left: in both movements

women ended up demanding that a male-led, coed movement live up to its own ideals and extend its principles of justice and equality to women. The labor movement gave feminists a vocabulary and an ideological framework within which to justify their own demands. It offered them institutional resources. Paradoxically, when it *failed* to live up to its own rhetoric of justice for all or only responded erratically, that too reinforced women's escalating calls for change.

"Women: There's Work to Be Done and a War to Be Won . . . Now!"[12]

What women judged as fair between the sexes changed dramatically during and after World War II. The attitudes of the 1930s labor movement toward women's rights came to seem tame, even conservative, and much in need of reconceptualization. So too did society's treatment of women, especially wage-earning women. The upheavals of the war contributed mightily to these changes.

The most celebrated gender pioneers of World War II are the Rosie the Riveters holding their hammer guns aloft, doing a man's job with gusto and finesse. The iconic 1940s images of Rosie the Riveter are upbeat, whether on government recruiting posters or taken from Norman Rockwell's celebratory 1943 Memorial Day cover of the *Saturday Evening Post*. Yet for twenty-first-century observers, the image of Rosie the Riveter may evoke a sense of loss as well as triumph. Many know that Rosie's wartime day in the sun—enjoying her boost in income, admired for her skill, and basking in societal approval—would not last. At the war's end, it is thought, Rosie the Riveter morphed into Rosie the Stay-at-Home Mom, surrounded by her children in a suburban dream home, cheerfully wielding a vacuum cleaner, not a rivet gun.

What often gets lost in both the wartime propaganda image and the popular narrative of Rosie's rise and fall is the experience of the

J. Howard Miller's 1942
recruitment poster for
Westinghouse later became
famous as "Rosie the Riveter,"
representing women's rights
and the millions of women
who performed wartime jobs
historically reserved for men.

majority of women war workers. Most Rosies were not new recruits
to the labor force but low-income workers. Women moved into men's
industrial jobs during the war, into some of the dirtiest and most
dangerous jobs in America, because they had few better options.
Most returned not to full-time domesticity but to their old jobs in
the blue- and pink-collar ghetto of low-paid, low-status women's
work. The baby boom at war's end was real enough, but so too was
another phenomenon: the rise of the Working Wife and Mother.

Still, their experiences of wartime employment were not forgotten. Rosie lost her riveting job, but her sense of what she deserved
and what was possible was forever changed. The experience of
doing a "man's job" and at times receiving respect and a "man's
pay" raised women's self-esteem and their expectations of what
they wanted on the job. More women now knew that they too could
do a "man's job" and that they too deserved the wages, respect, and
union protections all too often reserved for men. Carmen Chavez
of Albuquerque, for example, thought the women war workers in
her neighborhood "changed as much as the men who went to war.

We had a taste of independence we hadn't known before the war. We developed a feeling of self-confidence and a sense of worth."[13]

At the war's close, most women workers wanted to keep their higher-paying jobs, and many organized to fight for the right to do so. Although they generally thought it was fair for veterans to be able to get their old jobs back, they were infuriated by the presumption that *any* man, with or without seniority, whether in uniform or not, had a claim to their jobs. Equally grating for women war workers was the loss of pay and prestige when demoted to "women's work." Their unionized jobs gone, they were back in a work world of close supervision, speed-up, and low wages, without benefits or job protections.

Wartime gains and losses proved particularly bittersweet for minority women. In 1941, under pressure from civil rights organizations and a threatened March on Washington, President Roosevelt had signed Executive Order 8802, which set up the Fair Employment Practices Committee (FEPC) and barred job discrimination in the defense industry and among employers with government contracts. As a result, industrial jobs long closed to minority women opened up, bringing for some their first taste of economic independence. Yet the thrill of wartime employment opportunity turned to deep disappointment and anger in the war's aftermath. Women of color were the first laid off or demoted, and their brothers, husbands, and lovers returned from overseas to a second-class citizenship made more intolerable after their wartime sacrifices for their country. Jobs were scarce and discriminatory workplace practices commonplace, especially after the wartime FEPC turned out to be temporary. With government oversight gone, minority men and women had little recourse when faced with job loss or hiring discrimination.

No wonder Addie Wyatt doubted the union at her workplace would help her when she lost her job at Armour's meatpacking plant. Like many other minority women, Wyatt was just as likely to be replaced by a white woman as by a man. But when it happened to her, the union backed up her claims to the job. To her amazement, she regained her position. "This was moving to me, a black woman who had for a long time been discriminated against and unable to find a job. I finally had a job—and a better paying job than I ever dreamed I'd have. That the union could take my side and get results so that I was placed back in the job I enjoyed, this was moving to me." Just as surprising to her was the union's maternity policy, negotiated during the war. When the union steward promised Wyatt, pregnant with her first child, that she could take up to a one-year leave of absence and her job would be held for her, she didn't really believe him. But, Wyatt remembers, "I thought I'd try it." When she returned to the plant after three months, much to her surprise, the job was hers again. Once back on the line, Wyatt vowed to extend the union benefits she enjoyed to others.[14]

Wyatt was one of millions of women having babies in the war's aftermath. "After the war, my God! It was like a deluge of babies," former wartime riveter Lola Weixel told one interviewer. "When I went to have my first baby, there wasn't even room. People were doing labor in the halls. It was unbelievable. Oh yes, everybody, everybody and their sister was having a baby."[15] The famed baby boom continued for almost a decade, reversing the delayed marriage and small-family patterns of the Depression and early wartime years. An expanding economy made it financially feasible to have children again, and as Tillie Olsen saw it, having children helped restore faith in humanity and heal the wounds of war. But as many of these new moms also became wage earners, without the benefits Wyatt enjoyed, the stresses of the "double day" became commonplace, and women wanted relief from what was now becoming the new normal.

For women were not *only* having babies after the war ended. More than in previous generations, postwar women *combined* marriage, child rearing, and employment. They were having *more* children *and* spending *more* time in paid jobs. Stay-at-Home Mom was giving way to Working Mom and Working Wife. Employers preferred women as the postwar service economy soared, and more children and more consumer goods required more breadwinners. Fewer women quit working once they married; young mothers left their children sooner to take full- and part-time jobs; and as life expectancies increased, more middle-aged women sought employment once their children were grown. The dual responsibilities of home and job were now long-term realities for masses of women. Yet employers (and society too) seemed in denial about the changes in women's lives and the burdens of working two jobs: one inside the home, one outside.

Women's wartime experiences, the baby boom, and rising female labor force participation—all spurred a desire for change among women, particularly wage-earning women. Employed women in postwar America were indignant: they wanted better pay and more respect on the job; they wanted their family work acknowledged, valued, and accommodated. They believed things could and should be different, and many, like Addie Wyatt, chose to act on those beliefs in the war's aftermath. As the war drew to a close, the social justice feminist movement emerged even stronger than before.

A National Movement Crystallizes

The postwar social justice women's movement differed organizationally from its predecessors. All-female reform organizations like the WTUL continued to be active, but their memberships were smaller, and they were no longer the driving force of the movement politically or intellectually. Instead, the key leaders came largely from mixed-sex groups, primarily unions affiliated with the CIO-inspired labor movement. The U.S. Women's Bureau also remained a principal player, closely connected to women's movement activists outside government. At the war's end, it brought labor women together into a powerful national network and linked them with older women's organizations like the National Consumers' League, the League of Women Voters, and the National Council of Negro Women.

In 1944, Frieda Miller returned from England, where she had observed firsthand the gathering British support for new social welfare policies, to head the U.S. Women's Bureau. In one of her first acts, she set up a national advisory committee of labor women to formulate new gender and social policies for the postwar world and serve as an important pressure group to secure them nationally. The labor women's committee met frequently between 1945 and 1953 under Miller's leadership. When Miller lost the directorship after Eisenhower's election, the committee regrouped outside the auspices of the Women's Bureau, reconstituting itself as the National Committee on Equal Pay and other ad hoc coalitions. Its oldest committee members—like Miller's partner, Pauline Newman—were veterans of the suffrage, labor, and internationalist campaigns of the early twentieth century. But most were the young enthusiasts of the 1930s labor upsurge and the now rapidly expanding civil rights movement.

The women's movement of the 1940s broke new ground intellectually as well as organizationally. It still concerned itself with the full range of women's problems and sought the economic, political, and social rights of all women, but its sense of women's relationship to the family and to motherhood differed from what earlier women reformers had espoused. Heterosexual family roles remained central to most women's identity and were the source of some of women's greatest pleasures—a legacy in part of the 1920s cultural shifts. Still, midcentury social justice feminists knew that women had left home for paid work and were not going back. The

The 1946 U.S. Women's Bureau Labor Advisory Committee included, among others, Frieda Miller, chair (seated, third from left), Pauline Newman (standing, first from left), and Esther Peterson (standing, third from left). Library of Congress.

postwar realities of women's lives—combining caregiving and breadwinning—were here to stay. The reforms social justice feminists pursued in the decades ahead reflected these new postwar circumstances: they wanted to make it possible for all women to have both satisfying family lives *and* good jobs.

In pursuing these reforms, the new postwar women's movement remained attentive to how class and cultural differences shaped women's choices about home and employment. For low-income women, the choice was not between home and a satisfying professional career but, for example, between home and dealing with the crabby clientele at the local diner. Many would have loved to spend more time as housewives and mothers but could not afford to do so. Elite and professional women, by contrast, often saw housework as a worse option than the salaried careers they might find. In her 1963 blockbuster, *The Feminine Mystique*, Betty Friedan spoke for many college-educated women relegated to housework and denied the professional careers they hoped to obtain. Instead of a satisfying career, they felt reduced to being servants and maids.

Yet for those women who actually held jobs as maids, taking care of their own household and children rather than someone else's could seem like a liberatory step. Having the "opportunity" for a low-paying service or blue-collar job was not the feminist revolution low-income women had in mind. Postwar social justice feminists recognized that women had different ideas about what liberation meant, and they sought to create better options for nonprofessional women as well as more choice for all women. In their view, solving the "double day" for nonprofessional women meant creating more *good* jobs—jobs with higher wages and shorter hours—and greater access to them for all women. It also meant recognizing and revaluing mothering and the work of the home.

As the next chapter recounts, 1970s feminists would focus on the "feminine mystique" and on how certain ideals of womanhood kept women tethered to the home and created unachievable and undesirable expectations for them as mothers and wives. In contrast, midcentury social justice feminists criticized what can be called the "masculine mystique," or the valorizing of the qualities associated with masculinity and the male sphere of employment. They believed winning first-class citizenship for all women involved more than equal access to the market and to men's jobs. It required transforming the masculine work patterns, norms, and practices of the work world itself and rethinking how the traditional male and female spheres were valued. Jobs in postwar America had been designed with a man in mind, they claimed, and with the assumption he had or would have a full-time wife at home. Since men did not get pregnant or nurse, no parental leave policy was deemed necessary. Similarly, work hours were constructed without thought to the schedules of children or to any other family obligation outside of employment.

The CIO's top woman staffer, Vassar graduate Katherine (Kitty) Ellickson, who helped organize mineworkers in the early 1930s before graduate study in economics at Columbia, thought this work world a relic of a bygone era much in need of dismantling. Rather than ask women to adjust to an outmoded world of work, she wrote, the new postwar women's movement should insist that employers "adapt the man's world to women." That task, she believed, "transcend[ed] the efforts of isolated individuals" and demanded fundamental shifts in cultural norms, workplace practices, and social policy.[16]

The "masculine mystique" disadvantaged women at home as well as on the job. It reinforced a gender hierarchy in which the masculine was valued over the feminine. Qualities associated with femininity such as nurturance or collaboration were deemed less valuable, as was the work traditionally performed by women. The unpaid "reproductive" labor of caregiving took second place to the income-generating "productive" endeavors of the market. But why, labor feminists asked, shouldn't the work of caregiving and of service, whether paid or unpaid, be seen as valuable and worthy of respect? And why shouldn't the woman on the production line receive the same union protections and high pay as the supposedly more "skilled" male production worker next to her? These were the questions posed by social justice feminists at midcentury. By challenging the "masculine mystique" and the masculine norms embedded in workplace structures and social policy, they mounted a destabilizing assault on the gender order of their day.

Yet what postwar social justice feminists did not seek to change is as revealing as what they did. Certain things, they assumed, either did not need to change or were incapable of being remade. Unlike

1970s feminists, they did not view gender as a social construct. For the postwar feminists, sex differences were real, in part biological and unchangeable, and perhaps even desirable. Sex-based *hierarchies* needed dismantling, but less clear was whether gender *divisions* could or should be rearranged. Should men and women do the same jobs? Should men and women share equally in caregiving and the work of the home? These questions were asked but never really answered. Nor were they the burning concerns of the day. The midcentury priority was ending the unequal *valuing* of gender differences, not ending difference itself. If women's sphere and what women did could be equally valued, then half the battle had been won. It was this battle of equal worth that they fought.

To make progress on their ambitious reform agenda, social justice feminists launched legislative and workplace campaigns in the 1940s and 1950s in three broad areas: economic and social security for all Americans; an end to unfair discrimination against women as a sex; civil rights and first-class citizenship for minorities. They worked with men in the labor movement, the civil rights movement, and the Democratic Party. In addition, they organized separately with other women, working primarily through the U.S. Women's Bureau to form various coalitions with like-minded women's groups.

Backlash Against New Deal Reform

Beginning in 1943 and continuing into the early 1950s, left-liberal New Dealers and their allies in the labor movement introduced comprehensive "social security for all" bills intended to expand and improve the 1935 Social Security Act. The 1945 bill, for instance, called for universal national health insurance, extending old-age insurance to farm workers and domestic employees, raising the level of old-age, survivor, and unemployment benefits, and adding

new provisions for paid maternity leave. Social security, proponents explained, was not just for the elderly; nor was it only about
income in old age. Social justice feminists lobbied especially hard
for the provisions offering income support for new mothers. Frieda
Miller testified on behalf of the 1945 bill, for example, and continued her efforts into the early 1950s, working with the U.S. Children's Bureau to secure a federal law that would move the United
States closer to the family policies emerging in other industrial
countries: a minimum three-month paid maternity leave with job
security. Full social security, she and others proclaimed, could not
be achieved until society provided for the health and security of
mothers and children.

Although proponents of "social security for all" legislation made
little progress nationally, social justice feminists did secure modest victories at the state level benefiting mothers and children. In
a handful of states, for example, women mounted successful campaigns to keep open wartime childcare programs. In California, the
statewide CIO Women's Auxiliary spearheaded the effort, reaching
out to the Waitresses Union and other sizable women's and community groups to pressure the legislature. They won funding for
kindergartens, after-school programs, and other childcare programs. Led by its president, Tillie Olsen, the postwar California
CIO Women's Auxiliary, like most chapters across the country, lobbied actively for the progressive reform agenda adopted by the CIO's
national women's auxiliary, which included among its top priorities
public funds for childcare and child rearing, expanded social security protections, and an end to job and wage discrimination against
women and minorities. Labor auxiliaries admitted the wives, daughters, mothers, sisters, and, on occasion, "friends" of union men,
and by the 1940s some two million women belonged. Most of these
working-class women held or would hold paid jobs outside the home,
and their reform agenda reflected that postwar reality.

Although at the state level social justice feminists could claim some victories in securing funding for mothers and children, their efforts to expand New Deal wage-and-hour legislation to the majority of workers met with considerable frustration. While the Fair Labor Standards Act (FLSA), first passed in 1938, set wage floors and hour ceilings for industrial workers, many women and people of color fell outside its coverage. The majority of white women workers, concentrated in small retail and service jobs, lacked federal wage-and-hour protections, as did the mostly minority workforce in agriculture and domestic work. The lack of legal remedies and protections for domestic workers, who were treated more as servants or as "one of the family" dependent on paternal (or maternal) largess rather than as "employees" with adult rights and contractual guarantees, was particularly troubling. Esther Peterson, who worked as the Amalgamated Clothing Workers' Washington lobbyist from 1945 to 1948, devoted much of her time to the FLSA. Pregnant in 1946 with her fourth child, Peterson remembered the long weeks and months trying to change attitudes and convince male legislators that all workers, including women and minorities, deserved living wages and protection from overwork. One legislator, paying more attention to her ever-expanding stomach than to her economic arguments, joked that her child should be called Max for maximum hours if a boy and Minnie for minimum wages if a girl.

Peterson's FLSA efforts largely failed, as did most of the national campaigns to expand New Deal labor and social welfare legislation in the 1940s and 1950s. A hostile coalition of southern Democrats and conservative Republicans—-dubbed the "unholy alliance" by Pullman Porters union president A. Philip Randolph—gained new members after the 1946 election, and generous financial backing from newly coalesced business and professional associations bolstered forces bent on undoing the New Deal.

In 1947, Congress overrode President Harry Truman's veto and passed the Taft-Hartley Act, which amended key provisions of the 1935 Wagner Act, passed to ensure greater "equality of bargaining power" between labor and capital and thereby boost wages, consumer purchasing power, and economic growth. Taft-Hartley shifted economic power back to organized capital. By outlawing union recognition and sympathy strikes, mass picketing, secondary boycotts, and other forms of worker collective action, Taft-Hartley made it increasingly difficult for the labor movement to organize new workers in the private sector. It also narrowed the Wagner Act's protection of labor's right to organize and bargain to non-supervisory employees only, ensuring that, unlike in other developed nations, managers and white-collar workers in the United States would not be unionized.

New Deal reformers faced other hurdles as the "Iron Curtain" descended, dividing Europe and much of the world into two opposing camps. In the late 1940s and early 1950s, in the wake of deteriorating relations between the Soviet Union and the United States, fear of subversives within the U.S. government reached a fever pitch. FBI director J. Edgar Hoover and his allies fomented a witch hunt for Communists and others deemed un-American or a threat to national security. By the early 1950s, with Senator Joseph McCarthy (R-Wisconsin) whipping up public fear and anger, a wide range of New Deal liberals and leftists, including social democratic anti-Stalinists like Esther and Oliver Peterson, were subject to loyalty investigations and subpoenaed as potential subversives before congressional committees. These experiences left lasting scars even for those exonerated like the Petersons. Many prominent social justice feminists, including Tillie Olsen, withdrew from active political engagement.

Unable to extend New Deal reforms legislatively, the postwar labor movement sought enhanced social and economic security at individual workplaces. It met with some success, at least in mass production and other heavily organized sectors of the economy like mining, transportation, and construction. In the auto industry, for example, the UAW bargained for and won healthcare and pension coverage, supplemental benefits for laid-off, sick, and disabled workers, and paid vacations in addition to gains in wages and job control.

Social justice feminists, however, protested the sex bias of these new workplace policies. Many women, they rightly noted, failed to qualify for benefits because of their part-time status, interrupted careers, or shorter length of service. Even when they did qualify, their needs as caretakers and income earners often went unmet. Paid-leave language covered every sort of medical problem and disabling condition except pregnancy and childbirth. Sick leave provisions allowed time off for one's own illness but penalized workers when they stayed home to take care of a sick child or nurse an elderly parent. All workers, feminists patiently explained, did not have a wife at home who gave birth and cared for dependents. Sometimes the worker and the wife were the same person!

Moreover, the postwar employer-based welfare system provided only for that minority of workers lucky enough to have such benefits. Cognizant of the problem, UAW president Walter Reuther initially turned down employer offers of pensions and healthcare in the 1940s because the union favored universal coverage for all, a goal opposed by employers. Reuther finally agreed to employer-based health and welfare coverage in the 1950s, but he continued to hope that employers, saddled with high health and welfare costs for their employees, would drop their resistance to government programs. Such a shift would enhance American competitiveness with European and Japanese firms, he thought, where benefits came largely from the state, not the employer. Ideology trumped rationality, however, and U.S. employers opted for higher costs rather than what they labeled "socialized" benefits.

Sex Discrimination and Continuing Division
Among Feminists

The reforms social justice feminists sought in the 1940s and 1950s were more than just improvements on what the New Deal had achieved. They also introduced legislation and workplace reforms in new areas, notably ending sex-based wage discrimination and passing a broad women's rights bill, which they called the "Women's Status Bill."

To attack wage discrimination, social justice feminists introduced an "equal pay for comparable work" bill into Congress in 1945; they would reintroduce it every year until the early 1960s. CIO unions and women's organizations close to the U.S. Women's Bureau network were the prime backers. Some proponents, men and women, initially saw it as a way of preventing employers from lowering men's wages or replacing men with lower-paid women. Others, however, made a case for equal pay as a matter of simple justice and of fairness to women. These justice claims gradually became the dominant sentiment fueling the postwar drive for equal pay and ending wage discrimination against women.

The "equal pay for comparable work" bills of the postwar era advanced a broad idea of equal pay, continuing a transatlantic movement among women social reformers and trade unionists that picked up speed after World War I. Labor movement feminists and their allies believed it was discriminatory to pay women less than men when both held similar jobs; they also believed sex-based wage discrimination existed even when women held jobs very different from those of men. Winning "equal pay" for that small sliver of women in "men's jobs" would be a victory, of course, but it would fail to tackle the much broader problem of "sex bias" in wages. The wages in female-majority service and blue-collar jobs were lower than those in male-majority jobs because the skills, knowledge, and

productivity of women and of those doing "women's jobs" were sys-
tematically devalued. As Addie Wyatt saw it, in "women's departments the quality and the merit of the work was underrated because
it was considered a 'female job.' It had a sexist [wage] rate to it."[17]

Eradicating the "sex bias" in wages meant rethinking the value,
pay, and productivity of all jobs and understanding that women,
like men, deserved a wage capable of providing support for themselves and their dependents. The language of the legislation they
introduced reflected this expansive notion of "equal pay" and "sex
bias" in wages. The 1945 bill, for example, specified that it would
be "an unfair wage practice" to pay women less than men in jobs
with "comparable quantity and quality" or in jobs with "comparable
skills."[18] The jobs typically held by women were undervalued as to
their skill, responsibility, and productivity. Once reevaluated, advocates believed, the pay in most majority-female jobs would adjust
upward.

The movement succeeded in passing new equal pay laws in
eighteen states in the 1940s and 1950s, but federal legislation on
equal pay stalled, with the same forces arrayed against it that had
blocked social security. Employer policies, however, once again
proved more amenable to change than federal law, especially in
blue-collar industries, where powerful unions, pushed by women
members, decided to make equal pay part of their agenda.

The electrical unions conducted some of the most impressive
campaigns for women's wage justice in the 1940s and 1950s. The
battle opened during the war. With employers seeking to lower
men's wages and a governmental cap on wage hikes except in special circumstances, the United Electrical Workers Union (UE) made
a case before the War Labor Board for wage increases because of
discriminatory practices against women and minorities. After the
war, the UE made ending wage discrimination a central demand
when it struck GE and Westinghouse in 1946, joining telephone

operators, hospitality workers, department store employees, and thousands of others in the largest strike wave in U.S. history.

Westinghouse gave way first, agreeing to raise wages in almost all of the female-majority jobs. Over the next decade, other companies in the electrical industry complied as well. They reevaluated how they rated job skills and changed their policies to conform to the less biased rating systems put forward first by the UE and later by its anti-Communist rival, the International Union of Electrical Workers (IUE). As a result, Mary Callahan, a widowed mother, saw the paycheck from her job assembling radios at Philadelphia's RCA plant meet her family's basic needs for food and housing for the first time in sixteen years of employment. The RCA union's emphasis on wage equity and its success in securing maternity leave in the 1940s—not a benefit she enjoyed when her children were born in the 1930s—fueled Callahan's deep commitment to union activism. She acceded to the top position in her large majority-female local in 1946 and kept it for the next thirty years. By the 1950s, she was also the top female national officer in the IUE—a union of over three hundred thousand workers, 40 percent female—and chaired its national Women's Council. Pushed by Callahan and others (after Callahan retired in 1977), the IUE was a leading voice for ending sex-based discrimination in wages and benefits into the 1980s.

Particularly galling to social justice feminists trying to build support for equal pay was their inability to persuade the National Woman's Party to join in their campaigns either at the workplace or in Congress. The NWP did not oppose equal pay; it simply had its sights set on passing the ERA. The Republicans endorsed the ERA in 1940; in 1944, the Democrats joined them. By 1946, the ERA was ready for consideration in both houses, having been favorably reported out of committee for the first time since its introduction in the early 1920s, and the NWP was confident of finding the votes it needed. It had not reckoned, however, on the growing strength of

A cartoon by LeBaron Coakley from the *IUE News*, March 1, 1954, showing the IUE's support for equal pay for women. The caption "An Easter Bonnet She Deserves" was emblazoned across the original cartoon when it appeared. IUE Archives, Special Collections, Rutgers University Libraries.

its feminist adversaries. Social justice feminists, busy stirring up legislative support for equal pay in 1945, realized they needed an equal rights bill as well. Such a bill would serve as an alternative to the ERA and, of equal importance, be a rallying cry for their vision of women's rights.

In 1947, they introduced the Women's Status Bill into both houses of Congress, reflecting their abiding opposition to the NWP's version of equal rights. It also revealed their intellectual debt to Truman's 1947 President's Committee on Civil Rights and the United Nations' ongoing initiatives to assess women's status worldwide. The 1947 bill and the subsequent women's rights bills they championed in the 1950s sought "to eliminate unfair discrimination based on sex" but did not favor a constitutional amendment or a single legal intervention like the ERA. Rather, they proposed a Presidential Commission on the Status of Women as the first step in raising the overall "political, civil, economic, and social status of women." The commission would study "not just the legal status but the general status" of women, inaugurate a broad public conversation over how to ensure first-class citizenship for women, and recommend specific reforms to advance that goal.[19] Needed reforms, according to social justice feminists, included overturning laws that disadvantaged women, passing new "equal pay for comparable work" and civil rights laws, and changing employer and state policies to accommodate mothers and other caregivers.

In 1948, NWP and social justice feminists squared off against each other in a dramatic confrontation before the House Judiciary Committee, each group fighting for its own women's rights bill and each group defending its own larger political agenda and choice of allies. Social justice feminists, organized into a loose network of labor, civil rights, and women's groups led by former U.S. Women's Bureau director Mary Anderson, vigorously championed their bill, introduced by California Democratic congresswoman Helen Gahagan Douglas. The NWP, backed by powerful business groups and conservative Republicans, fought equally hard for their bill.

The two sides disagreed over what "women's equality" and "sex discrimination" meant and what kind of legislation met the needs of the majority of women. NWP feminists favored strict legal equality between men and women in labor laws as well as in laws affecting marriage, divorce, and child custody. As NWP's Nina Horton Avery asserted, "All adults should be treated alike." New York Republican congresswoman and ERA supporter Katharine St. George backed her up, asserting that women "want to be free to work as equals asking for no special privileges." Educated in Europe and "presented at the Kaiser's Court" before her stint as executive vice president and treasurer of her husband's coal brokerage company, St. George saw few obstacles facing women except laws discriminating on the basis of sex.[20]

Social justice feminists thought otherwise. They opposed the uniform, gender-neutral legal approach, which they feared the ERA

would inaugurate. Instead of a blanket amendment instituting formal legal equality, they called for a review of laws affecting women
and a determination on a case-by-case basis of whether they disadvantaged women. The laws deemed to advantage women, such
as job-protected leave after childbirth, even if they treated men
and women differently, should be retained. As Frieda Miller put
it, "identity of treatment" is not the same as equality.[21] Sometimes
it was necessary to treat men and women differently in order to
advance women's equality. To insist upon women's legal rights in
relation to men without regard to what happened to women's other
rights could result in less overall progress for women.

Class and Cold War politics were on full display in the 1948
hearings. Pauline Newman accused ERA proponents of being
"selfish careerists" without concern for the needs of low-income
women. Food and Tobacco Workers leader Elizabeth Sasuly agreed:
she characterized the ERA as "an empty concept of equality" offering women "the right to be exploited." As the male legislators
looked on, a few chortling at the squabbling women, NWP feminists returned the vitriol in kind. They called their opponents "lady
bountiful" sentimentalists and "lackeys" of male-led unions. They
defended the ERA as "vital to the American way of life" and dismissed the unions opposed to it as "communist."[22]

The Communist label would also soon be used to great effect
against the principal legislative sponsor of the 1947 Women's Status Bill. In 1950, Helen Gahagan Douglas, a consistent ally of the
social justice women's movement and a frequent sponsor of "equal
pay for equal work" bills as well as other progressive legislation,
lost her Senate bid in California to Richard Nixon. In a vicious
smear campaign, Nixon questioned her loyalty and that of her Jewish husband, Hollywood actor Melvyn Douglas, and claimed the
"Pink Lady" was "pink right down to her underwear."[23]

Needless to say, neither bill advanced very far in 1948 or in the decade following. But that did not mean the battle between social feminists and equal rights feminists subsided. Indeed, it raged on throughout the 1950s and would culminate in confrontations over equal pay and civil rights legislation in the early 1960s, with lasting consequences for women and for the nation's well-being.

Advances on the Civil Rights Front

Social justice feminists experienced more success on the civil rights front in the 1940s and 1950s than in their campaigns for extending social welfare or women's rights. As African Americans continued their mass exodus from the South in the 1940s and 1950s, settling primarily in the industrial cities of the North and Midwest, many exercised their voting rights for the first time and pulled the lever for Democrats. As African American political power grew, so too did momentum for a federal legislative response to racial violence and discrimination.

Politicians felt pressure as well from the rising swell of African American protest, individual and collective, in communities across the country. In 1942, Maida Springer, Pauli Murray, and laundry worker organizer and Amalgamated Clothing Workers official Dorothy Lowther Robinson led one of New York's first mass street protests against lynching and race segregation, a "silent parade" of five hundred marchers down Seventh Avenue. The three women carried a huge cloth banner, JIM CROW HAS GOT TO GO.[24] Four years later, the Garment Workers released Springer to organize a Madison Square Garden rally on behalf of replacing the defunct wartime fair employment agency with a permanent Fair Employment Practices Commission (FEPC) to prevent racial and religious discrimination in employment. The event drew seventeen thousand people.

The conservative minority in Congress, however, repeatedly shot down anti-lynching legislation and other civil rights measures, including calls for a permanent FEPC, a proposal strongly backed by the labor movement. Frustrated with Congress, civil rights activists turned to President Truman. Feeling pressure from an increasingly militant civil rights movement and aware too of the Cold War context—how U.S. aspirations to spread democracy abroad could be undercut by the nation's own domestic record of limited citizenship—Truman issued an executive order in 1946, establishing the President's Committee on Civil Rights. A year later, the committee's report, *To Secure These Rights,* condemned the denial of first-class citizenship to African Americans and other minorities and called for government action to ensure "the elimination of segregation based on race, color, creed, or national origin, from American life."[25] Truman endorsed the report and urged Congress to heed the committee's call for equal opportunity, an end to Jim Crow, anti-lynching laws, and abolition of poll taxes. Congress failed to respond. After A. Philip Randolph's coalition of unions and civil rights groups vowed once again to march on Washington, however, Truman issued executive orders in July 1948 desegregating the federal workforce and the armed services.

At the local level, some of the earliest and most successful struggles for civil rights occurred in unionized workplaces, with left-leaning industrial unions, especially those with large numbers of minority members, leading the way. These postwar assaults on the racial order of the workplace, campaigns that involved dismantling racial hierarchies in women's jobs as well as in men's, are often overlooked in histories of civil rights and women's rights. In the Packinghouse Workers, for example, Addie Wyatt and other black women formed a coalition with black men and other sympathetic workers, including whites as well as Mexican Americans and other minorities, to mount a series of workplace actions in the 1940s and 1950s that changed race relations on the job and in the community.

Historically, the jobs processing the bacon, hot dogs, chicken, and hamburgers consumed by millions of Americans were rigidly segregated by sex and race. The easier and cleaner jobs were reserved for white women. After the animal had been killed, cut into sections, and cleaned, white women trimmed the meat and then weighed, packed, and wrapped it. Black women could be found in the offal department, flushing worms and feces from animal intestines. As one white UPWA activist who worked on the line slicing bacon explained to an interviewer in 1939: "I'm in Sliced Bacon. That's supposed to be the lightest, cleanest place to work. They wouldn't take on a Negro girl if she was a college graduate."[26] With the backing of the union's white male leadership, women like Wyatt set out to change this state of affairs. Their first goal was not moving women into men's jobs but ending racial discrimination in female hiring.

Gaining the support of black men was a necessity. Black men were responsible for the first step in the meat production process: killing the animals. If they refused to do so, the plant shut down. In the late 1940s they did just that, bringing work to a halt in support of ending the racial segregation of "women's jobs." Breakthroughs occurred first in Chicago at Swift's after years of organizing by a multi-racial women's committee. Then other locals stepped up their anti-discrimination efforts. In Waterloo, Iowa, when the Rath Company hired black women in the sliced bacon department for the first time, white women threatened a walkout. Only when black men in the hog-kill department countered by refusing to work did the company decide to retain its new hires. By 1954, in meatpacking plants across the country, white and minority women now stood next to each other on the line, used the same rest rooms and locker rooms, ate in the same cafeteria, and were entitled to the same union rights and benefits.

Blue-collar workers, like those in the Packinghouse Union, also fought racial segregation in the community, integrating restau-

Caroline Davis (far left), Lillian Hatcher (standing), and William Oliver of the UAW
Fair Practices Department welcome Dorothy Height of the National Council of Negro
Women to the 1955 UAW Convention. Archives of Labor and Urban Affairs, Wayne State University.

rants near the plant and forming community organizations to agi-
tate for better housing, credit, and other basic necessities. In the
UAW, for example, African American Lillian Hatcher and white
southerner Caroline Davis, whose friendship deepened after their

arrest for eating together in a Jim Crow Detroit restaurant, sought similar kinds of reforms. As leaders of an influential multi-racial group of men and women linked to the union's Women's Department and its Civil Rights Division, they pressed the UAW to fight for the rights of all women to job security, promotional opportunities, and just wages. They lobbied within the UAW for more attention to workplace discrimination against married women, women of color, and mothers. They also partnered with civil rights organizations like the National Council of Negro Women and urged the UAW to throw its considerable political and financial weight behind the 1955 Montgomery bus boycotts and the other mass civil rights protests that would follow.

The Partial Victories of the 1960s

In 1960, with the election of John F. Kennedy as president and Democratic majorities in both the House and Senate, hope for New Deal–style reform at the federal level stirred once again. Like many other progressive reformers who had weathered the postwar conservative backlash and the political lull of the Eisenhower years, social justice feminists believed their agenda would finally get the hearing it deserved. The civil rights movement was now inspiring millions to action on behalf of the right of African Americans to education, jobs, and other basic needs. In addition, social justice feminists had played key and highly visible roles in Kennedy's presidential campaign, as had the labor movement as a whole. In 1960, the UAW's Lillian Hatcher, along with other women labor leaders, for example, had helped mobilize labor's ranks—including women trade unionists, then a quarter of all union members, as well as large numbers of working-class wives, mothers, and daughters in women's auxiliaries—to elect Kennedy and other Democrats to office.

Lillian Hatcher with a group of UAW volunteers during the 1960 presidential election.
Archives of Labor and Urban Affairs, Wayne State University.

Of equal importance, Esther Peterson had renewed her friendship with Kennedy in 1958 as she made the rounds in her new job as the Washington lobbyist for the AFL-CIO, the fifteen-million-member labor federation. Peterson voiced her support of Kennedy's candidacy early, before many other labor people. Later, she handled the labor desk for him at the Democratic Party national headquarters and put together a national three-hundred-member "Committee of Labor Women for Kennedy and Johnson" to coordinate labor support across the country. Peterson had gotten to know Kennedy when they worked together on minimum wage legislation after he was first elected to Congress in 1946. As she often laughingly recounted, in 1945, when her fellow labor lobbyists, all men from the big industrial unions—steel, auto, rubber—met her for the first time, they didn't know what to do with her. Finally someone said, "Oh, give her to Kennedy, he won't amount to much." But he did, and he remembered Peterson, her command of facts, and their compatibility in crafting legislative options in the 1940s as well as her substantial efforts on his behalf during the presidential campaigns. Kennedy appointed her director of the U.S. Women's Bureau and a few months later, in early 1961, promoted her to assistant secretary of labor, making her the most influential woman in the Kennedy administration. A thirty-year veteran of the labor movement and of social justice feminist politics, Peterson brought a long-standing reform agenda with her, and she moved quickly to act on it.

Shortly after Kennedy's inaugural, Peterson met with trade union women to discuss reviving the idea for a presidential commission on the status of women. She then formed a committee, including her longtime collaborator Kitty Ellickson, then AFL-CIO Social Security expert, as well as former laundry worker leader Dollie Robinson, to draft a proposal. Before approaching Kennedy, Peterson lined up her old friend Secretary of Labor Arthur Goldberg, a former labor counsel to the Steelworkers and the CIO, and other government officials. She also made sure she had the support of her base: women in labor organizations, in the Democratic Party, and in the social feminist women's organizations grouped around the Women's Bureau. In December 1961, Kennedy signed Executive Order 10980, setting up the President's Commission on the Status of Women (PCSW).

The two-year PCSW process involved hundreds of participants. Peterson served as executive vice chair and convinced Eleanor Roosevelt to act as chair, a largely honorary position. For the day-to-day coordination and the drafting of the commission's final report, she turned once again to Kitty Ellickson, who took a leave from the AFL-CIO. To the commission itself, Peterson persuaded Kennedy to appoint a mix of twenty-six powerful figures from government, business, labor, education, and the community, including her friends Mary Callahan of the Electrical Workers, National Council of Negro Women president Dorothy Height, and social historian and New Dealer Caroline Ware. Caroline Davis, Addie Wyatt, Bessie Hillman, Pauli Murray, and others in Peterson's circle of women reformers sat on the seven subcommittees advising the commission.

The commission's report, *American Women,* presented to the president on October 11, 1963, Eleanor Roosevelt's birthday, would be overshadowed by the tragedy of President Kennedy's assassination the following month. Nevertheless, within a year of its release, *American Women* sold sixty-four thousand copies, and governors across the country, surprised at the outcry it generated from women, formed state commissions on the status of women. Involving thousands of participants from all walks of life, these commissions, created an expanded and energized national network dedicated to women's reform. The commission's report, like the other 1963 feminist salvo, Betty Friedan's *Feminine Mystique,* was thus key in sparking the rise of a new mass women's movement.

The final report of the PCSW reflected many of the concerns and sensibilities of the postwar labor feminist network. "Full equality of rights" had been denied women, the report proclaimed, and government had an obligation to rectify the situation. The PCSW called for revaluing household and reproductive labor through social supports, including paid maternity leave, universal childcare services for women "whether they were working outside the home or not," and changes in Social Security that would allow housewives to build up equity as if they were earning wages. The commission insisted unequivocally on the right of *all* women to employment and noted the need to eliminate the "special discriminations" faced by low-income mothers and minority women. It favored opening up educational and training opportunities for women so that women could move into jobs traditionally held by men. At the same time, it recommended upgrading the jobs in which the vast majority of women worked. As part of that effort, *American Women* endorsed raising the minimum wage, equal pay for comparable work legislation, and the extension of New Deal statutes to cover those left out. Finally, the commission asked for a stronger governmental commitment to the right of workers to organize and bargain collectively and to programs enhancing women's political and civil leadership.[27]

American Women generated considerable controversy. In 1963, most commentators, at least those who took the report seriously, worried that by affirming women's rights to employment the report encouraged women to abandon their home responsibilities. In contrast, a decade later, critics faulted the commission for paying too much attention to the needs of mothers and homemakers and not enough to women's employment rights. By the 1970s, with a new feminist movement in full bloom, the PCSW report began to be described as timid and maternalist, meaning it overemphasized women's domestic identities. Some saw it as an anti-feminist document sponsored by an administration hostile to the ERA and to women's rights.

It is true that the PCSW did not endorse the ERA. It sidestepped the issue by relying on Pauli Murray's contention that women's equality of rights under the law could be advanced through the Fourteenth Amendment and thus the ERA "need not now be sought."[28] Murray's judgment carried particular weight among the commissioners because of her long and fierce advocacy against the twin evils of race and sex discrimination. (In 1965, while finishing her studies at Yale Law School—and becoming the first African American to receive a JSD from Yale—she would refine her legal theories further and publish a famous article on "Jane Crow," making explicit the parallels between sex- and race-based systems of exclusion.)[29]

Nevertheless, as the new feminist movement took up the ERA mantle in the 1970s, the commission's failure to endorse the proposed amendment made it appear conservative to many feminists. Its heavy reliance on state action and top-down solutions seemed dated as well. But perhaps most damning was the misreading of the report as a conservative document reinforcing the gender status quo. Quite the opposite was true. *American Women* assumed women's family and marketplace identities were equally valid and should be accommodated through major and "long overdue" change in government policy and employer practice. The report asserted that women deserved full equality—economic, political, and social. That was a bold and progressive formulation in 1963, and it remains so in the twenty-first century.

The 1963 Equal Pay Act

By the time Esther Peterson presented the commission's report to Kennedy in October, its recommendation of equal pay for comparable work legislation was moot. President Kennedy had signed the Equal Pay Act on June 10, 1963. For many on the commission, however, the new law was at best a mixed blessing. Peterson called it a first step but worried, and rightly so, that the crucial next steps would be long in coming.

Social justice feminists had been optimistic in 1962 when Caroline Davis and other UAW women lobbied Congress on behalf of equal pay. As Davis testified, the bill they supported conceived of equal pay in a capacious way. The majority of women would benefit whether they were the few in traditionally male jobs or the many in the pink-collar world. A legislative priority for social justice feminists since 1945, the 1962 equal pay bill had the backing of the AFL-CIO and many prominent Democrats, including Oregon congresswoman Edith Green.

President John F. Kennedy signing the Equal Pay Act, June 10, 1963. Peterson is fifth from the left in the front row. John F. Kennedy Library.

The global movement for equal pay was flourishing as well in the early 1960s. Maida Springer had cheered in 1951 in Geneva, sitting next to Esther Peterson, when the International Labor Organization approved its one hundredth international labor standard, the Convention on Equal Remuneration, which contained the broad comparable work language familiar to trade union women. By the early 1960s, over thirty nations around the world had adopted the convention as law. The United States, however, had not signed the international equal pay convention (and as of 2014 still has not); nor would it meet the convention's international norm in its own domestic equal pay legislation. In 1962, as the labor-backed equal pay bill inched along the tortuous route to becoming law, it met formidable opposition from the U.S. Chamber of Commerce, the National Association of Manufacturers, and key conservative legislators, women and men.

The opponents' strategy was not to block "equal pay" legislation altogether but to narrow it, ensuring that it affected only a small subset of women: those doing substantially the same job as men.

The defining moment occurred in the House debate. Katharine St. George, the same Republican congresswoman who had opposed the Women's Status Bill in 1947, rose to amend the bill, proposing to strike out "for work of comparable character" and substitute "for equal work." To St. George, the path to equality lay through "equal treatment," and women could only lay claim to first-class citizenship based on being the same as men.

Others jumped into the fray, arguing that "equal may mean exactly alike," and "if you put in the word 'equal,' we will have no equal pay bill at all." St. George rebutted that charge with a bow to a version of feminism that many would eventually conflate with feminism itself. "We do not want favors," she claimed. "What we really want is equality," and that "implies no difference."[30] St. George's amendment passed, and the Equal Pay Act, approved by both the House and the Senate the next year, retained her amendment.

Substituting "equal" for "comparable" limited the law's effectiveness dramatically. The 1963 Equal Pay Act only allowed for equalizing wages when men and women performed substantially similar tasks. By denying the sex bias in wage setting in female-majority jobs and the need for more broad-based comparisons, the law left pay in the majority of women's jobs unchanged. Many of these jobs would continue to pay poverty wages into the twenty-first century, even though, as with childcare, they were among some of the most valuable, demanding, and responsible jobs in society.

The 1964 Civil Rights Act and the "Sex" Amendment

By 1963, the top priority for social justice feminists was civil rights legislation. No woman gave a major speech that summer at the famous 1963 March on Washington for Jobs and Freedom; and although National Council of Negro Women president Dorothy Height was included in the leadership group for the march and sat on the podium looking out at the quarter of a million march-ers, there were no women or women's organizations represented in the march's official "big ten" organizing committee. Neverthe-less, countless women had long made securing first-class citi-zenship for all people a priority. Myra Wolfgang, Addie Wyatt, Maida Springer, Lillian Hatcher, Caroline Davis, Pauli Murray, and many others, as we have seen, had campaigned to bring an end to Jim Crow in the workplace, the military, schools, and other settings for decades. They helped pass fair employment practice laws prohibiting employment discrimination in the majority of states, and in 1961, they had been part of a powerful coalition of labor and civil rights groups that successfully con-vinced President Kennedy to sign an executive order banning "discrimination because of race, creed, color, or national origin" in businesses with federal contracts, a quarter of all private sector companies.

In 1963, however, what social justice reformers wanted was a com-prehensive federal civil rights law. Working with Dorothy Height and others, Esther Peterson had organized a national women's committee on civil rights to press for passage of federal civil rights legislation soon after she assumed her White House appointment, and at last, victory seemed achievable. In the wake of the march, civil rights legislation advanced, and following Kennedy's death in November, it made rapid strides in both houses, encountering few surprises. But on February 8, Democratic congressman Howard W. Smith, the influential southern conservative from Virginia and a sponsor of the ERA since 1945, introduced an amendment to what he called "this iniquitous piece of legislation" that threw the liberal forces, particularly the women, into turmoil.[31] With considerable jocularity and to much laughter, Smith proposed adding "sex" to Title VII of the civil rights bill, making it illegal to discriminate on the basis of sex as well as on the basis of race, ethnicity, religion, and national origin. Feminists divided on Smith's proposal, falling into camps that looked remarkably similar to those bedeviling the women's movement since the 1920s.

For the NWP leaders who asked Smith to introduce the amendment, women's rights were not a joke: they favored the passage of legislation outlawing discrimination on the basis of sex. At the same time, they remained divided over race and federal civil rights policy. Some in the NWP, including Alice Paul, may have sympathized with the proposed civil rights legislation and hoped that the addition of the sex amendment would not jeopardize the bill's passage. Indeed, Paul characterized the maneuverings over the sex amendment proposal as "sideshows" to the ERA.[32] Nevertheless, even for those like Paul who generally favored civil rights, the defeat of the civil rights bill was a risk worth taking if the issue of women's rights could be advanced.

Others, however, including Nina Horton Avery and Butler Franklin, the two NWP lieutenants who proposed the sex amendment to Smith, saw it not only as a way of advancing women's rights but also as a means to delay if not defeat civil rights legislation. They opposed the civil rights bill because it involved government regulation; in addition, they favored maintaining the racial status quo. Avery, long active in southern segregationist politics, wrote Smith in January 1964, explaining that adding the sex amendment was "from the standpoint of the NWP . . . merely a tool of strategy to take the pressure off the passage of any CRB [civil rights bill]." Thank God for members of Congress, she continued, "who will use their brains and energies to prevent a mongrel race in the U.S. and who will fight for the rights of white citizens in order that discrimination against them may be stopped."[33]

Esther Peterson and other social justice feminists were caught off guard by Smith's proposal. They too supported women's rights and saw sex discrimination in employment as a problem needing legislative intervention, but the question was how to balance that commitment with other concerns such as addressing race and class injustices. The sex amendment, they feared, like the ERA, would jeopardize woman-only labor laws. Moreover, adding the amendment might make it harder to pass the civil rights bill. Peterson called the possible defeat of the civil rights bill her "primary fear," and she did not initially support the sex amendment. Neither did most other social justice feminists. Peterson later elaborated, "I for one was not willing to risk advancing the rights of all women at the expense of the redress due black men and women."[34] For social justice feminists, lessening discrimination on the basis of sex did not always have priority over lessening other injustices.

In the raucous debate on the House floor over the sex amendment, its proponents relied unashamedly on race prejudice to boost their positions. Former NWP member and Democratic congresswoman from Michigan Martha Griffiths argued that without it, "white women will be last at the hiring gate." Her speech closed with a final racial appeal: "A vote against this amendment today by a white man is a vote against his wife, or his widow, or his daughter, or his sister." Midway through the debate, Republican congresswoman Catherine Dean May read a letter from NWP chair Emma Guffey Miller expressing alarm that without "any reference to civil rights for women" in this bill, the "white native-born American women of Christian religion" would be "discriminated against." Male congressmen from Alabama, South Carolina, and Arkansas now joined in, echoing the idea that the civil rights bill, if not amended, put white women at a disadvantage.[35]

The only congresswoman who spoke against the amendment was Edith Green, veteran Democrat from Oregon and perpetual sponsor of equal pay legislation. She favored women's rights but opposed the sex amendment because she believed it would "be used to help destroy the bill." As a "white woman" she had "been discriminated against," she volunteered, but "the Negro woman has suffered ten times the amount of discrimination." She concluded: "If I have to wait a few years to end this discrimination against me, [I am willing] if the rank discrimination against Negroes will be finally ended."[36]

In the end, the sex amendment passed. Although many supporters of the original civil rights bill voted against it, Southern senators and others not known for their advocacy of women's equality or civil rights voted in favor. Many then switched sides when the bill—which now included prohibitions against employment discrimination on the basis of sex as well as race, religion, and national origins—came up for its final vote. An overwhelming majority of liberals and moderates in both parties now endorsed the legislation with the blessing of their labor, civil rights, and women's movement allies; most conservative representatives, including Howard Smith, voted no.

After the passage of the 1964 Civil Rights Act, other legislative victories followed. In 1965, the Voting Rights Act struck down barriers to political participation across the country, including land and property ownership requirements for voting as well as the infamous literacy tests and "grandfather clauses," which by limiting suffrage to those whose grandfathers cast ballots disenfranchised descendants of slaves. Women's suffrage had finally been extended to the many left out in 1920. In 1966, Congress raised the minimum wage and at long last broadened the wage-and-hour provisions of the 1938 Fair Labor Standards Act to cover the majority of workers, including the majority of women, though still excluding domestic and agricultural workers who were mainly people of color. In subsequent years, a similar alliance of labor, civil rights, and poor people's movements would achieve additional gains. Despite overheated rhetoric about welfare state dependency from a rising conservative opposition, over the course of the 1970s Congress would expand aid to the poor, primarily mothers and their children, raise minimum wage levels several times, and make new groups, including domestic workers, eligible for Social Security and other benefits.

The Torch Passes

Nineteen sixty-six marked the high point of legislative unity for social justice feminism. That summer, at the annual meeting in Washington of the state commissions on the status of women, close allies for a quarter century found themselves on opposing sides. A new feminism, with new organizations, leadership, and priorities, was surfacing.

Even before the meeting commenced, tensions flared. The two most prominent feminists in the Johnson administration, Peterson and U.S. Women's Bureau director Mary Dublin Keyserling, a stalwart New Dealer and former National Consumers' League leader, felt under siege from those on the outside who in their view lacked sufficient sympathy for a liberal administration attacked from the right and left. Some of the strain among women activists reflected the seismic shift under way in the political culture: President Lyndon B. Johnson's 1965 escalation of the Vietnam War created bitter animosities among progressives; older interracial and cross-class alliances were breaking apart; the liberal commitment to worker organization and class-based policies was waning. The New Deal generation with its politics of social solidarity and security, forged in economic depression and world war, was being eclipsed.

Tension over tactics—whether to pursue older strategies of gradualism and loyalty to the Democratic Party or adopt more confrontational and politically independent approaches—was palpable as women activists descended on Washington. Frustration with the Johnson administration's foot-dragging on women's rights was just as evident: proposals from the national and state commissions on the status of women were languishing; the Equal Employment Opportunities Commission (EEOC), charged with enforcing the 1964 Civil Rights Act, was not doing its job. It had ignored the complaints of flight attendants who charged the airlines with unfairly firing them at age thirty-two; it failed to see the problem with sex-segregated "Help Wanted—Male" and "Help Wanted—Female" job advertisements or with hiring policies funneling men into managerial positions and women into dead-end clerical jobs. One male commissioner called the sexual integration of the workplace the "Bunny problem," referring to the absurdity of men being Playboy Bunnies, and labeled the idea of a work world in which men and women held the same jobs as "ridiculous." The only woman on the EEOC, Aileen Hernandez, a Howard University–educated daughter of Jamaican immigrants and a former organizer for the International Ladies' Garment Workers' Union in California, would soon resign, disgusted with the commission's failure to take sex discrimination seriously.

As those gathered at the annual meeting debated what to do, Keyserling, chairing the conference, tried to keep order. She acknowledged the various complaints but cautioned against undermining and embarrassing the Democratic administration. She also warned that the EEOC needed to proceed slowly lest state laws protecting low-income women be lost in the rush to open up opportunity. Betty Friedan and Pauli Murray disagreed, as did other influential women such as political scientist Kathryn (Kay) Clarenbach, the chair of Wisconsin's state commission on the status of women, and, in a surprising break with their union sisters, UAW leaders Caroline Davis and Dorothy Haener.

At lunch, as speakers droned on, the dissidents finalized their overturning woman-only labor standards legislation, a stance that infuriated many of their old allies. Addie Wyatt too embraced the new women's movement, joining NOW early on and, in 1974, founding the Coalition of Labor Union Women, which put abortion rights, women's leadership in unions, and equal rights for women in hiring, promotion, and pay among its top priorities.

By the early 1970s, only Myra Wolfgang and a few other hold-outs actively opposed the new feminism. Wolfgang testified against the ERA before the Senate in May 1970, claiming that for "Tillie the Toiler" the ERA would bring "an equality of mistreatment." Betty Friedan, representing the pro-ERA forces, roared back, "I accuse the male labor establishment of gross neglect and blindness to the problems of working women." The "Aunt Toms" who agree with them, she added, with a nod to Wolfgang, didn't help matters either. Wolfgang and Friedan traded insults again a few months later at a Women's Teach-in at Wayne State University. This time when Friedan trotted out the "Aunt Tom" label, Wolfgang exploded. "Look who's calling who 'Aunt Tom,'" she retorted. She turned to the audience and pointed to Friedan. "She's the real Aunt Tom, the Chamber of Commerce's Aunt Tom. Anyone who tries to repeal women's protective legislation is doing the bosses' work." Wolfgang's objections to the new women's movement went beyond the ERA or her personal squabbles with Betty Friedan. In a 1971 address before the American Association of University Women, Wolfgang challenged the new feminism's claim to universalism and to represent all women. "I disagree with the approach that calls for the unity of women under the nebulous slogan that 'Sisterhood is Powerful,'" she began. Then, with a sly rewriting of a phrase from Rudyard Kipling's poem "The Ladies," in which the male protagonist judges all the many women with whom he has consorted as alike, as "sisters under the skin," she begged to differ: "The Colonel's Lady and Judy O'Grady may be

Attendees at NOW's Organizing Conference, October 1966. This group, along with the women who gathered in June 1966, are honored as NOW's founders. Courtesy of the Natio Organization for Women.

plan, hatched the night before in Friedan's hotel room, for new organization: an "NAACP for women," devoted to women rights much the same way as the NAACP pursued the rights of African Americans. The National Organization for Women, the leading national organization of the new feminism, was born In its 1966 Statement of Purpose, drafted by Friedan and Pauli Murray and adopted at the founding convention in October, NOW vowed to advance the "unfinished revolution toward true equality, now."[37]

Social justice feminists divided in their response to NOW and to the new women's movements gathering power among college students and others. Caroline Davis and Dorothy Haener, among NOW's founding members, embraced the new feminism whole-heartedly. They convinced the UAW to support NOW financially and give it office space its first year. Although they and other UAW women left NOW briefly in 1968, objecting to its endorsement of the ERA, they eagerly returned a year later, having convinced the UAW to change its position on the ERA—the first union to do so. Davis and other UAW labor feminists also urged the EEOC to pursue sex discrimination claims aggressively, even if it meant sisters under the skin but their lives, concerns, and needs are radically different."[38]

A third group, best exemplified by Esther Peterson and Kitty Ellickson, took a middle path: they were neither enthusiastic nor hostile to the new feminism. In 1971, Peterson dropped her opposition to the ERA. Few woman-only state laws remained, she reasoned, and "now I believe we should direct our efforts toward replacing discriminatory state laws with good labor standards that will protect both men and women. . . . History is moving in this direction," she added, and "women must move with it." Relieved because she thought a century of acrimony over the ERA had finally come to an end, Peterson urged her political allies to move on and put the old battles behind them. At the same time, she worried that in a new unified feminist movement, the needs of low-income women and women of color might be lost. Don't forget, she cautioned, the many women not well positioned to take advantage of opportunity.[39]

Ellickson too had mixed feelings about the changes taking place. She had spent her life arguing for women's rights and trying to make sure that the labor movement, employers, and government took women seriously. Now thousands of women were taking up the cause, continuing the struggle for women's equality and freedom. She welcomed what she called a "different wave in the long struggle for women's equality" and marveled at the new movement's bold attack on the psychological underpinnings of women's oppression.[40] Young women, she wrote, were digging deep into their own psyches and asking whether they should be sacrificing for others and putting the needs of others first; these questions were important and must be asked and answered. Yet she too worried that other issues would be pushed aside and forgotten. The younger generation of activists, born in prosperity and educated for success, might find it hard to understand those without such advantages. Economic disparities must not be ignored, she warned, nor should the caregiving, perhaps even self-sacrifice, necessary for societal survival be underestimated.

In 1971, Anne Draper, a 1938 Hunter College graduate turned garment worker organizer, had a similar set of concerns as she stood before the California Industrial Welfare Commission, testifying on behalf of raising the minimum wage, and held aloft a tattered Woolworth's bra. She was speaking not just for Woolworth workers as Myra Wolfgang did in 1937 but for Woolworth shoppers. Yet she too identified as a social justice feminist, and she too was a veteran of the 1930s and the upheavals that followed. Many women today, given their paltry income, could afford at best one bra every couple of years, she informed the state commissioners. This one, sad to say, lasted six months. It was time for a raise.

As the next chapter tells, a new women's movement famously stuffed bras, girdles, and other intimate items in a "Freedom Trash Can" on the Atlantic City boardwalk in 1968 as they demonstrated against the Miss America Pageant. They wanted the freedom to define their own sexuality and beauty and not have it determined by the judges. But for Draper and those she represented, the bra was a potent symbol as well. Women deserved better than a tattered bra, she argued, whether they sewed it or bought it.

Today's low-wage workers shop at WalMart. The last Woolworth's closed in 1997. And while the issues of Woolworth's workers and shoppers could be dismissed as belonging to another era, they remain far more relevant than often realized. Anne Draper's call for a living wage still resonates in the twenty-first century, as does the larger reform agenda of her generation of social justice feminists. They believed in sex equality and would have applauded the progress women today have made toward that goal. At the same time, they remind us that the women's movement needs to be about more than sex equality. Economic disparities among women are extreme in the twenty-first century, and without decent jobs and sufficient income, dignity and real freedom for most women will remain elusive. They wanted to make it possible for women and men to have fuller, more satisfying lives at home and on the job. It's still not too much to ask.

1. Dorothy Sue Cobble, *Dishing It Out: Waitresses and Their Unions in the Twentieth Century* (Urbana: University of Illinois Press, 1991), 97–98; Dana Frank, "Girl Strikers Occupy Chain Store, Win Big," in Howard Zinn, Dana Frank, and Robin D. G. Kelley, *Three Strikes: Miners, Musicians, Salesgirls, and the Fighting Spirit of Labor's Last Century* (Boston: Beacon Press, 2001), 57–118, quote 98.
2. Quotes from Dorothy Sue Cobble, *The Other Women's Movement: Workplace Justice and Social Rights in Modern America* (Princeton: Princeton University Press, 2004), 2–3, and Jean Maddern Pitrone, *Myra: The Life and Times of Myra Wolfgang, Trade Union Leader* (Wyandotte, MI: Calibre Books, 1980), 124.
3. Interview with Caroline Davis by Ruth Meyerowitz, July 23, 1976, Twentieth Century Trade Union Woman: Vehicle for Social Change Oral History Project, Institute of Labor and Industrial Relations, University of Michigan–Wayne State University (TUWOHP), 83, 112–14.
4. "Lady Labor Leader: To Keep Labor Peace and Prosperity in an Indiana Factory, the Boss of Local 764 Just Acts like a Woman," *Life*, June 30, 1947, 83–85.
5. Quote from Addie Wyatt, " 'An Injury to One Is an Injury to All': Addie Wyatt Remembers the Packinghouse Workers Union," *Labor Heritage* 12 (Winter/Spring 2003): 27. See also interview with Addie Wyatt by Rick Halpern and Roger Horowitz, January 30, 1986, United Packinghouse Workers of America Oral History Project, State Historical Society of Wisconsin, Madison, and Cobble, *The Other Women's Movement*, 31–33, 201–03.
6. Mary Anderson, "Should There be Labor Laws for Women? . . . Yes, Says Mary Anderson," *Good Housekeeping*, September 1925, 52.
7. The identity of the child's father is not known. At times the two women spoke of their daughter as adopted, but other historical documents point to Miller's pregnancy.
8. Thomas Piketty and Emmanuel Saez, "Income Inequality in the US, 1913-2002," *Quarterly Journal of Economics* 118, no. 1 (2003): 1–41.
9. Cobble, *The Other Women's Movement*, 34; Esther Peterson with Winifred Conkling, *Restless: The Memoirs of Labor and Consumer Activist Esther Peterson* (Washington, DC: Caring Publishing, 1995), 13–15; Esther Peterson, "The World Beyond the Valley," *Sunstone* 15:5, issue 85 (November 1991): 23.
10. Interview with Maida Springer, TUWOHP, 141–42.

11. Rita R. Heller, "*Women of Summer: The Bryn Mawr Summer School for Women Workers, 1921–1938*" (Ph.D. diss., Rutgers University, 1986), 70–73.

12. Slogan from U.S. Employment Service War Manpower Division recruitment poster designed by Vernon Grant, 1944.

13. Carmen R. Chavez, "Coming of Age During the War: Reminiscences of an Albuquerque Hispana," *New Mexico Historical Review* 70, no. 4 (October 1995): 396–97.

14. Wyatt, " 'An Injury to One Is an Injury to All,' " 26–27.

15. In the documentary film by Connie Field, *The Life and Times of Rosie the Riveter*, Clarity Productions, 1980.

16. Cobble, *The Other Women's Movement*, 121–22.

17. Wyatt, " 'An Injury to One Is an Injury to All,' " 29.

18. Cobble, *The Other Women's Movement*, 106.

19. Cobble, *The Other Women's Movement*, 64.

20. Cobble, *The Other Women's Movement*, 65.

21. Cobble, *The Other Women's Movement*, 65.

22. Cobble, *The Other Women's Movement*, 62, 66.

23. Sally Denton, *The Pink Lady: The Many Lives of Helen Gahagan Douglas* (New York: Bloomsbury Press, 2009), 158.

24. Springer interview, TUWOHP, 141–42; Yevette Richards, *Conversations with Maida Springer: A Personal History of Labor, Race, and International Relations* (Pittsburgh: University of Pittsburgh Press, 2004), 124.

25. *To Secure These Rights: The Report of President Harry S. Truman's Committee on Civil Rights*, edited and with an introduction by Steven Lawson (Boston: Bedford/St. Martin's Press, 2004), iv.

26. "Interview with Mary Hammond" and "Interview with Anna Novak" in *First-Person America*, ed. Ann Banks (New York: Vintage Books, 1980), 54, 64.

27. President's Commission on the Status of Women (PCSW), *American Women* (Washington, DC: Government Publications Office, 1963).

28. For the ERA quote and the argument that the U.S. Constitution "now embodies equality of rights for men and women," see PCSW, *American Women*, 45–46.

29. Pauli Murray and Mary O. Eastwood, "Jane Crow and the Law: Sex Discrimination and Title VII," *George Washington Law Review* 43, no. 2 (1965): 232–56.

30. Cobble, *The Other Women's Movement*, 165.

31. Jo Freeman, "How 'Sex' Got into Title VII: Persistent Opportunism as a Maker of Public Policy," *Law and Inequality: A Journal of Theory and Practice* 9, no. 2 (March 1991): 163–184; for quote, 171.

32. Freeman, "How 'Sex' Got into Title VII," 174.

33. Cobble, *The Other Women's Movement*, 175.

34. Esther Peterson, "The Kennedy Commission," in *Women in Washington*, ed. Irene Tinker (Beverly Hills, CA: Sage Publications, 1983), 31.

35. *Congressional Record, House,* vol. 110, pt. 2, February 8, 1964, 2578–80, 2582–84.

36. *Congressional Record, House,* vol. 110, pt. 2, February 8, 1964, 2581–82.

37. 1966 NOW Statement of Purpose available at www.now.org/history/purpos66.html accessed July 6, 2013.

38. Cobble, *The Other Women's Movement,* 192–93.

39. Cobble, *The Other Women's Movement,* 191.

40. Cobble, *The Other Women's Movement,* 196.

Stewardesses on strike against TWA, 1970. Photograph by Cathy Cade, courtesy of the Bancroft Library, University of California, Berkeley.

THE WOMEN'S LIBERATION MOVEMENT

Linda Gordon

T he young feminists' protest at the 1968 Miss America contest symbolized women's enslavement to beauty by throwing items such as hair curlers, girdles, and a bra into a garbage can. But it was probably not a ragged bra, for these protesters could afford new ones. The difference between the two bras can represent both the strength and the weakness of their movement: strength because the protest symbolized a feminist critique that reached beyond economic discrimination to encompass an entire culture; weakness because the protesters were largely (though not completely) middle-class women whose own economic security made it hard for them—although they tried—to create a movement that included less privileged women.

In that year it seemed there might be two women's movements, separate and somewhat suspicious of each other. NOW, founded in 1966, had pulled together labor union, professional, and political women to mount campaigns for equal opportunity for employed women. Between 1967 and 1969 a younger generation of women, influenced by the civil rights struggle and the anti–Vietnam War campaign, came together to form what was soon called the wom-

Cartoonist and date unknown.

en's liberation movement. They sought a more holistic transformation of the society, one that would do away with male dominance in every sphere—in private as well as public—and would challenge all the older gender patterns. Like all the other radicals of the New

Left, they tended to be somewhat disdainful of their elders for not being militant enough. But this separation of the feminist generations did not last long, and for many women outside the big cities, the separation never existed, because the movement quickly became vastly larger and more varied than the sum of its organizations. By the early 1970s, these women collectively created the largest social movement in U.S. history.

Many writers have labeled the protest at the 1968 Miss America beauty pageant as the founding event of the women's liberation movement. Identifying dramatic episodes as discrete beginnings creates a discursive trope that lives on in collective memory. The civil rights movement is said to begin when Rosa Parks wouldn't give up her bus seat to a white man. The gay rights movement is said to begin when patrons at the Stonewall bar resisted a police raid. Similarly with the 1968 Miss America pageant. All these events were vivid and photogenic, and by attracting media coverage brought attention to the movement, but to credit them with setting off mass movements is misleading. Rosa Parks was a member of a group that had been planning action for several years. Gay rights advocates had been organizing for over a decade. The women's liberation movement had already conducted several national meetings and invented consciousness raising before the Miss America event, and immediately afterward that protest was criticized by other feminists for seeming to blame the women who entered beauty contests, without spelling out how the mainstream culture socialized women into feeling that beauty was their most important trait.

To get even an inkling of the range of feminisms, we could identify many founding events. Here are a few. Every one of them illustrates a major area of women's movement activism, every one energized many further developments, and every one—in a style typical of the movement's diversity—stimulated disagreement, criticism, and new tactics.

- The National Welfare Rights Organization, established in 1966, was equally part of the civil rights and women's movements. Although led at first by an African American man, George Wiley, by 1973 it was headed by Johnnie Tillmon—a sharecropper's daughter who worked in a California industrial laundry (where she was the union's shop steward) until she became ill and was forced to turn to welfare to support her children. She advanced a feminist view of the work of raising children and analyzed the problem of single mothers as derived from the low wages that made it impossible for them to simultaneously earn for and care for their children.

- In 1968, Fran Beal published "Double Jeopardy: To Be Black and Female," which became a founding document of the Black Women's Alliance. She had been an NAACP member in college at the University of Wisconsin, and then lived for seven years in Paris, where she was educated by the movement against French colonialism in Algeria. The "Double Jeopardy" article laid out some of the foundational arguments of African American feminism: the doubled oppression—racial and sexual—of black women, the economic exploitation based on class, race, and sex, and the coercive sterilization of women of color.

- In 1969, New York was moving toward legalizing abortion— seventeen states would do so by the time of *Roe v. Wade* four years later—and as part of that legislative process, a committee of the state legislature held hearings on abortion. The committee was all male, and the "experts" testifying were fourteen men and a nun. Kathie Sarachild was so furious when she saw the lineup of "experts" on women's reproductive needs that she stood up at the hearing and demanded a chance to speak. She was, unsurprisingly, refused, but a month later the New York City feminist group Redstockings held a public speakout on abortion at the Washington Square Methodist Church. To an audience of nine hundred, twelve women spoke of having had illegal abortions, explaining their reasons and their experiences, refusing guilt or apology. To understand the impact of the event, one needs to understand how some women's travails were made worse by being, literally, unspeakable. Breast cancer was one: it wasn't polite to speak of breasts in mixed company, and cancer in a breast seemed to stigmatize the woman herself, much as rape did (and still does in many places). Abortion was equally unadmittable: it marked a woman as not respectable.

- Also in 1969, members of the Boston women's liberation organization Bread and Roses produced the first version of *Our Bodies, Ourselves*, the pioneer women's health manual. Originally a 190-page stapled booklet, printed on cheap newsprint paper, sold for seventy-five cents, and distributed by a New Left underground press, it became a commercial-press bestseller ten years later—with all profits going into the women's health movement. At least 4.5 million copies in thirty-one different languages have now been sold. Its information on diet, alcohol and other drugs, occupational health and safety, birth control, violence, childbirth, and parenting is now not even recognized as feminist because it has become so mainstream. But take note: at first it was banned by schools and public libraries and denounced as "obscene trash" by conservatives.

- In 1970, a hundred feminists conducted an eleven-hour "takeover" of the *Ladies' Home Journal*, the country's biggest-circulation (at fourteen million) women's magazine, to protest its discriminatory hiring and promotion—its senior editors were almost all male—and its articles that assumed women were incapable of serious reading. They demanded equal pay and promotion for women and, in particular, hiring African American women. The editor, John Mack Carter, was at first furious and stubborn but ultimately caved, agreeing that the magazine would publish a women's liberation supplement. Looking back years later, he remarked, "Confrontation is certainly effective on the confrontee"—something that the women's movement was rapidly learning.[1]

- In 1971, a thousand women from all over North America met with women leaders from Vietnam in Vancouver, Canada. Most members of women's liberation opposed the U.S. intervention in Vietnam (and later Cambodia). American women in particular, infuriated and agonized by the napalm, herbicides, firebombing, village razing, and massacres of women and children to which Vietnam was being subjected, flocked to Vancouver to express solidarity with the Vietnamese struggle for independence. They had cathected emotionally with Vietnamese heroines portrayed in the news and were eager to meet them and express sisterhood.

- In 1971, a female janitor at Chicago's city hall contacted the Chicago Women's Liberation Union (CWLU) to ask for help. She did the same work as the male janitors but received lower pay, and although she had more seniority than the men, she was passed over when it came time to get daytime as opposed to night work. The CWLU then researched the civil service codes, anti-discrimination laws, and city budgets, worked with a progressive alderman to publish a study, and set off a campaign by marching on the mayor's office. Success didn't come easily, but the feminist group created an ongoing project, DARE, or Direct Action for Rights in Employment, and eventually won.

- In 1972, women at the University of Massachusetts in Boston, both students and faculty, had been agitating for a daycare center for several years. (The school enrolled many "returning" women students, working-class mothers who could not afford commercial childcare.) When the university repeatedly promised to consider the need but did nothing, a group of about a dozen mothers arrived unannounced at the president's office, with their toddlers, asking to speak with him. When he once again said he would consider the request in due time, they conducted a mother-child sit-in. The president left. The mothers then told his secretary that they were staying and might supply the children with crayons—but not paper. That grabbed his attention, and before long there was a daycare center.

These "firsts" could have been multiplied many times.

There were no "lasts," no swan songs or concluding events; social movements fade out gradually. But the fade-outs are by no means failures. It is the nature of social movements not to endure. They make their impact through intense, mass participation, periods when participants spend prodigious energy and devote a great deal of time to activism. Except for those who can earn a living through advocacy, few people can maintain these levels of dynamism and time commitment indefinitely. Students graduate and get jobs; adults become parents; energies flag. By the 1980s activism was shrinking, vigor weakening. Like a powerful and fast-flowing river, though, it had radically changed the terrain. It moved rocks, carved out new courses, and deposited new soil, producing new gender structures. The new riverbed was felt everywhere: in health, reproductive choices, media and culture, employment, parenting, education, sex, and man-woman, woman-woman, and parent-child relations. The changes were self-perpetuating, as women sensed new opportunities and used them to make further changes.

This chapter examines the women's liberation movement that flourished from 1967 to the mid-1980s. It discusses its organizing methods, its theory, its problems, and above all its activism. But first, let me introduce some of its leaders, who may provide a taste of the movement's diversity of political identities and backgrounds.

Elizabeth Martínez, known as Betita, was born in Chevy Chase, Maryland, a suburb of segregated Washington, D.C., in 1925, the only child of a Mexican father and a Euro-American mother. Her father, Manuel Guillermo Martínez, who spoke proudly of the Mexican revolution, had moved up into the middle class, becoming a professor of Spanish literature at Georgetown University. But in Washington, she and her dark-skinned father had to sit in the back of the buses. The girl next door was not allowed to play with the Mexican girl. A superb student, she became the first Latina to attend Swarthmore College. After graduating in 1946 she worked in New York City for a publisher, for the UN, and for *The Nation* magazine. Taking on her mother's Anglo maiden name, Sutherland, because she knew she would be unable to get an editorial job with the name Martínez, she became a skilled writer and editor and a member of New York's literati. She married the well-known writer Hans Koningsberger (later he called himself Hans Koning). Nevertheless, in 1965, already almost forty, she quit her job and joined the staff of the civil rights group SNCC (Student Nonviolent Coordinating Committee). She had already demonstrated her interest in Left politics by persuading her employers at Simon and Schuster to publish a photographic book on civil rights, *The Movement* (1964). Then a book of her own, as Elizabeth Sutherland of SNCC, the gripping *Letters from Mississippi*. The two books together were immensely influential in mobilizing white support for civil rights.

Increasingly aware of the sexism of the literary world and the New Left, Sutherland returned to New York in 1968 and joined a small women's group, where she was often the only woman of color. She began writing feminist pieces including a humorous one organized as questions and answers. "Don't some women naturally want to be housewives? A: Anyone who thinks she feels good . . . after washing the 14,789th batch of sparkling dishes isn't being 'natural'; she's literally lost her mind."[2] The group happened to be meeting on the day Martin Luther King Jr. was assassinated, and Elizabeth could think of nothing else; the others wanted to continue with the previously planned topic. She was shocked and angry. "This is just too white for me. . . . I'm outta here!" She never went back.[3] This was not, however, a break with feminism. Instead she became a Chicana feminist, an identity she acted on for the rest of her life. She is eighty-nine as we write.

Born twenty-five years later than Betita Martínez, in 1950 in Chicago, Karen Nussbaum was the daughter of middle-class Jews with progressive politics. She got involved in the movement against the Vietnam War in high school and at the University of Chicago and dropped out of school in her second year: college paled compared to the thrill of the movement. In 1970, she went as a volunteer to Cuba in the Venceremos Brigade, a project of young New Leftists who tried to help the Cuban economy by harvesting sugarcane. Afterward she moved to Boston, where the women's liberation movement was at full gallop. To support herself, she got a job as a clerical worker at Harvard, a job she initially thought of as temporary but which ultimately led to her life's work. She got involved first in typical women's liberation activities—silk-screening posters, studying karate, setting up free classes for women in everything from auto mechanics to political theory. Bread and Roses, the Boston women's liberation movement organization, had joined in community protests against Harvard's taking over more and more of working- and middle-class Cambridge. In 1971, Bread and Roses women executed a dramatic takeover of an abandoned Harvard building, hoping to make it a women's center. Karen joined hundreds of other young feminists who camped out there for a week; she would head for her job at Harvard during the day, then return to the building to sleep. (Harvard capitulated by buying a house for the movement, where the Cambridge Women's Center still operates. More importantly, the takeover demonstrated the power of militant collective action.)

Soon Karen began to resent the low pay and indignities of her Harvard job and sense the discontent among other clericals. With feminist friends she formed a lunchtime discussion group among these workers, which grew into the famous "9to5" organization of clerical workers, honored in a major 1980 film by that name; in the film three clericals (played by Jane Fonda, comedian Lily Tomlin, and country-western icon Dolly Parton) carry out revenge against an egotistical, lying, harassing sexist boss. From 9to5 the union 925, SEIU, was born, and Nussbaum became a career fighter for working women. President of the union until 1993, she was then appointed by President Bill Clinton to heard the Women's Bureau of the U.S. Department of Labor, then moved to head the Working Women's Department of the AFL-CIO. In 2003, she founded Working America, the community affiliate of the AFL-CIO, representing workers who do not have a union on the job.

Martínez and Nussbaum had the advantage of parents sympathetic to their progressive values. Shulamith Firestone did not. She was born Shulamith Bath Shmuel Ben Ari Feuerstein, the second of six children of Orthodox Jewish parents, in Ottawa, Canada, in 1945. Her father soon moved the family to Kansas City and changed their name to Firestone. He ruled them all in an authoritarian, censorious manner, creating a home "riddled with accusations, guilt and violence," in the words of one obituary. (Firestone died in 2013.) Temperamentally assertive, Shulie was perpetually in conflict with her father, particularly by defying his religious strictures; her sister recalled that he "threw his rage at Shulie."[4] First sent to a yeshiva, she later attended the Art Institute of Chicago, where she met young women's liberationists. She moved to New York City in 1967. A charismatic woman, she soon founded New York Radical Women (NYRW, with Elizabeth Sutherland Martínez as its only nonwhite member), at first a small consciousness-raising group, and her personal magnetism attracted followers; they remember her as "firebrand" and "incandescent." NYRW was one of a succession of New York City feminist groups that arose and disappeared, but Firestone began to study the history of the women's rights movement and to write. With amazing commitment and speed, she wrote *The Dialectic of Sex*, published in 1970 while the women's liberation period of the movement was still in its babyhood.

The book was calculatedly provocative. Firestone even advocated laboratory, rather than sexual, reproduction as a means of liberating women—a proposal ignored by other feminists. She had a deep-seated and highly individualist need to be always walking the most radical edge. But her appreciation of the nineteenth-century women's rights movement and her brave attempt to analyze how women's subordination was carried out through every aspect of society were extremely influential. Had she not burned out so quickly, she might have fulfilled her dream of becoming another Simone de Beauvoir, the French partner of Jean-Paul Sartre and author of the globally influential 1949 feminist book *The Second Sex*.

Consciousness Raising

These three prominent feminists represent different feminist streams. But the energy behind all the streams arose from a common ground: consciousness raising (CR), a process named in 1968 that spread throughout the United States and then the world. Subordinated groups had been forever practicing CR without the name, discussing and airing their grievances—"speaking bitterness," as the Chinese revolutionaries called the process. By institutionalizing consciousness raising as a method of organizing and developing social analysis, however, women's liberation made a unique contribution to political activism. Pam Allen of the San Francisco group Sudsofloppen—a nonsensical and lighthearted name chosen to signify their open, exploratory discussions—identified four processes in consciousness raising: opening up, sharing, analyzing, and abstracting. Although some critics accused con-

"Breaking Out," 1970, author unknown.

sciousness raising of narcissism and do-nothing-ism, in its first years it was, to the contrary, laying the groundwork for activism. In fact, it *was* activism, for in changing consciousness, it made social change.

The consciousness-raising route to change involved opening

up to a small group of women about personal matters. One set of sample questions for discussion included, Are you a "nice" girl? Have you ever faked an orgasm? Do you feel guilty if your house is dirty or messy? Do you worry about being truly feminine? How do you think men see you? Do you feel competitive with other women? As one woman wrote about consciousness raising, "Nothing upside-downed my world as much. . . . I learned that maybe I wasn't so odd after all, because maybe, just maybe, patriarchal social constructions had caused the various forms of discrimination I'd experienced all my life, both as a woman and as a person of color. I was overjoyed. I embraced my new *friend, feminism*."[5] Another wrote, "The light was blinding, and then illuminating— and, I must say, the illumination was an astonishing comfort. . . . To be a feminist in the early 1970s—bliss was it in that dawn, to be alive."[6] When others belittled consciousness-raising groups, calling them "coffee klatches, hen parties or bitch sessions . . . we responded by saying, 'Yes, bitch, sisters, bitch.'" In fact, one woman pointed out that coffee klatches were "a historic form of women's resistance."[7]

By changing women, consciousness raising changed all sorts of relations, often without conscious plan. Women's raised consciousness changed everyday experience, transforming relations with fathers, mothers, siblings, boyfriends, husbands, children, bosses, supervisors, teachers, auto mechanics, shop clerks . . . It was consciousness raising that made the women's liberation movement different from NOW: the younger women first grasped and exposed the ubiquitousness of the relationships, both public and personal, that structure domination and inequality. Within a few years, the differences between the older and younger streams of feminism began to fade.

Feminist organizing differed from that of the civil rights and labor movements, because unlike members of those movements, who knew that they were discriminated against and exploited, many white middle-class women were unconscious of their own oppression and limited opportunities. This was partly because many of them had spent most of their years in school, where sex discrimination was less marked than in the worlds of employment and housewifery. But their lack of consciousness also arose from accepting the gender system as a "natural" and inevitable out-growth of their sex. They had to unlearn what Marxists call a false consciousness. The impact of consciousness-raising groups can be seen in the fact that most Americans today understand the differ-ence between "sex," a biological category, and "gender," a matter of socialization. This was a distinction entirely new in 1969.

Exploring the hidden injuries of gender had to be accomplished in small and women-only groups. The groups provided permis-sion to complain and vent anger without fear of consequences and offered freedom to explore the intimate. They also provided com-parisons that gave rise to analyses. As Amy Kesselman recalled, "It replaced self-hatred with both anger and political analysis; it made sense of the world, reconnected me with other women, and gave shape to a host of unformed thoughts and feelings that had lurked for years in the shadows of my consciousness."[8]

Women were learning by questioning *all* the conventions of gen-der and male dominance. As one consciousness-raising group mem-ber put it, "In the sixties I knew, successful women were successful at pleasing men."[9] It was as if they became anthropologists, study-ing themselves and their communities, unearthing the processes of gender and male dominance. They were claiming that they were the experts on their own lives, refusing to defer any longer to the doc-tors and preachers and politicians who declaimed about what was normal for women. Their meetings were not therapy, although they were supportive; they were not bitch sessions, although plenty of anger and pain was let loose. For most, they were exhilarating and empowering. As poet and journalist Susan Sutheim wrote:

today
i lost my temper.

temper, when one talks of metal
means make strong,
perfect.

temper, for humans, means angry
irrational
bad

today i found my temper.
i said,
you step on my head . . .
today i think
i prefer my head to your clumsiness.

today i begin
to find
myself.

tomorrow
perhaps
i will begin
to find
you.[10]

They were making themselves the heroes of their own lives. But they sensed that this process could only happen collectively. When women trade experiences and emotions, much depends on the responses they get. A classic example: If a woman hinted at being abused, she might get sympathy, an empathic "Aren't men hard to put up with at times?" If instead the response was "That's awful, did you call the police?" or "That's awful, you shouldn't have to put up with that," the sympathy remains but the message changes. Suddenly women saw men with new eyes: his inconsiderate ways of making love, his refusal to share housework, his assumption that his work was more important than hers.[11] When consciousness raising worked well, it gave rise to the slogan "The personal is political," because it created the discovery that sexism—another word created by the movement and now universally understood—operated in every sphere, including kitchen and bedroom. As Pam Allen wrote, reflecting her background in the civil rights movement, "Personal liberation will happen simultaneously with the changing of society, not independently."[12]

Feminist Theory

In developing feminist theory, women in consciousness-raising groups were to some extent *re*inventing an analysis of women's subordination. Women were not just ignorant of previous feminist theory—they had been denied access to it by their education, just as African Americans had been denied their history. By the end of the nineteenth century feminists like Elizabeth Cady Stanton had elaborated a radical, sophisticated critique of male dominance and, occasionally, of gender itself. Yet the younger women were equally unfamiliar with it and with the work of New Deal–influenced feminists discussed in the previous chapter.

Ignorant of their heritage, the consciousness-raising groups did not read. Rather they started with the evidence at hand—their own lives in the 1950s and 1960s. Ignoring the past also freed them to be creative and to examine everything anew. Their process rested on existing gender characteristics, notably women's socialization toward intimate and emotional talk with other women, and then subjected those very characteristics to critique. Women's liberation founders realized that many women considered their problems to be personal and that this misconception isolated them; as in Katz and Allport's concept of pluralistic ignorance,[13] many a woman tended to feel that she was the only one who didn't like her looks, her body, her sexual activity, her housework, and so on. Enunciating their discontents, consciousness-raising group members soon recognized that those feelings were widespread and reclassified them as social, not personal. Once that was understood, they began to analyze them, asking questions like: Who benefits from sexism? Are men in general the enemy? How does sexism relate to and interact with other forms of discrimination?

The single most important feminist theoretical contribution to social theory was the concept of gender, i.e., the social structures and meanings attributed to sex difference. Distinguishing social from biological factors, "gender" would ultimately give rise to many other challenges to practices once believed to be natural. Even discriminatory practices were often considered the inevitable consequences of being a woman. When Jean Tepperman worked in a commercial bakery on a 4 p.m. to 12 midnight shift, for example, her best work friend, Mary Ann, thought it was "cute and masculine" that her husband refused to "help her" with housework and childcare.[14] To speak of gender signaled that women's subordinate position was not natural but socially, economically, and culturally constructed. Understanding sexism as *learned*—taught, like racism, to children from their earliest years—meant that it could be unlearned. It followed that what had been constructed by humans could be deconstructed and replaced with greater freedom and equality.

"The personal is political" slogan encapsulated the idea that many problems previously considered individual and private were created by social structures: for example, the fact that women, even when employed full-time, did all the housework and childcare; the fact that few women believed they could achieve the standards of beauty and self-sacrificing motherhood—these were political issues created by sex inequality. Even the most intimate of practices, such as sexual activity, reflected political power. Feminists argued that what was considered "natural" in heterosexual intercourse was that which brought men to climax most easily, while what gave women pleasure had been labeled abnormal. One of the most widely read essays of the day was Anne Koedt's "The Myth of the Vaginal Orgasm," and for many women, the idea that the clitoris, not the vagina, was the primary seat of female sexual pleasure came as a welcome surprise because it explained that what they had once considered their own sexual inadequacy was in fact the product of ignorance.

From here feminists began to challenge a wide range of institutions that had been labeled natural. One was marriage, but it was already being affected by cultural changes that began long before the women's liberation movement: starting in 1950 the average age of marriage increased, and the proportion of those never marrying grew, while the divorce rate had been growing throughout the century. Sex outside of marriage started becoming more acceptable as early as 1920, and that trend grew further after about 1950. Feminism gave new meaning to these trends, sending a message of female economic and social independence. Young feminists concluded that women could function well and happily without marriage, that women friends might be at least as important a source of support and contentment as a husband, that loving sexual partnerships need not be legalized by the state or the church.

There soon followed a challenge to the assumption that only heterosexuality was natural. While small numbers of gays and lesbians had been trying for several decades to counter the widespread condemnation of homosexuality, it was women's liberation's rejection of the alleged naturalness of heterosexual marriage and "missionary position" sex that opened up the common imagination to accept nonstandard sexual acts and romantic relationships. Prior to the 1970s, it seems likely that most women who were attracted to women were nevertheless married to men, because their economic security and social status required it. Women's liberation did not create lesbians but did create the space in which they could live their lives without hiding, suppressing their emotions, or denying themselves fulfilling partnerships. Less directly but equally the women's movement helped gay men to free themselves from stigma.

These challenges to the "natural" extended to sex segregation in the job market, which had rested on assumptions of what came naturally to women and men. Feminists understood that men could be nurses and nursery school teachers, and women could be politicians, surgeons, priests.

From the civil rights concept of "structural racism," the new feminists came to understand structural sexism: that is, discrimination against women did not necessarily arise from sexist or misogynist *attitudes* but from *structures*, i.e., the most basic organization and institutions of the economy, society, and culture. The fact that a man earned more for the same job was not his fault, and he could not individually opt out of that situation. Unequal pay was an economic structure practiced by employers on the basis of calculations about profit and preventing worker organizing, as well as dominant social assumptions about women—such as that women worked for "pin money"* and were mainly supported by

*The phrase "pin money," from the French *epingles*, originally referred to an allowance a man gave his wife for her domestic needs, as for sewing pins. The phrase then morphed to refer to a small, inconsequential amount.

husbands' wages, that women couldn't handle machines, or that women couldn't assume authority.

The most interesting theoretical questions were those that provoked disagreements, even anger, among feminists. Starting in about 1969, Shulamith Firestone and several New York City groups, and Roxanne Dunbar's Cell 16 in Boston, labeled radical feminists,[*] argued that the oppression of women by men was the oldest and most basic form of injustice and emphasized that women's oppression created direct benefits to men—such as wives who provided sex and housekeeping services. Their analyses of male dominance tended to position women as victims and to assume that men were unlikely to change. By articulating direct conflict between women and men in this provocative manner, they helped all women to acknowledge their own anger. Some radical feminists even experimented with attempting to cut themselves off from men. This emphasis on male-female antagonism gave birth to a separatist stream of feminism, which somewhat unrealistically discussed seceding from male-dominated institutions altogether. Some thus defined lesbianism as a political choice—indeed, the only truly feminist political choice—rather than an innate sexual orientation. A less radical but related stream of thought, cultural feminism, sought to replace male superiority with female superiority, on the grounds that women were a kinder, more cooperative sex, and that if women ruled, the world would be freer of conflict and other ills. Convinced that women's institutions and communities would naturally be less competitive and aggressive than men's, cultural feminists thought it a high priority to get women into positions of authority, in both private and public sectors. Cultural feminists were often the builders of small women's enterprises,

---

[*] It is worth noting that "radical feminism" in England meant something different.

such as bookstores, coffeehouses, country retreats, and communes. Many of this stream became eco-feminists, arguing that the history of humanity's ruthless drive to dominate nature—and despoil it—stemmed from male aggressiveness. A key problem of cultural feminist analysis, however, was assuming that all women were alike and denying women's own capacity for aggression and exploitation.

Boston's Bread and Roses, Chicago's Women's Liberation Union, and several other organizations called themselves socialist feminists, although by socialist they did not refer to any of the socialisms of the Communist bloc. They also distinguished themselves from Marxist feminists because, while they respected Marxist analysis of class exploitation, they did not believe that Marxism contained adequate explanations for race and gender hierarchies. While they recognized that capitalism and the rule of the profit motive was one major source of injustice, along with sexism and racism, they believed feminists needed new analyses to understand how sexism worked. Many activists in this stream did not accept the socialist label but sought a modified, regulated capitalism, like what Europeans call social democracy. These feminists were at first called "politicos," because they emphasized collective political engagement with the "male" world of activism, rather than withdrawal from it. The Combahee River Collective of African American feminists, which arose in Boston in the mid-1970s, insisted that feminism was not about individual success but involved changing conditions for all women. These groups argued that many aspects of injustice came together and required complex, situationally specific explanations: they did not assume that gender discrimination was the major issue in all situations. They tended to emphasize structural sexism and to deemphasize the sexism of individual men, assuming that men could change, could even benefit from equality with women, could be feminist themselves. They did not assume that putting women into power would automatically solve problems, reasoning that it was power itself that created ruthlessness; they pointed to Margaret Thatcher, the 1980s British prime minister, as Exhibit A, because her conservative policies rolled back many of women's gains. They also recognized that many men stood against injustice. In short, they were continuing the social justice feminist tradition discussed in the previous chapter.

Although most feminists recognized that many men, both individually and in the aggregate, gained material benefits from women's subordination—men got someone to do the housework and raise the children, higher wages, greater chances at promotion, and sexual gratification that was not necessarily reciprocal—the majority was optimistic that the movement could defeat sexism. They believed that men also stood to gain from women's liberation, that men would experience pleasure from egalitarian love and friendship, and liberation from the often demanding gendered constraints of normative masculinity. (And many men did.)

Meanwhile, NOW continued a liberal feminist orientation, focusing primarily on changing laws and creating equality between the sexes. By the early 1970s, however, the various streams of feminism converged, in a unity created in part by the virulent anti-feminist backlash. And in many parts of the United States, especially outside the biggest cities, feminists were typically unaware of or dismissive of these theoretical differences. They knew only that women were rising up.

All these theoretical tendencies prized women's relationships with women. Women have always cherished and leaned on mothers, daughters, sisters, friends, but the strongly heterosexual and heterosexist culture of the mid-twentieth century had cast women's relationships with other women into the shadow of the romantic heterosexual bonding that was, supposedly, a woman's chief desire and destiny. The women's movement brought female friendship into a position of honor, not in second place after heterosexual dating and marriage.

Then there was the lesbian question—and little else about this history has been so distorted by the media. Women's liberation contributed mightily to the large-scale "coming out" of lesbians through shattering assumptions about what was natural, in sex, in love, in family life, and by viewing marriage as an option, not a necessity. By disrupting the myths about women's sexual desire and pleasure, it deposed the penis from its position as necessary for women's sexual pleasure. Some in the women's movement, particularly among the older generation, feared that their movement could be stigmatized if it were associated with lesbians, and Betty Friedan, a leader of NOW, announced at a 1970 NOW meeting that a "lavender menace" was threatening the movement. Her fear reflected in part her anxiety about her own potentially stigmatizing background as a "Red," which she hid—understandably, given the frenzied repression of leftists she had lived through. Friedan's homophobic statement is widely remembered, but few note that later that year at a Congress to Unite Women, the whole audience laughed and cheered when a group proudly wearing T-shirts reading LAVENDER MENACE took over the stage.[15] Friedan soon reversed herself, and in 1971 NOW adopted a resolution supporting gay rights; besides, Friedan's attitude was never widespread in women's liberation. Gay and straight women worked together in camaraderie and friendship in most women's liberation groups, and many women first came out as lesbians in consciousness-raising groups. Lesbians formed separate groups, such as the Washington, D.C., Furies, but lesbians were often persevering activists in causes of greater concern to straight women, such as birth control and abortion rights. Lesbian feminists, never a monolithic group, divided in their analyses of what their sexual preference meant. Some argued, extending the cultural-feminist perspective, that lesbianism was the highest form of feminism, and that heterosexual women were compromisers; to them lesbianism was a political choice. Others believed that their sexual attraction to women was intrinsic and had little to do with their politics.

Race, Class and Feminism

By the late 1970s, many of these differences came to seem trivial—a remnant of an overly ideological moment of the past. As the backlash against the women's movement arose, to be discussed further below, feminists tended to shed concerns with doctrinal differences and to understand themselves as members of a general liberal/progressive swath of Americans.

One fissure within women's liberation, however, was never bridged: its dominant white and middle-class composition gave rise to accusations of racism and privilege directed at it. The confidence, the articulateness, even the vocabularies of the college-educated women who dominated many feminist groups in the 1970s often functioned to silence working-class women. One working woman's complaint poignantly illustrated that class divide: in Bread and Roses, the middle-class majority, whether students, housewives, or professionals, usually wore pants or jeans; when she arrived, directly from her job, wearing skirts and nylons, she felt the majority regarding her as if she were unfeminist! But the problem was not merely one of style. Sisterhood talk and a one-size-fits-all feminist program were not harmless; in reflecting the class and race upbringings and cultures of those who dominated the movement, middle-class women built walls around themselves. Despite their best intentions and despite their conscious opposition to racism, their priorities and assumptions sometimes blinded them to the situation of women of color and poorer women. The bonding produced by small-group consciousness raising led many white women to assume that all women had the same grievances and priorities. Middle-class whites did not take sufficiently into account the situation of women who experienced racism, low wages, ill health, and dangerous neighborhoods. Those poor and working-class women, in turn, frequently felt that the women's liberation movement did not represent them—even though many of them were feminist in the generic sense that they recognized women as disadvantaged. Moreover, many were activists on issues that reflected their interests as women, as we will also see below.

Many other feminists of color shared Elizabeth Martínez's experience—that white feminists were oblivious to the depth and strength of racism in the United States, and to the need to put civil rights foremost. Less well articulated but equally prevalent was the middle-class domination of the movement and the obliviousness it sometimes produced to the experience of working-class and poor women. These perceptions and resentments often took the form of mistaken accusations that the movement excluded women of color. (In fact, middle-class white feminists, feeling guilty about their privileges, made many of these accusations.) There was never exclusion; feminist groups badly wanted nonwhite and poorer members. But their experiences and priorities were at times so different, and their conversations so insular, that their groups *felt* exclusionary to women of color. As Barbara Emerson, who grew up saturated in civil rights activism—she is the daughter of Hosea Williams, a civil rights leader who was close to Martin Luther King Jr.—put it, "It was a white women's movement, not necessarily because it was exclusionary of women of color, but simply because the agenda was a white women's agenda."[16]

Many women's groups focused projects on the urgent needs of working-class and low-income women, such as healthcare, welfare, daycare, and working conditions. However, the white-dominated groups sometimes made the mistake of formulating projects first and *then* trying to recruit working-class women, oblivious to the arrogance implied in that process. At the same time, many white feminists allowed their guilt feelings to insult people of color in an opposite way, through automatic agreement with any black opinion, a deference that was actually disrespectful.

Nothing illustrates this pattern, and a problem faced by African American feminists, better than the uncritical support white feminists gave to the Black Panther Party. This urban northern Black Power group, founded in 1966 in Oakland, California, arose in response to police brutality. Their protests sometimes took the form of armed posturing, beginning with a notorious march on the state capitol in Sacramento with guns in hand. Centuries of white oppression had prevented African American men from inhabiting the positions of authority that white men took for granted; to this was added, as African American feminist historian Robyn Spencer points out, a theory of black "emasculation at the hands of superpowerful black women,"[17] a theory promoted as much by self-appointed white experts on black poverty and crime as by black nationalists.[18] Although the Black Panther Party's original agenda could have been written by a feminist group, calling for full employment, decent housing, and education, its early practice was as much about gender as about race, asking black women to step back into the protection of their men. Numerous male civil rights activists charged that feminism was an attempt to impose "white" values, although, as Fran Beal pointed out, "when it comes to women he [the black man] seems to take his guidelines from . . . *Ladies Home Journal.*"[19]

While the need for race solidarity led some women of color to accept the doctrine that they should "step back," others resisted male dominance in the movement. From the beginning female Panthers pressed for power. Sixteen-year-old Tarika Lewis walked into the Black Panther Party office, asked to join, and demanded her own gun. It was Panther women who created the positive programs

that brought the party widespread respect: free breakfasts, clothing, medical care, and classes on politics and economics. Women
in the Puerto Rican Young Lords Party, which had grown out of
a Chicago turf gang, became incensed when they observed the
position (literally) of women in Amiri Baraka's Afrocentric group:
his female followers were required to approach him on hands and
knees. Denise Oliver, who observed this, told other female Lords
that "if we didn't do something we would end up on our hands
and knees" like them. So they conducted a "sex strike," refusing
to have sex with their male partners until the Lords agreed to add
women to the leadership and get rid of the call for "revolutionary
machismo," among other demands.[20]

Black feminism and other feminisms of color emerged from

A Boston demonstration, 1979, led by the Combahee River Collective. Photograph by Ellen Shub.

both male-dominated and autonomous women's groups. One pioneer was the Third World Women's Alliance, which developed when a black women's group started by Fran Beal in 1968 wanted to reach out to Latinas. The name reflected the New Left notion that people of color in the United States shared the oppression of "Third World" people, and that Western imperialist domination over the "underdeveloped" world was of a piece with domestic racism. The group's core analysis—that women of color had to struggle against race, class, and gender domination at the same time—was common among all feminists of color, but there was no more homogeneity among them than among white women. Moreover, many African American women, like Barbara Emerson, did not feel disadvantaged as women, but rather asserted the strength and leadership of black women—at least until black nationalism became the dominant stream of the black movement.

The development of separate feminisms among African Americans, Latinas, Asian Americans, and American Indians did not weaken the overall force of the women's movement. Political scientist S. Laurel Weldon has shown, in fact, that women's movements were stronger and more successful when there were multiple groups organized by racial/ethnic and other identities.

Feminist activism among women of color and white working-class women often took forms rather different from the white and middle-class projects that are usually identified as feminist. Some developed as labor struggles, such as the victorious two-year strike (1972–74) of garment workers at the Farah Company in El Paso, Texas; four thousand Chicana workers defied violent intimidation, sparked a national boycott of Farah clothing, and won union recognition. In 1969, four hundred hospital workers in Charleston, South Carolina, won a dramatic 116-day strike sparked by the firing of twelve black aides for attending a grievance meeting. As one striker, Bessie Polite, said, "We was women and we didn't have no weapons. . . . I felt like they wouldn't hardly hit us with those big clubs." To which Ernestine Bryant added, "When you're working around people who discriminate against you . . . they call you like 'hey, girl,' . . . you just really feel like—you know—fighting."[21] These labor struggles and other feminist campaigns by working-class women gained support from the Coalition of Labor Union Women; founded in 1974, the group arose from the intersection of long-term pressure by women within the AFL-CIO with the influence of women's liberation.

Much women's activism focused on children, and the converse is also true: movements for children are typically women's movements. This kind of activism was not new, but the women's movement energized it. Women campaigned for better garbage collection, traffic lights, guards at school crossings, parks and playgrounds and swimming pools. Women were frequently the leaders of campaigns against toxic wastes in their neighborhoods. In 1978, Lois Gibbs, a working-class mother only twenty-seven years old, discovered that her son's elementary school was built on top of a toxic waste dump. At first she thought that she "just had to go to the right person in government and he would take care of it." She remembered being very upset to find that "democracy isn't democracy," and added, speaking with familial feelings of betrayal, "It's like finding out your mother was fooling around on your father." She then started a movement that forced the cleanup of Love Canal and led to the creation of the "Superfund" for environmental safety.[22] Not all women-led campaigns were praiseworthy, for it was also women who protested public housing, halfway houses, school desegregation and busing, and even harassed people of color moving into their neighborhoods. In fact, conservative women modeled some of their tactics on feminist activity, as when anti-abortion protesters copied New Left tactics such as sit-ins and chaining themselves to fences.

Although Chicano (male) activists stubbornly resisted Chicana feminism, that did not stop the development of feminist consciousness among Chicanas. At the 1971 Mujeres por la Raza conference in Houston, a survey of the six hundred in attendance showed that 84 percent resented not receiving equal pay for equal work, and 72 percent felt discriminated against within the Raza movement. In Chicago at a meeting of a Latino/a American student group, one woman rebelled when the group's president announced, "'The girls are going to go and prepare something [to eat] while we discuss this political question.' . . . I was single. I didn't even cook. . . . Why the heck was I going to cook for some guys? Cristina and I didn't budge. . . . The rumor thereafter was that Cristina and I were lovers. . . . Then, they started saying that we weren't heavy chested and that made us more masculine. . . . From then on, we raised issues . . . related to Chicanas." They called a Latina women's conference, La Mujer Despierta (Women Awake), in 1973.[23]

American Indian women had a history of leadership greater than that of other ethnic groups; women led, for example, the first Indian activism of the civil rights era—the 1960s "fish-ins" defending tribal rights. But with the Indian seizure and occupation of Alcatraz Island in 1969–71, and then the 1973 occupation of Wounded Knee, male violent rhetoric and armed posturing, much like that of the Black Panthers, accelerated, and women got sidelined—and began to criticize the men. After the Wounded Knee defeat, Indian women founded Women of All Red Nations and campaigned against coerced sterilization (see below) as well as sexism.

Asian American women traveled a different trajectory: the Vietnam War affected them strongly and intensified their commitments to Asian American civil rights and anti-imperialist activity. They created fewer distinctly feminist organizations but many centers and projects for women—cultural centers, health clinics, battered women's shelters; moreover, the Asian American New Left was less sexist and less violent than were the black and Indian New Lefts.[24]

Still, the nonwhite feminist groups also shared strategies: fighting racial/ethnic as well as gender discrimination; pushing bread-and-butter issues. Major concerns crossed all racial ethnic lines: ending rape, harassment and domestic violence; making reproduction control accessible to all; criticizing sexist representations of women; honoring divergent family forms and sexual preference; insisting that women get equal access to professions, jobs, salaries and promotions.

Another thing all feminists of color shared: denunciations by their racial/ethnic brothers. They accused women of undermining already fragile male egos, fragmenting and thereby weakening civil rights efforts, destroying families and damaging their children, losing their own culture, threatening community solidarity, and accepting white women's values. When Elizabeth Sutherland reclaimed her Mexican American identity and her father's name—Martínez—and moved to New Mexico to join a movement for her own people, some of her *compañero/as* charged she was *agringada* (whitened) because of her feminism. (This was a bitter irony for the girl who had had to sit in the back of the bus in Washington.) She criticized the use of images of *"our women/ in postures of maternity, sadness, devotion/ tears for the lost husband or son/ our women*, nothing but shadows/reflections of someone else's existence/ BASTA!"[25] She saw, moreover, that her sister Chicanas had plenty of resentment about their own experience of male dominance; in rejecting feminism they were primarily rejecting a movement they saw as white and middle-class, and they also saw the need for male-female solidarity in fighting anti-Mexican racism. The relative strength of feminism among women of color seems to have been correlated with the degree of nationalism in the New Left group they were embedded in: Asian American women had an easier time promoting gender concerns because the Asian American New Left was not particularly nation-

alist. Anti-feminist attacks were also virulent among whites, however, usually on the similar ground that the women were playing
"identity politics" and thereby fragmenting progressive unity.

Feminism and the New Left

In the early 1970s, almost all the younger participants in the
women's liberation movement had previously participated in other
parts of the New Left. Most writers have narrowed their understanding of the "New Left" by referring exclusively to the white
student-intellectual movement that coalesced around campus and
anti-war activism in the 1960s, then broke up into sectarian frag-
ments from 1968 to 1970. A closer look shows the New Left as a
developing, interlocked chain of social movements that began in
the 1950s with civil rights, extended through campus protests, the
anti–Vietnam War campaign, the women's liberation and then gay
liberation movements, taking in also the environmentalism that
continued throughout. These movements shared anti-authoritarian
impulses, a recognition of the need for new analyses of injustice and
exploitation, strategic orientation toward defiance, tactical reliance
on direct action and civil disobedience, rejection of conformist culture, and creativity in pioneering new cultural and communitarian
forms and innovative tactics. Recognizing this "long New Left" is
vital for understanding the women's liberation movement.

From the constricted, predominantly white, male and heterosexual misconception of the New Left flowed another misconception: that feminism arose by "breaking off" from the New Left.
True, women had been criticizing their treatment in the labor, civil
rights, peace, and environmental movements for decades, but that
criticism did not usually mean divorce, any more than does criticism of family or friends. In fact, women's liberation grew from
and remained an integral part of the New Left. Participation in

earlier movements sharpened feminists' analyses of injustice and their confidence that collective action could create change.

The single greatest influence on women's liberation was civil rights, and many early feminists were veterans of that movement. Elizabeth Martínez's life's work shows it clearly. From her childhood experiences of racism through her writing and editing work in New York, she was gripped by the southern civil rights movement, despite not being an African American. Though she wasn't typical—not many people will quit their jobs to join a dangerous struggle in alien territory at age forty—her integration of feminism with civil rights and other progressive causes was typical. Pam Allen, the first codifier of consciousness raising, also came from civil rights. She went to Mississippi in 1964 a devout Christian, convinced that God would protect her, but that was before the killings of three of her fellow civil rights workers; twenty-five years later she found a letter her father wrote to his congressman saying, "Get her the hell out of there," and she was grateful that the letter did not succeed.[26] As Catherine Stimpson, noted scholar and founder of the feminist journal *Signs*, wrote, the civil rights movement "scoured the rust off the national conscience."[27] By exposing the mechanisms of white domination and proving that a social movement could defeat some of those centuries-old mechanisms, it shaped and invigorated feminism. In one way the civil rights influence was too great, because feminists compared women's oppression to African Americans'—an extremely limited and misleading analogy. True, both race and sex inequality are profitable for others: employers who could pay low wages and husbands and boyfriends who received domestic services. (If husbands had to pay for domestic services, not to mention the labor of child raising, the great majority of them would not have been able to live on their wages.) But the differences between race and sex inequality are far greater: almost all women live with and love

men, as fathers, brothers, husbands, sons; and women's subordination was naturalized far more deeply than that of blacks. Furthermore, in the rhetoric of analogizing women to blacks, black
women dropped out of the picture. (One classic feminist book put
the hidden exclusion behind the analogy perfectly: *All the Women
Are White, All the Blacks Are Men.*)

Within the civil rights movement, SNCC exerted the greatest
influence on the rest of the New Left. Hundreds of northern students, white and black, volunteered for the summers of 1963 and
1964. Although not many stayed for two years, as Betita Martínez
did, even a summer was intense enough to change them forever.
SNCC's commitment to internal democracy, nonviolent resistance,
and grassroots organizing, along with the extraordinary patience
and bravery of its staff and supporters, showed that even the least
powerful people could make social change. The horrific rage and
violence of the southern white resistance also produced an impact:
volunteers experienced vicious beatings in Selma, saw cross burn-
ings and firebombings by the White Citizens Councils in Mississippi, and experienced the murders of their friends. Many other
women watched this violence on TV. They were learning the inten-
sity with which those who held power would resist sharing it. Sexual attacks on black women were commonplace, as white men had
virtually never been prosecuted for these crimes. In 1959, in the
first case to lead to a conviction, Betty Jean Owens was pulled out
of a car in Tallahassee by a crowd of white men who had decided to
"go out and get a nigger girl," then raped seven times.[28]

As civil rights advocates were winning major legal and legislative victories, most young feminists were also participating in the
anti–Vietnam War movement. This campaign was sparked by Students for a Democratic Society, a national campus organization that
grew rapidly in the mid-1960s, and the draft resistance movement.
Both were even more male dominated than civil rights, for two

Anti–Vietnam War leaflet, 1970, Bread and Roses.

reasons: only men could be drafted, so only men could resist the draft; and SDS gained mass support largely through big demonstrations, public "teach-ins," and charismatic speeches—at a time when most women were too diffident, due to their conventionally feminine upbringing, to take on assertive public roles. Karen Nussbaum was active in SDS and Black Panther support activity at the University of Chicago, and her older brother was a draft resister. Betita Martínez was no longer a student, but she and virtually all civil rights supporters saw U.S. imperialism—especially the United States' invasion of small, distant, and entirely unthreatening Vietnam to impose the kind of political system it wanted—as a global extension of racism. That war turned "peaceniks" into critics of American economic and military imperialism.

In all these movements, men dominated the leadership (though SNCC was more sexually egalitarian than SDS), while women did the organizational maintenance work. Men seemed to assume control "naturally," while women deferred to them. That deference reflected the sexual objectification and subordination of women, problems that had permeated male culture for eons. Women who had written brilliant political and historical analyses in their college courses were afraid to speak in large meetings mainly because of their awareness of being seen but not heard and of being evaluated by their sexual desirability. It was not only men's "ways of seeing," in John Berger's sense, but also men's ways of hearing: a woman might make a point, then a man might make the same point, and the point was thereafter referred to as his. Men automatically regarded other men as their audience, comrades, co-strategists, or adversaries. For many women, becoming a feminist grew out of a process of recognizing how men—often unconsciously—could render women invisible as subjects, only visible as bodies.

Still, feminists' growing understanding of the depth and, often, subtlety of sexism rarely removed them from these other New Left causes. Women's libbers, both individually and through their organizations, continued to work on anti-war, civil rights, and civil liberties issues. They marched against the Vietnam War carrying banners like FEMINISTS FOR PEACE or WOMEN AGAINST IMPERIAL-

ISM. They introduced feminist analyses of the motives behind the arms race, military interventions, and support for dictatorships like those in Vietnam, Chile, El Salvador, and Uruguay. Eco-feminists, adopting a term from French feminist Françoise d'Eaubonne, connected male domination over women with the destruction of nature. Many flocked to organizations fighting nuclear power, such as the Clamshell Alliance. African American and American Indian women were particularly prominent in environmentalist protest, in part because toxic projects are so frequently sited in the neighborhoods of poor people of color. Many were shy at first, not accustomed to speaking in public or even to speaking to strangers. One environmental activist explained, "Twenty years ago I couldn't do this. . . . I had to really know you to talk with you. Now I talked. . . . I waited until my fifties to go to jail. . . . I never went to no university or college but I'm going in there and making speeches." Some were even frightened at first; one American Indian woman opposing a landfill on the Los Coyotes Reservation said, "People here fear the government. . . . When I became involved in opposing the garbage, my people told me to be careful . . . they annihilate people like me."[29] Not all became lifelong activists like Martínez and Nussbaum, and many never owned any of the common labels, such as "feminist," "peacenik," or "environmentalist," but the majority supported the progressive causes of the New Left for the rest of their lives.

Feminism was not always welcomed by male leftists. Some of them not only criticized but cursed the early feminist spokeswomen. When Marilyn Webb and Shulamith Firestone took the stage to speak at an anti-war rally in 1969, male hecklers shouted, "Take her off the stage and fuck her," and the legendary pacifist leader Dave Dellinger responded by trying to get the women off the stage rather than admonishing the hecklers. Angela Davis was called domineering by black men who feared she would "rob them of their manhood."[30] Kathleen Cleaver felt she had to "genuflect" to the male Black Panthers.[31] Even supportive men assumed that women's liberation should aim at mobilizing women to support the older New Left issues, and when confronted with criticism about sexism, they often became defensive. To convince men to listen to women sometimes required arduous and repetitive pressure, while others took in the lessons quickly and began to act on them. What is important here is that most feminists blamed not men in general, or the left in general, but *the structure* of sexism, and continued to press from within the Left.

Women's Liberation Organizations

Just as earlier New Left movements influenced feminist practice, so they influenced women's liberation's organizational preferences. From SNCC came the principle that social change required personal transformation and empowerment, which in turn required face-to-face organizing. From both the civil rights and anti-war movements came the understanding that the United States was not thoroughly democratic but was governed by politicians whose greatest loyalty and accountability were to wealthy donors and lobbyists. So they disdained representative democracy. They favored decisions made by groups in which everyone participated in full discussion of issues and options.

This radical egalitarianism may have been the perfect form for the content being produced, i.e, consciousness raising. Small groups allowed all the assembled experiences to be added to the discussion, provided the group was small enough that everyone could contribute but just large enough to include a range of experience. Meeting in living rooms, some crowded onto sofas, others sprawled on the floor, often nibbling snacks, less often drinking wine since the typical members had little money, the participants experienced not a meeting as much as a late-night intimate conversation. The size meant that everyone spoke because there was no pressure to be articulate or to have an "analysis." The analysis came after, not before, exchanging experiences.

Most women's liberation activists felt no inclination to create larger organizations: they created none on the national or state level and only some citywide. This decentralization resulted in extraordinarily productive bursts of creativity. Small groups could engender quick decision making and action. They could dream up projects and act on them without first seeking approval from larger organizations; rather than sit through long meetings discussing the pros and cons of different proposals, or prioritizing among competing proposals, the small groups could simply begin. Even the citywide groups, such as Chicago's CWLU and Boston's Bread and Roses, divided among smaller project groups. Over time these projects *were* the women's liberation movement.

Some believe, however, that the movement would have been stronger had it created more multi-issue organizations. In contrast to NOW, an organization with fifty years of staying power, women's liberation harbored extreme suspicion of formal pyramidal structures. One scholar labeled NOW the "bureaucratic" and women's liberation the "collectivist" branch of the movement.[32] Although that distinction did not apply universally—some NOW chapters were like women's liberation groups, and vice versa—it is true that most of the younger feminists were allergic to hierarchical organization and leadership. Their groups rarely elected officers and usually rotated jobs, a pattern that made it harder to hold people responsible for the tasks they undertook and accountable to the membership. (It was not uncommon for someone to volunteer for a task and then fail to attend the next meeting, leaving the group in the dark about whether the task was accomplished.) Few organizations established membership requirements, such as dues or initial orientation or committee assignments. Decisions were not final because new members could challenge them at any time. One exception to this pattern was the long-lasting Chicago Women's Liberation Union (1969–77). Its relative longevity derived from its ability to compromise between effectiveness and democracy, its insistence that all members be actively engaged in at least one project, and its creation of respect for leadership.

True, the movement might have accomplished even more had it integrated the freewheeling creativity of decentralization with the strategically targeted clout of a disciplined national organization. But movements can only grow from the longings of their activists, and this generation of feminists acted not only out of passion for social justice but also out of rejection of authority. As it was, they wrought massive change.

It may be, however, that decentralization and consciousness change have their greatest impact only in the pioneering moments of movements, and that staying power requires stronger organization. Luckily NOW, the National Organization for Women, continued to hold together a national network. As the last chapter showed, NOW was more diverse than women's liberation: labor union leaders and women of color helped start it; Caroline Davis of the United Auto Workers and Jamaican American Aileen Hernandez of the International Ladies' Garment Workers were among its first officers. Focused primarily on employment discrimination, it was able to campaign for reforms that benefited working women of all classes. NOW consistently supported civil rights legislation.

While most women's liberation members de-emphasized electoral campaigns, NOW threw its energies into the two-party official political system. As it began its work, there were thirteen women in Congress; in 2013 there were ninety-eight. With NOW's support, New York's Shirley Chisholm (1924–2005) became the first African American woman in Congress, in 1969. She was a feminist heroine who deserves far more recognition than she has received. Born in Brooklyn to West Indian immigrants, her father a factory worker and her mother a domestic, she went to Brooklyn College, worked as a schoolteacher, and ran her campaign on the slogan "Unbought and Unbossed," signaling her independence from the Democratic Party political machine. When she won, she told her constituents, "There may be some fireworks," and she set them off herself, by immediately challenging the seniority system in the House, which had assigned her to the Agriculture Committee— hardly relevant to her Brooklyn constituents. She became skilled at rounding up Republican support for her priorities, as in a bill to extend the minimum wage law to domestic workers. An expert on child welfare and education, she was responsible for the country's first federal legislation providing comprehensive childcare assistance to needy families and managed to get it passed with bipartisan support—only to have President Nixon veto it, surprising even members of his own Republican Party.

NOW's chapters were autonomous and diverse, but its national office initiated both lobbying and demonstrations on issues as diverse as getting women appointed to federal commissions, responding to rape, and impeaching Nixon. NOW's Legal Defense and Education Fund, founded in 1970, became a powerhouse of expertise and litigation for judicial and legislative victories. It won the famed Title IX of the Education Amendments of 1972, which virtually revolutionized women's sports. In 2013 college women began using it to combat campus rapes. It pressured the mass media to be more responsive to and respectful of women. It trained feminist lawyers, produced the Rape Shield Law, and in alliance with union women won the Pregnancy Discrimination Act of 1978.

Through the 1970s NOW was increasingly deploying its "troops" in the battle for the Equal Rights Amendment. In earlier decades many social justice feminists had opposed the amendment on the grounds that it might cancel legislation that supported women's needs, such as pregnancy benefits, as chapter 1 explained. Now labor unions were part of the pro-ERA alliance as well. Women's numbers and positions in the wage labor force had changed so much that the potential loss of protective legislation was less threatening to women than the continued discrimination against them. By the time the amendment passed in Congress in 1972, the lay of the land had shifted: the opposition came no longer from the social justice feminists and labor unions but from the right wing. The anti-ERA lobby gained massive corporate and conservative religious funding and propagandized by appealing to people's fears: opponents argued that the ERA would destroy the family, free husbands from having to support wives and children, send women into combat, end separate women's and men's toilets, uphold abortion rights and homosexual marriages and destroy businesses. Although a majority of the states ratified it, a constitutional amendment required approval by three-fifths, and this hurdle the movement could not vault. Conservatives were able to keep the United States as one of the only nations not to guarantee women equal rights, a bitter disappointment to millions and a foretaste of the power of the backlash, to be discussed at the end of this chapter.

In retrospect, many feminists came to believe that it was a mistake for NOW to focus so exclusively on this single project. In fact, the NOW and women's liberation branches of the feminist movement carried on with campaigns about many other issues. It would take a multivolume book to discuss them all, so this chapter focuses on a few of the most striking.

Bodily Health and Harm

Paradoxically, the issue with which women's liberation has been most identified, abortion rights, is where it actually had little success. After the initial limited legalization of abortion through *Roe v. Wade* in 1973, the anti-abortion-rights movement made abortions steadily less accessible. The history of this conflict merits careful attention because the opposition made it symbolize the whole movement.

All known human societies have tried to control reproduction, and abortion was a common means. It was legal in the three great monotheistic religions—Judaism, Christianity, and Islam— provided it was accomplished before "quickening," the old term for the moment when a pregnant woman could first feel a fetus move. The same women who assisted in childbirth usually performed abortions. In the mid-nineteenth century, moral reformers in the United States and Europe initiated a campaign to ban reproduction control, and they made little distinction between what we today call contraception and abortion. Between about 1840 and 1890, all U.S. states banned *all* methods of reproduction control, and in 1873, a federal law did likewise. By the early twentieth century, however, the changing economy made those restrictions unacceptable, especially for those who could not afford large families. A grassroots campaign to legalize contraception, now called birth control, produced a compromise: legalizing contraception but continuing to prohibit abortion. In the 1960s, several new factors—such as the medical ability to detect fetal pathologies and the growing acceptability of sex outside of marriage—made the ban on abortion unacceptable. The very fact that people had grown accustomed to being able to plan their reproductive lives intensified women's demands for abortion: if contraception failed, they needed a Plan B.

At first, *Roe v. Wade* brought significant gains to women and their families: greater safety, lower costs, an end to stigma, and greater opportunity in education and employment. In 1965, illegal abortion was responsible for 17 percent of pregnancy-related deaths; by 1999, only 0.3 percent of women having legal abortions suffered any serious complications. In the four years between 1972 and 1976, deaths from abortion went from thirty-nine to two per million. Equally important was that women who aborted could be guaranteed not only sterile, safe procedures, but also discussions with sympathetic female counselors who made sure that pregnant women considered all their options, and accurate medical information as opposed to dishonest propaganda—for example, that abortion caused cancer or sterility, that fetuses feel pain, or that all unwanted children can be adopted.

Agitation to repeal the abortion prohibitions began well before women's liberation became a mass movement. Seventeen states had liberalized their abortion laws *before Roe v. Wade,* and observers believed the reform wave would soon spread throughout the country. Once the powerful women's movement took up the cause, however, feminism became the face of abortion, and that allowed abortion opponents to brand it as radical and not traditional. The Catholic hierarchy, of course, opposed it from the outset, as it opposed contraception. Evangelical Protestants endorsed abortion rights until secular Republican Party strategists pulled the evangelical leadership into the anti-abortion campaign. These creators of the "New Right" sought to break the Democratic Party's electoral majority. By de-emphasizing traditional Republican issues (conservative economic policy and anti-Communism) and focusing instead on "social" issues (gender and sexual matters), they planned to win over some traditional Democratic voters. They painted abortion as a tool of radical feminists who were using it to "destroy the family."

The plan worked, for two reasons. First, while the nineteenth-century anti-abortion campaign argued that abortion allowed women to evade their God-dictated destiny for motherhood and domesticity, that argument could never have gained traction in the mid-twentieth century. So the new campaign focused on the fetus and its "right to life," an issue almost never mentioned in the previous century. Second, Republican funders threw massive resources into the anti-abortion-rights cause. The opposition succeeded in limiting abortion through burdensome restrictions, especially by prohibiting the use of Medicaid funds for abortion—so that the poor, who most needed to reduce their childbearing, could not do so—and by driving out abortion providers through a terrifying campaign of violence. The American Coalition of Life Activists circulated "Wanted" posters—mimicking official police placards identifying suspected criminals—with the photographs and, often, *home addresses* of physicians who performed abortions, identifying them as "war criminals" and, recalling the Nuremberg Laws, guilty of "crimes against humanity."[33] These posters contributed to a terrifying wave of violence against abortion personnel. From 1977 through 2001, assailants in this campaign murdered 3 doctors, 2 clinic employees, 1 clinic escort and 1 security guard; attempted 71 other murders; executed 41 bombings, 165 arson attacks, 82 attempted bombings, and 372 clinic invasions; and caused $8.5 million in damage. This was enough to drive even staunch supporters of reproductive rights out of the practice, and those who remained were heroes indeed.

Anti-abortion advocates also labeled abortion rights as a white people's cause, which is not the case. Women of all races were and are divided on the issue, just like men, but black feminists were staunchly in favor. Blacks have a higher abortion rate than whites, because they have more unintended pregnancies and because they are poorer, according to a poll by the Public Religion Research Institute, and in 2012, two-thirds believed that abortion should be legal in all or most cases, despite anti-abortion sermons by some black ministers. Immigrant Hispanics supported abortion rights in smaller numbers, 41 percent, but among those born in the United States, 55 to 57 percent agreed that abortion should be legal in all or most cases. Numerous prominent women of color led in the campaign for abortion rights, including Dr. Helen Rodríguez-Trias, Congresswoman Shirley Chisholm, National Council of Negro Women president Dorothy Height, NOW president Aileen Hernandez, and many more.

Because of the strength of the anti-abortion movement, over the last forty years many feminists had to devote time and money to defending reproduction rights exclusively. This need to concentrate on a single issue contributed to the decline of multi-issue feminist organizations. Still, other campaigns to protect women's bodily safety gained successes.

One, the movement for free choice in sterilization, won significant victories. About sterilization, women of different classes had different complaints. When prosperous women sought sterilization, physicians could arbitrarily refuse their requests on the grounds that they were too young or hadn't yet had "enough" children (on the assumption that physicians knew better than the women what was in their best interest), while poor women, and particularly people of color, had been frequently subjected to involuntary sterilization—a practice used since early in the twentieth century. State authorities could threaten to cut women off welfare if they did not agree to be sterilized, or get them to sign consent forms at moments of painful labor and delivery. One egregious case gave the widespread practice publicity in 1973: Alabama authorities sterilized Minnie Lee and Mary Alice Relf, African Americans aged fourteen and twelve, not only without consent but without even their or their mother's knowledge, on the grounds that they were "at risk" of early sexual activity. The National Welfare Rights Organization and the women's movement protested loudly enough to get a federal investigation into what were widely known as "Mississippi appendectomies."

Latinas were in the lead in this campaign. In the mid-1970s

in Los Angeles, ten low-income, Mexican-origin women filed suit against obstetricians who had coerced them into sterilization within hours of giving birth. Their stories showed the abuse clearly: Helena Orozco testified that a "doctor said that if I did not consent to the tubal ligation that the doctor repairing my hernia would use an inferior type of stitching material which would break the next time I became pregnant, but that if I consented to the tubal ligation that the stitches would hold as proper string would be used." Jovita Rivera testified that "while I was in advanced labor . . . and in great pain, the doctor told me that I had too many children, that I was poor, and a burden to the government and I should sign a paper not to have more children . . . that my tubes could be untied at a later time and I could still have children."[34] Nevertheless, the judge ruled against them. They continued to organize and soon found over a hundred similar victims. Sterilization had been pushed on women in Puerto Rico without informing them of other, temporary birth control methods, and this was happening in New York as well. Dr. Helen Rodríguez-Trias, a Puerto Rican, founded the Committee to End Sterilization Abuse in New York City in 1973. Then women of the Puerto Rican Young Lords Party also joined the campaign, which they situated within a larger program for reproductive rights. Instead of following the nationalist line, that birth control itself was a form of genocide against Puerto Ricans, the Lords women developed a holistic program calling for reproductive rights, including abortion, but also including the right to bear children.

Soon these activists formed a national organization, the Committee for Abortion Rights and Against Sterilization Abuse (CARASA), based on a simple but radical premise: that women should have the right to decide their reproductive options without coercion. CARASA argued that women needed not only legal but also economic and social rights. Giving women true choice, the

Poster, probably from CARASA (Committee fo Abortion Rights and Against Sterilization Abuse), probably 1974–75, designer unknown.

group argued, should include economic help in raising children when necessary and in accessing contraception and abortion when desired. CARASA was able to get the federal government to issue stringent regulations designed to prevent involuntary sterilization in 1979, including notably a required thirty-day waiting period to ensure that women were not pressured into a decision under stress. It never succeeded, however, in repealing the federal ban on Medicaid funding for abortion.

Women's bodies have been violated for centuries by rape, harassment, and assault, and by the relative impunity of so many male culprits. The size of the problem before the women's liberation movement is unknown, precisely because so few women complained, which was, in turn, because they knew their chances of getting justice were slim. The all-out feminist campaign against domestic violence generated a sea change in public opinion. Women as well as men once regarded male "punishment" of wives as acceptable and did not categorize such aggressions as pushing, slapping, or threatening as constituting domestic violence, let alone criminal assault. Shortly before the women's liberation movement, anywhere from one-quarter to two-thirds of Americans thought such "mild" assaults acceptable or even, in male opinion, necessary or good. Today very few Americans would admit such an attitude to a pollster. Still, the problem has not disappeared by any means. The Domestic Violence Resource Center estimates that one in four women has been attacked by a partner or ex-partner and three out of four women know someone who has been. Every day in the United States, three women and one man are killed by partners or ex-partners. Of course, these figures represent both greater consciousness that these assaults are crimes and greater willingness to report them.[35]

One approach to domestic violence was the establishment of battered women's shelters throughout the United States. In 2012, on an average day, some 1,900 shelters served an average of sixty-four thousand women and children, and twenty-nine thousand more were counseled. African American women are disproportionately likely to use shelters because they lack the resources to find housing on their own when they leave abusive partners. No such refuges existed before the women's liberation movement created them, and no physical space ever met a greater need. Many abused women had previously had no place they could go with their children— and few mothers were willing to leave marriages without their children. A program originating in England, shelters were opened by American feminist groups starting in 1967. Thousands of women volunteered to staff these facilities and to raise money for them. National coordination produced shared policies: no men allowed; locations not made public; no drugs or alcohol; all residents cooperating in cleaning and maintenance; and consciousness-raising sessions aimed to expose residents to the feminist understanding that domestic violence was a means of enforcing male dominance and erupted most often when that dominance was threatened.

"Hotlines" also proliferated, allowing women to learn that support was available. Feminist groups pressured medical clinics to
post information about getting help, and doctors to raise questions
about injuries they would once have ignored—or accepted pretexts
about, such as "I ran into a door." Feminist pressure caused police
forces to change their responses to domestic violence calls: instead
of acting to separate the couple and pacify the man—or, worse,
sympathize with man's complaints about the woman—most police
departments have revised their procedures, and twenty-two states
have made arrests mandatory.

A marker of the feminist achievement was the Family Violence
Prevention and Services Act of 1984, which provided federal
grants. (Since then there has been a political seesaw: Democratic administrations supported the program, and the Clinton
administration added the Violence Against Women Act; Republican administrations cut the funding and tried to repeal the
laws.) Although these government commitments represented
major feminist victories, their funding does not match the need.
Every day approximately ten thousand needy women and children ask for help but cannot get it because of inadequate funding. Twenty-three thousand calls come in to anti-violence hotlines
every day. An additional problem is that accepting federal money
requires shelters and hotlines to conform to guidelines that often
prohibit feminist discussions with victims, which many activists
believe weakens their ability to help women permanently free
themselves from violence through understanding its roots and
symptoms. Men can also be victims, especially gay men, and it
has often been difficult for male victims to report this, because it
makes them feel humiliated and weak; about two thousand several networks have been established to support them, such as the
Gay Men's Domestic Violence Project.[36]

The feminist campaign against violence against women worked

Leaflet by Women Office Workers of New York, 1979.

not only to protect women and children but also to support research and analysis of the problem. For example, it is now well known that abuse often occurs when a woman tries to separate from her partner; and that many abusive relationships begin with a very controlling, even imprisoning, partner. One woman's story: The husband of a woman I'll call Sheila would not permit her to work outside the home or do anything independent. Each day when he left for work, he recorded the odometer reading on the car and took the phone with him. His need to control became so extreme that he started to dish out her food portions, telling her that she needed to lose weight. He became violent when he suspected any resistance from her. She finally prepared to escape with her three children after getting advice from a feminist hotline in rural California, whose staff told her to gather up her important papers, such as the kids' medical records, bank and insurance information, and personal keepsakes in case she could not go back to the house, which turned out to be true.

The feminist impact against rape may well have been even greater. For this form of violence the historical data are even sparser, because for centuries the cost of reporting was trivial for the culprit and massive for the victim. We learn more by looking at definitions. Before the women's liberation movement, the dominant notion of rape was an assault by a stranger on the street, and rape of children was widely considered a one-in-a-million occurrence, also done by strangers—"dirty old men." So the women's movement had to redefine rape itself: by making people aware not only that the majority of rapes are perpetrated by people who know the victim, and those of children by male family members, but also that rape includes marital rape, homosexual rape, and rape without intercourse. As early as 1971, at least four big cities had rape crisis centers, and soon it was impossible to keep up with the momentum—speakouts, support groups, hotlines, counseling, training for police and medical personnel. There were some fifteen hundred antirape projects by 1976.

One feminist tactic against violence was the "Take Back the Night" march. The first one was probably held in Philadelphia in 1975, sparked by the murder of a young woman walking home from work. That march "went viral," even though there was no Internet then. The phrase and the events were picked up the following year at an international tribunal in Brussels, and soon there were marches across the globe. These marches repudiated, both symbolically and in practice, the widespread acceptance of the view that women should not move through a city alone at night, and that it was at least partly their fault if they were assaulted. "Take Back the Night" represented putting the blame for violence against women where it belonged: on male assailants.

Women's liberation's impact on bodies was probably strongest not in struggling against harm but in working for health. *Our Bodies, Ourselves*, first published in 1971, inaugurated a sea change in women's knowledge of their own bodies. Its major impact was not in communicating information but in promoting new attitudes—that women should learn about their bodies and should face health questions with the understanding that they need not defer to physicians or other moral authorities in making decisions. Out of this first publication and countless local projects arose the National Women's Health Network, now almost forty years old and thriving. One aspect of this influence was the geometric increase in female doctors as women flooded the medical schools, partly out of desire to practice medicine in a woman-friendly way. (In 1905, 4 percent of physicians were women, and that number was virtually unchanged until 1970; in 2011, women were 48.3 percent of med school graduates.) The movement forced changes in medical research, making it no longer acceptable to study only male diseases or use only male subjects in drug testing. The women's movement particularly transformed childbirth, through insisting on women's choices about where, when, and how to deliver babies and—perhaps surprising to many—winning a difficult battle to include fathers in childbirth, in or out of hospitals.

Discrimination in health care is by no means gone. Females earn less than male physicians, are less often promoted, and are less often appointed to medical school professorial or leadership positions. Female physicians cluster in lower-status fields of medicine—such as pediatrics—not so much because these fields require less expertise as because they reflect political values, e.g., that caring for children and women is less prestigious than caring for men. Female patients, particularly poor ones, frequently receive less aggressive treatment when they need it. With these problems continuing, it is hardly surprising that in the 1970s some feminists wanted to reject mainstream medicine altogether. Some learned to do their own cervical examinations, and many experimented with holistic, nonstandard practices, from herbal medicines to rejecting vaccination.

Two issues divided feminists in the 1970s and 1980s: pornography and sex work, especially prostitution. The disagreements show once again that there is no single feminist analysis or program. The pornography issue provoked an angry, name-calling conflict, the "sex wars," at a 1982 conference at Barnard College, which aimed to generate feminist discussion about sexuality (outside the pro- and anti-abortion framework that so dominated the public discourse). Organized in the provocative spirit of the early women's liberation movement by feminists who adopted what came to be called a "pro-sex" line, the conference included speakers who opposed the censorship of pornography (on the basis of a civil liberties principle of free speech and because they doubted that porn was any more insulting or dangerous to women than nonsexual media that depicted women in subordinate roles), criticized a stream of prudery within the women's movement, and affirmed a human right to sexual pleasure. Even more controversial, the conference included Gayle Rubin and Pat Califia, who defended S-M (sadomasochist role-playing) sex.

Providing a platform for these defenders of pornography infuriated another stream of the women's movement. Anti-pornography activists, such as Andrea Dworkin, attacked the conference as promoting patriarchal values and convinced Barnard College to confiscate the conference program on the grounds that it contained some pro-sex statements as well as conference information. These feminists considered pornography to be inevitably coercive, exploitive, and denigrating toward women. "Male sexual aggression is the unifying thematic and behavioral reality of male sexuality," Dworkin wrote. "Pornography is the essential sexuality of male power: of hate, of ownership, of hierarchy; of sadism, of dominance."[37] A Dworkin ally, law professor Catharine MacKinnon, who had earlier been key in expanding federal anti-discrimination laws to include sexual harassment, wrote model bills that criminalized pornography by defining it as a violation of the civil rights of women, a form of sex discrimination, and an abuse of human rights. These bills provided that those who claimed to be harmed by pornography would be entitled to sue for sex discrimination (although, clearly, substantiating that harm would be most difficult). The "pro-sex" feminists criticized this legal strategy as well as the fact that the anti-porn activists allied with Christian conservatives in proposing and supporting these laws; such ordinances were enacted by several city governments but overturned by the courts. This controversy has subsided, but feminists' differences about pornography remain.

Sex work, from Playboy bunnies to prostitution, never produced strong antagonism, but feminists did differ—and continue to differ—about it. Each of three different policies toward prostitution—prohibition, legalization, and decriminalization—had advocates. Among prostitutes themselves, some supported legalization, which exists in some rural areas of Nevada, whereby prostitutes are licensed and inspected; supporters believed that this system provided greater safety. The majority of prostitutes, however, called for decriminalization, the repeal of all laws governing the practice. They argue that sex work is a form of labor that any individual should be free to undertake. Some even asserted that sex work could empower women and increase their autonomy. Influenced by women's liberation, some sex workers began to organize. The earliest and best-known group was COYOTE, "Call Off Your Old Tired Ethics," founded in 1973 by the flamboyant and glamorous feminist sex worker Margo St. James in San Francisco. None of these groups managed to change local laws, however, even though freer sexual norms were simultaneously reducing moralistic outrage. Many 1970s feminists hoped to abolish prostitution entirely, since they considered it always damaging to women and degrading to all, through its commercializing of an activity that should be free of economic pressure. They argued that women and girls are often coerced into sex work, sometimes by men, and often by an economy that deprives women of opportunity for better jobs. They also pointed to the fact that sex workers were far more vulnerable to abuse than other working women.

Still, all feminists and sex workers agreed about fundamental principles and problems. All condemned policies that criminalize the sex workers as opposed to their clients or employers. All believed that sex workers need legal and social protection from violence, exploitation, and other hazards of the occupation, including disease. All condemned coercing people into sex work, of course. Defining coercion, however, exposes the complexity of the issue. Obviously "trafficking" is coercive, when women (or men) are duped, kidnapped, imprisoned, or otherwise forced into prostitution. The data show, however, that the incidence of sex trafficking has been exaggerated (while the incidence of nonsexual trafficking of low-wage workers has been underemphasized). But when poverty and the lack of other work force people into only sex work, is that not coercion? When sex work pays a living wage, or just a higher wage than other jobs, is that not coercion? When we consider what conditions make free choice impossible, we see that sex work becomes a microcosm of the more universal problems of inequality—gender inequality and all other forms of inequality and poverty as well.

Work

The single greatest factor changing women's lives in the twentieth century was that most had to earn wages. Some chose employment because it offered a stimulating career; for most, however, jobs were necessary to support themselves and their families. In part because men's real wages—that is, their buying power—were falling, more families needed women's wages. Women's employment was a major factor strengthening feminism: there is nothing like seeing one's hard work and competence disregarded to make women notice the inequality of the sexes.

But 1970s feminism also involved rethinking and redefining what counted as work. The notion that women were naturally oriented toward housework and child raising had held sway for centuries, and in capitalist society, where work was redefined as earning money, domestic labor had lost its status as work. While most women recognized the labor involved, many contributed to maintaining the assumption that it was "naturally" women's responsibility. By retaining that responsibility, women also retained control over it—no small value. In practice, many men had long contributed to household labor, but the ideal, that the family should consist of male breadwinner and nonemployed wife/mother, remained.

Feminists retheorized domestic labor, in part by identifying its economic value. A "wages for housework" campaign never produced practical demands; who would or could pay these wages? Most men could never afford to hire a housewife, even at minimum wage. Still, the "wages for housework" idea illustrated how the economy depended on women's unpaid labor. Moreover, the majority of women in couples continued to do the bulk of the work even if their hours of employment equaled those of the men they lived with. So feminists began insisting that men share the domestic work, with some success. Men's response affords an example of how consciousness change became behavior change: as more women expected this sharing, more men accommodated to it—and often found they enjoyed it.

Recognizing domestic work as work underlay feminist support for what was then called "welfare," Aid to Families with Dependent Children. A part of the Social Security Act of 1935, this program guaranteed, in principle, aid to the children of poor single parents. Over the years the grants became steadily lower (the usual way that conservatives sought to undercut social programs they opposed but did not wish to to condemn publicly), discriminatory (subjecting recipients to privacy-invading eligibility tests), and stigmatized (recipients being labeled lazy and criminal). In the mid-1960s, a

Welfare rights demonstration, 1977. Photograph by Diana Mara Henry. Copyright © 1977 by Diana Mara Henry/www.dianamarahenry.com.

largely African American welfare rights movement began asserting rights to fair and respectful treatment. Though its members
would not have called themselves feminists—associating that label
with privileged white women—they often *were* feminists, in that
their analysis focused on the disrespect for women's domestic
labor. Some women's liberation groups sought alliances with welfare recipients, as Mothers for Adequate Welfare did in Boston, and
supported the national welfare rights movement.

Backing welfare rights was an attempt by women's liberation
to support the different needs of poor women of color. However,
welfare issues exposed a disagreement within the women's movement, a disagreement that reflected different concerns. NOW, with
its base among employed women, at first saw wage work as the
route to gains for women, so it pushed for subsidized childcare to
enable women to take out-of-home employment and did not offer
support for the welfare rights movement. By contrast, many poor
lone mothers wanted to be able to care for young children themselves, as prosperous mothers could, and fought requirements that
they should be forced into the low-wage labor market and then pay
those same low wages to babysitters. They received support from
the more left-wing women's liberation movement, which wanted
to support poor women and to make the point that domestic labor
was an honorable vocation.

That women were traditionally responsible for all housework
and childcare is a large part of the reason for their lower wages:
paying women less had been justified by the notion that they took
jobs only for "pin money," to afford "extras," while fathers or husbands supported them. This assumption had never been true for
all women, and as the marriage age rose, as separation and divorce
increased, and as children grew more expensive, most women's
wages became vitally necessary to their families. Paying women
less increased profits for employers, lowered men's wages, and

weakened labor's collective power in bargaining with employers—yet many working men still supported this inequality, conditioned by assumptions about women's "natural" role. Besides, the labor market was sexually segregated, so women were slotted into "women's jobs," which paid less. (Even in 2013, female-dominated jobs paid an average of $408 per week and male-dominated jobs $553 per week.) A self-reinforcing logic operated here: women's jobs paid less because women did them, and women did them because the jobs paid less. The women's movement challenged all these aspects of employment discrimination, with considerable success.

An early campaign targeted the sex segregation of job announcements and advertisements. Heretofore they were listed in separate newspaper columns. For example, these ads appeared in the 1968 *Raleigh News and Observer*:

HELP WANTED MALE

Wanted: Office Supervisor. Wholesale distribution office offers rapid financial advancement to young man who learns over-all operation quickly. Start $400.

HELP WANTED FEMALE

Wanted, settled white lady to work nights in rest home. Some experience and transportation.

Wanted, General Office "Gal Friday" type job for stable, personable lady in one girl office. Starting $80.

Attorney Sylvia Roberts, a founder of NOW, won the first sex-discrimination victory under the EEOC in 1969, arguing for Lorena Weeks, who was banned from a better job because it required being able to lift more than thirty pounds. Women laughed about that, since they carried kids and groceries weighing much more. So

Weeks came into court with her heavy manual typewriter—which she often had to move around in her workplace—and indeed, it weighed more than thirty pounds. In 1973, after NOW women had been picketing city newspapers for several years, the Supreme Court, still all male, finally ruled 5–4 that segregated employment ads constituted unlawful discrimination. (Chief Justice Warren Burger's dissent charged that the decision opened a "treacherous path" toward government regulation.)[38]

Desegregating want ads would have achieved little, however, without women's increasing ambitions and assertiveness in pursuing the jobs. As the value of most men's earnings fell, and fewer husbands could single-handedly support a whole family, more women recognized that they would be permanently employed. With aspirations raised by the women's movement, they made gains because they *used* the anti-discrimination laws to bring grievances that forced the EEOC to act. In 1970, women earned on average 59 percent of men's wages; in 2011, 77 percent. (This differential exists today *despite* women having more education than men.) The improved ratio narrowed the gap considerably but did not always improve women's standard of living. Women's earnings in comparison to men's rose in large part because men's real wages fell (now $22 per week *lower* on average than in 1980)—thus many women gained relatively but became poorer in absolute terms.

Employed women's grievances went far beyond wages. Sexual harassment had hounded employed women for centuries. Some of their first strikes, two hundred years ago, protested lewd behavior by foremen. Women in the armed forces had been slotted into the worst jobs with the least benefits and subjected to widespread rape and harassment. In the 1970s, waitresses and saleswomen typically had to buy uniforms or clothing that conformed to standards of appearance imposed by employers and sometimes highly sexualized. Lack-

59 Cents, A Woman's Dollar

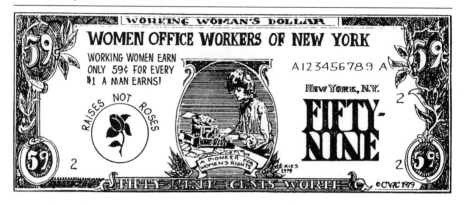

Leaflet by Women Office Workers of New York, 1979.

ing clear job descriptions, they were often called upon to perform arbitrary and insulting tasks, to put in exceptionally long hours, or to give up breaks and holidays at the whim of employers. They were called "girls," whatever their age, and addressed by first names, while a male superior was always "Mr." Women found this disrespect galling. For clericals, nothing symbolized the disrespect they felt more than being asked to make coffee—and their resentment emanated directly from feminist consciousness raising. That their bosses felt entitled to make this demand expressed their expectation that women "naturally" performed domestic chores. Expectations spilled from their homes into their offices; clerical work appeared not only as a job category but also as an emanation of femininity. It was not accidental that Aretha Franklin's 1967 hit "R.E.S.P.E.C.T." became the virtual anthem of the women's movement.

Women's liberation generated a wave of organizing in female-dominated jobs, and it was here that Karen Nussbaum found her life's work. College-educated women were still limited to jobs as secretaries, for which they were usually overqualified, and brought organizing campaigns into job categories that male-dominated labor unions had neglected. The most famous of them, 9to5, began in 1972 when Karen Nussbaum and Ellen Cassedy, both Harvard University clericals, started the office workers group 9to5, which created a sister organization, the union SEIU 925. Women Employed (WE), an offshoot of the CWLU, began in 1973. One of its early studies of clerical work—which WE, cleverly, managed to get funded by the Playboy Foundation—began with this telling anecdote from a receptionist: "A client came onto the floor . . . looked directly at me and asked, 'Isn't anyone here?' "[39]

All these organizing projects flowed from consciousness raising, as well as feminism's osmosis into the consciousness of many who had never experienced consciousness-raising groups: the strategies reflected, first, interrelated and quite possibly inseparable demands for tangible gains and respectful treatment, and second, personal relationships as the basis of organizing. 9to5's first ten members spent a year just talking, venting resentments, and musing about how to bring in more workers. They began a newsletter that focused on disrespect as well as the male/female wage gap. They began to offer services such as workshops providing free legal advice and courses on leadership skills. In 1973 the group sent Ellen Cassedy to Chicago to attend the Midwest Academy, run by Heather Booth of the CWLU. What she learned confirmed a personalized recruitment method: before anyone could become a 9to5 member, she had a private lunch with an older member. This provided an orientation and created a personal relationship. New members were then immediately given some responsibility, a task to accomplish; this method not only enabled the group to identify potential activists but also made the new person feel needed—a vital part of becoming part of a community.

Even the services 9to5 provided to individuals who never became active members served to educate and raise consciousness. Many workers complained about workplace problems but did not identify them as sex discrimination—for example, a service representative at New England Telephone who said she was "treated like a child" or one at an engineering firm who thought it natural that the draftsmen were all men. By taking such cases to the EEOC, the complainants were learning about sex discrimination. By asking questions that stimulated thinking, 9to5's surveys functioned as a form of consciousness raising.

When office-worker organizers tried to reach clericals in the banking and insurance industries, however, those mega-corporations struck back with massive anti-union publicity, threats, and firings and successfully held off unionization. The early successes of clerical organizing, ironically, rested on discrimination against women, which put middle-class and working-class women into the same clerical jobs and thus created a cross-class alliance. When feminist pressure opened managerial and professional jobs to educated women, that class alliance was broken, and the union movement weakened accordingly. As throughout the labor movement, unionizing achieved only limited gains with respect to overall social justice issues. 9to5 organizers found that women responded less positively when they brought in other issues, such as the Vietnam War, so kept their focus specific to clerical work. Many workers were afraid of the labels "feminist" and "union," and 9to5 did not use them.

Nevertheless, 9to5 and similar women's organizing influenced thousands, perhaps even millions, of women workers toward increased self-respect; and when these efforts combined with the massive cultural transformations wrought by the rest of the women's movement, they brought higher wages and made supervisors understand that office workers were not their wives. By parodying "National Secretaries Day" with slogans like "Raises, Not Roses," the movement hammered in the understanding that clericals were workers who would not be bought off with one day a year of thanks. But the movement soon changed the slogan to "Raises *and* Roses"!

For employed mothers, childcare was an absolute necessity.

(Fathers—there were few single fathers then—were not typically held responsible for their children.) Working-class women, whose wages were usually not high enough to pay for daycare centers, relied on family members or "home daycare," done by other working-class women who cared for a few children other than their own in their homes. In the World War II period, the need for women to work in defense plants had led to government-subsidized childcare; after the war these programs were usually cut, despite women's agitation to keep them. Now women's liberation groups took up the fight— especially at universities and other large employers. Elsewhere daycare cooperatives arose, sometimes staffed entirely by parents, sometimes with professional staff paid through a sliding scale in which those who could afford higher fees subsidized those who couldn't. Responding to women's pressure, federal programs begun in the early 1970s offered limited numbers of very poor families some childcare help. On the whole, however, the women's movement did not make a major dent in the childcare problem, and low-wage women workers cannot usually afford high-quality daycare centers providing children with safe and stimulating play environments.

Meanwhile, women pushed their way into professions that discriminated or even excluded them: law, medicine, and the university professoriate most visibly, and even the ministry. In 1970, Barbara Andrews, a woman disabled from cerebral palsy who used a wheelchair, became the first pastor ordained in an American Lutheran church. In 1972, Sally Priesand became the first female rabbi, but only after being repeatedly rejected by a rabbinical school; she finally earned her degree as the lone woman among thirty-five men, many of whom claimed she was only there to find a husband. When the Episcopal Church refused to accept female ministers, a group of women deacons and bishops conducted an "irregular" ordination in 1974, and just two years later the official church capitulated. Evangelicals started a feminist journal. Seminaries filled with women.

Major denominations began rewriting liturgies, changing "man-kind" to "humankind" or "people of faith" and even removing "He" for God and replacing it with "Our Lord" or the like.

Culture

Cultural change happens particularly slowly, with few precise milestones, so we may not notice it or what created it. In fact, femi-nism transformed popular culture, though often it took decades for everyone to see the results.

The influence of women's liberation was most visible in cloth-ing. Before the 1970s, working women had to wear stockings, garter belts or girdles, high heels, and dresses. By 1980, a gen-eration of feminists had legitimated comfortable low-heeled shoes, rejected girdles, and made pants acceptable for all occasions. Many women still love heels and skirts, but they have a choice. The 1970s radicals tended also to reject makeup and the carefully coiffed hair of the 1950s, but this by no means meant a rejection of beauty; it merely changed standards of what *was* beautiful. Civil rights had similarly made "natural" black hair beautiful and fashionable, and white women with curly hair adopted a version for themselves.

Feminist influence likewise affected attitudes toward female bodies, for which delicacy had once been the norm. Much of the credit for this transformation should go to Patsy Mink, congress-woman from Hawaii, who brought us Title IX of the Education Amendments of 1972, prohibiting sex discrimination in schools. Title IX drew tens of thousands of women into active sports, and they then redefined strong, muscled bodies as beautiful. Of course, merchants soon capitalized on these new norms, and, as always in a consumerist society, styles that were once rebellious and counter-cultural soon became new standards, sometimes as conformist or even coercive as the old.

The Fat Chance Performance Group, celebrating "real" women's bodies. Photograph by Cathy Cade, courtesy of the Bancroft Library, University of California, Berkeley.

The feminist health movement contributed mightily to new prac-tices of eating and cooking, by promoting whole grains, fresh pro-duce, and organic food. Feminists were often active in starting food co-ops, and their presence stimulated for-profit stores to compete by offering healthier foods. But these new standards were deeply stratified by social class and race. Vegetarianism, whole-grain food, and organic produce were simultaneously products of cultural feminism and of gentrification, and these changing tastes became markers of privilege among those with the time to do fine cook-ing and to keep their children's diets pure. Working-class women, by contrast, often unable to afford healthier food, were more often involved in campaigns to nourish children through improving school lunches and providing school breakfasts.

Many women's liberation groups created cultural projects. The CWLU created a graphics collective that made beautiful silk-screened posters, on global as well as American issues. Poetry

poured out of the movement. Women's rock bands formed and
played at "women's lib" dances, encouraging women previously
confined to singing to play instruments. Naomi Weisstein started
a band in Chicago because she was enraged by the Rolling Stones'
glee that a girlfriend was "under my thumb." With her sister musicians she began writing lyrics that allowed feminists to rock out,
such as these:

> *Poppa don't lay that shit on me,*
> *I can't accommodate.*
> *You bring me down,*
> *It makes you cool.*
> *You think I like it?*
> *You're a goddamn fool.*

These bands were the pioneers. There were hugely popular
women's singing groups previously, like the Supremes and the

Women's Liberation Rock Band, 1972–73. Photograph by Virginia Blaisdell.

Andrews Sisters, but almost never female instrumentalists. Feminism made women's rock commercial, from the 1970s all-"girl" rock band the Runaways to Madonna in the 1980s and the riot grrrls in the 1990s. Some feminist cultural projects became institutionalized, such as the national women's music festivals and the "womyn's music" they promoted.

Television incorporated some feminist themes quickly. At times feminism was negatively caricatured: *Maude,* a sitcom that ran from 1972 to 1978, featured an overbearing, hectoring social worker/therapist who preached women's equality. But *The Mary Tyler Moore Show* offered a more complex and more daring group of people. CBS told the show's creators that "American audiences won't tolerate divorce in a series lead any more than they will tolerate Jews, people with mustaches, and people who live in New York," but the show broke all these rules. Moore was single, committed to her job, and not seeking marriage; what's more, she had strong female and workplace friendships but was not afraid to be in charge. It took until the 1980s to get the first big-time female-buddies cop show, *Cagney and Lacey,* which ran through 125 episodes with thirty-six Emmy nominations and fourteen wins; Helen Mirren's breakthrough role as the star of *Prime Suspect* could not have happened without this predecessor. One African American woman, Teresa Graves, played a cop in *Get Christie Love!,* but the series did not last, and the few sitcoms that showed blacks with respect, like the Cosby show, remained headed by men.

Hollywood roles for women had long presented only two main options for whites—beautiful "good girl" or evil seductress. For women of color there was only one—faithful servant. Katharine Hepburn had been an attorney, but she was unique. By the mid-1970s this changed. The stars still had to be young, white, and beautiful, but their strength, independence, and complexity increased. Overtly feminist Hollywood films did not appear until the 1980s;

the most striking of them was 1988's *The Accused*. In it Jodie Foster, who got her start playing a teenage prostitute in 1976's *Taxi Driver*, showed us a real working-class rape victim. Based on an actual gang rape in a working-class bar that had prompted major feminist protest, the film presented a feminist view of rape without polite euphemisms. It proclaimed that neither flirtation nor sexy dress justifies rape, that the victimized woman need feel no shame, and that the right response is to press charges and refuse to be intimidated by public stigma—making the woman a hero rather than a victim.

It was far more difficult for the women's movement to break into the male-dominated fine arts. The witty feminist art group Guerrilla Girls created parodic posters and donned gorilla masks to ask, Why are there so few female artists in the museums? Even in the second decade of the twenty-first century, the gains have been small. While women conductors and composers are becoming more common, men continue to dominate all the major orchestras. Women had long been iconic stars in dance, and leaders in modern dance, but in ballet women choreographers are still hard to find, with the exception of that crossover from jazz dance Twyla Tharp. Judy Chicago created a sensation with her 1974–79 *Dinner Party* ceramic installation that featured many vagina-like images, smoothing the way for Eve Ensler's *Vagina Monologues* in 1996. Perhaps the most influential group of women visual artists were Chicana muralists working in the Southwest: Judy Baca, Barbara Carrasco, Sonya Fe, Carmen Lomas Garza, Ester Hernández, Judithe Hernández, Yolanda López, Patricia Rodríguez, and others produced a virtual explosion of grassroots feminist imagery. The greatest gains have been literary. Female novelists, short-story writers, poets, and essayists of all racial/ethnic groups now abound, although the most influential book review outlets still disproportionately ignore them, and "chick lit" is still a category inviting disdain. Slowly female playwrights are getting work produced even on Broadway.

Perhaps the biggest gender change in high culture was the transformative impact feminism had on the universities. Women now earn more BAs and PhDs than men do, and this resulted in part from a change in who is teaching them. The young feminists of the 1970s and before rarely met a female professor, and that mattered: even the kindliest male professors rarely mentored their female students equally with their male students. All three of us college professors writing this book, like all professional women and college students, benefited directly from feminism and the affirmative action programs pushed by the movement. I never had a female college or university instructor, and was never taken seriously as a student. In graduate school I was one of two women studying history, and we two, unlike the men, were never invited to the dinners with visiting scholars and never recommended for jobs. As I write, in 2013, I work for a department that is half female, and women receiving PhDs in history outnumber the men. Similar gains now show in most humanities fields, while women remain minorities, even small minorities, in the sciences.

This change happened on two levels. First, women students, armed with the feminist critique of androcentric—often called patriarchal—curricula, demanded change, and already in 1970 the first women's studies program opened. Before long there were hundreds, and today it is rare for a college or university not to have a women's studies program. Second, women began earning higher degrees and, thanks to anti-discrimination complaints and women's caucuses within professional organizations, got hired as faculty. Once in universities, they soon made it impossible for traditionalists to maintain that they were inferior scholars, and they also began to mentor women students, which in turn created more professional women.

Academic women transformed not only who taught but also what was taught. In anthropology and sociology, some gendered research had been traditional, but economics, history, and literature ignored gender. For a scholar to write about women was to write about something unimportant, while men took on the "big questions." In literature, women's writing, with a few exceptions, was a marginal genre. The generation entering the universities in the 1970s changed that. Scholarship about women and gender flourished to the extent that by the 1980s, students often learned at school what the previous cohort of feminists had reinvented. The bottom-up demand for women's studies courses created, in a feedback loop, more jobs for women in the colleges and universities. Women's studies in turn nurtured gay, now LGBT, studies programs and scholarship. Soon scholars and courses began to examine masculinity as a gendered construction as well.

Much of "women's studies" happened outside academic institutions. Throughout the country 1970s women's liberation activists created "women's schools," and many still continue. They reflected women's desire to learn material that had previously been offered only to men—classes in auto mechanics and self-defense were ubiquitous—but also material that would develop their movement: classes in women's history, feminist theory, and economics. They both reflected and strengthened women's confidence that they could take on "male" work, from biology to truck driving. Many of the classes at women's liberation schools differed only slightly from consciousness raising, because they provided opportunities for women to meet in small groups, while other classes involved extensive reading and study.

One of the most enduring material achievements of 1970s feminism is *Ms.* magazine, founded and symbolized by the formidable Gloria Steinem. At age twenty-nine, in 1963, she was already a journalist who not only wrote the news but also featured in the news, because of her article about going undercover as a Playboy Bunny. Her beauty helped smooth the path for her ambitions, but her unfaltering commitment has by now guided them for over forty years. She too was a product of women's liberation, having been deeply influenced by the 1969 speakout on abortion mentioned at the beginning of this chapter. She continued that speakout in print, in the 1972 first issue of *Ms.*, by publishing the names of women who had had illegal abortions. (One writer listed that as one of the "100 Media Moments that Changed America.")[40] The editors originally intended to publish a newsletter until Steinem raised some major funds and the first three hundred thousand copies of a real magazine sold out in eight days. Its success was one measure of feminist enthusiasm, at a time when even women's magazines were edited by men and when most female journalists were confined to "human interest" rather than news assignments. Over its history *Ms.* has been attacked for being too radical and not radical enough, and weathered intense debates about what advertising to accept, if any; but it has managed to maintain its coverage of issues important to women of all classes, ethnicities, races and ages. In 2001 the Feminist Majority Foundation took ownership of the magazine, whose banner reads, "More than a Magazine—A Movement!"

THERE IS NO definitive end point for the women's liberation movement, especially since many organizations and projects begun in the 1970s are ongoing. The National Organization for Women continues strong to this day. Indeed, some feminist activities accelerated just as others slowed. But several phenomena marked an important transition. By the mid-1980s, a critical mass of college graduates had studied with feminist professors, often in women's studies courses. By the late 1980s, even larger groups of young people, both male and female, had been raised by feminist parents. Moreover, some of the mass media presented feminist characters and communities—even if that f-word was not mentioned— which presented alternatives to the majority representations that remained organized around male authority figures and heroes. In other words, feminism was moving to new generations in three ways: formal education, parental upbringing, and mass culture. So it should come as no surprise that a revival of feminist energy appeared early in the 1990s.

That renewed energy was also responding to an angry backlash. Led by conservatives, parts of the Republican Party, and Christian fundamentalists, the anti-feminist opposition was funded by massive corporate donations. The backlash also pulled in millions who imagined that feminism would somehow destroy families. It attacked affirmative action, gay and lesbian rights, and women in politics; it challenged and sometimes weakened laws against sex discrimination; it promoted commercial products, from movies to advertisements, that featured women in traditional roles and suggested that women who stepped out of them would suffer. It moved most Republicans and Protestant evangelicals from accepting abortion rights to opposing them, and its intensive propaganda made many women who needed abortions suffer from guilt. Ultimately the backlash even attempted to attack contraception, which almost all Americans considered a basic necessity of life as long ago as the 1930s. The next chapter discusses women's activism since the 1980s in the context of that opposition.

1. Flora Davis, *Moving the Mountain* (New York: Simon & Schuster, 1991), 113.

2. Carol Hanisch and Elizabeth Sutherland in *Notes from the First Year* (New York: New York Radical Women, 1968).

3. Loretta Ross, interview with Elizabeth Martínez, Voices of Feminism Oral History Project, Sophia Smith Collection, Smith College, 9–10.

4. Susan Faludi, "Death of a Revolutionary," *The New Yorker*, April 15, 2013.

5. Stacey K. Sowards and Valerie R. Renegar, "The Rhetorical Functions of Consciousness-Raising in Third Wave Feminism," *Communication Studies* 55, no. 4 (Winter 2004): 543.

6. Vivian Gornick, *The Solitude of Self: Thinking About Elizabeth Cady Stanton* (New York: Farrar, Straus & Giroux, 2005), 14.

7. Kathy Sarachild (née Amatniek), speech to First National Conference of Stewardesses for Women's Rights, 1973, available at https://organizingforwo mensliberation.wordpress.com/2012/09/25/consciousness-raising-a-radical-weapon/, accessed June 19, 2013.

8. Amy Kesselman, "Our Gang of Four: Friendship and Women's Liberation," in *The Feminist Memoir Project: Voices from Women's Liberation*, ed. Rachel Blau DuPlessis and Ann Snitow (New York: Three Rivers Press, 1998), 25.

9. Priscilla Long, "We Called Ourselves Sisters," in DuPlessis and Snitow, *Feminist Memoir Project*, 327.

10. Susan Sutheim, "For Witches," in *Sisterhood Is Powerful*, ed. Robin Morgan (New York: Random House, 1970), 557–58.

11. Rosalyn Fraad Baxandall, "Catching the Fire," in DuPlessis and Snitow, *Feminist Memoir Project*, 210–11.

12. Pam Allen, *Free Space: A Perspective on the Small Group in Women's Liberation* (Albany, CA: Women's Liberation Basement Press, 1970), 7.

13. Pluralistic ignorance, a term coined by Floyd H. Allport in 1931, describes "a situation where a majority of group members privately reject a norm, but assume (incorrectly) that most others accept it." Daniel Katz and Floyd H. Allport, *Student Attitudes* (Syracuse, NY: Craftsman, 1931).

14. Jean Tepperman, "Two Jobs: Women Who Work in Factories," quoted in Morgan, *Sisterhood Is Powerful*, 133.

15. Karla Jay, *Tales of the Lavender Menace: A Memoir of Liberation* (New York: Basic Books, 1999).

16. Barbara Emerson, "Coming of Age: Civil Rights and Feminism," in DuPlessis and Snitow, *The Feminist Memoir Project*, 69.

17. Robyn Ceanne Spencer, "Engendering the Black Freedom Struggle," *Journal of Women's History* 20, no. 1, (2008): 91.

18. On white pronouncements blaming black "matriarchy," see Daniel Patrick Moynihan, *The Negro Family: The Case for National Action* (Washington: U.S. Dept. of Labor, 1965).

19. Frances Beal, "Double Jeopardy: To Be Black and Female," in Morgan, *Sisterhood Is Powerful*, 343, available at http://www.hartford-hwp.com/archives/45a/196.html.

20. Jennifer Nelson, "'Abortions Under Community Control': Feminism, Nationalism, and the Politics of Reproduction Among New York City's Young Lords," *Journal of Women's History* 13, no. 1, (Spring 2001): 161–62.

21. Excerpts from film script "I Am Somebody," Local 1199, quoted in *America's Working Women*, ed. Rosalyn Baxandall and Linda Gordon (New York: Norton, 1995), 359–60.

22. Celene Krauss, "Women and Toxic Waste Protests: Race, Class and Gender as Resources of Resistance," *Qualitative Sociology* 16, no. 3 (1993): 254–55.

23. Magda Ramírez-Castaneda, "A Proud Daughter of a Mexican Worker," in *Chicanas of 18th Street: Narratives of a Movement from Latino Chicago* (Urbana: University of Illinois Press, 2011), 153.

24. Laura Pulido, *Black, Brown, Yellow, and Left: Radical Activism in Los Angeles* (Berkeley and Los Angeles: University of California Press, 2006), chapter 7.

25. Elizabeth Martínez, "History Makes Us, We Make History," in DuPlessis and Snitow, *Feminist Memoir Project*, 120.

26. Chude Pam Parker Allen, "Loneliness in the Circle of Trust," at http://www.crmvet.org/info/chudexp.htm, accessed September 23, 2013.

27. Catherine Stimpson, *Where the Meanings Are: Feminism and Cultural Spaces* (New York: Routledge, 1988), 32–33.

28. Danielle L. McGuire, *At the Dark End of the Street: Black Women, Rape, and Resistance* (New York: Knopf, 2010), chapter 5.

29. Quoted in Krauss, "Women and Toxic Waste Protests," 258.

30. Quoted in Paula Giddings, *When and Where I Enter: The Impact of Black Women on Race and Sex in America* (New York: Morrow, 1984), 316.

31. Quoted in Alice Echols, *Daring to Be Bad: Radical Feminism in America, 1967–1975* (Minneapolis: University of Minnesota Press, 1989), 106.

32. Myra Marx Ferree, *Controversy and Coalition: the New Feminist Movement* (Boston: Twayne, 1985).

33. Eugene Volokh, UCLA School of Law, "Menacing Speech, Today and During the Civil Rights Movement," *Wall Street Journal*, April 3, 2001, available at http://www2.law.ucla.edu/volokh/nurember.htm, accessed March 30, 2012. A Ninth Circuit Court of Appeals decision finally shut the site down in 2002 after a prolonged debate. The *Nuremberg Files* case, which is officially titled *Planned Parenthood v. American Coalition of Life Activists*, is available online at http://laws.findlaw.com/9th/9935320.html.

34. *Madrigal v. Quilligan*, no. 75-2057, U.S. District Court for the Central District of California, June 30, 1978, 25, 35–36.

35. California survey reported at http://www.huffingtonpost.com/2012/11/12/domestic-violence-survey-_n_2115528.html and http://californiawatch.org/dailyreport/domestic-violence-survey-finds-shift-attitudes-awareness-18653, accessed September 23, 2013.

36. Gay Men's Domestic Violence Project website, http://gmdvp.org/about-us/, accessed September 23, 2013.

37. Andrea Dworkin, *Pornography: Men Possessing Women* (New York: Dutton, 1981), 57, xxxix.

38. The case was *Pittsburgh Press Co. v. Pittsburgh Commission on Human Relations*, 413 U.S. 376 (1973).

39. "The ~~Girls~~ Women in the Office: The Economic Status of Clerical Workers" (Chicago: Women Employed Institute, n.d.).

40. Jim Willis, *100 Media Moments That Changed America* (Santa Barbara, CA: Greenwood Press, 2010), 121–22.

March for Women's Lives, Washington D.C., April 2004. Photograph by Nikki Kahn, Getty Images.

FROM A MINDSET TO A MOVEMENT

FEMINISM SINCE 1990

by Astrid Henry

I n the fall of 1991, Rebecca Walker, daughter of renowned author Alice Walker, was a twenty-two-year-old senior at Yale University, fed up with the stereotype that Generation X—the post-baby-boomer generation born after 1964—was politically apathetic. Having started a magazine for people of color and worked on AIDS activism, Rebecca was involved with a number of progressive causes while an undergraduate. But it wasn't until October of 1991 that her generation, as she put it, "found a place to enter the political fray and share our passion for change."[1] For many, the incentive to step onto a public political stage was watching Anita Hill, a law professor and former lawyer at the Equal Employment Opportunity Commission (EEOC), come forward to accuse Supreme Court nominee Clarence Thomas of sexual harassment—and then subsequently seeing Hill disparaged by an all-white male group of U.S. senators.

The retirement of Supreme Court Justice Thurgood Marshall four months earlier had unexpectedly created a resurgence of feminist activism, coinciding with the creation of the term "third wave" to describe new feminists. Marshall was a liberal icon: he had served as the chief counsel to the NAACP from 1940 to 1961, during which time he argued many cases before the court on which he would later serve, including most famously *Brown v. Board of Education of Topeka*, the 1954 case desegregating U.S. public schools. When named to the Supreme Court by Democratic president Lyndon Johnson in 1967, Marshall became the first African American justice. His career on the Court had made him an ally to feminists. His retirement was therefore met with trepidation from those on the left, who awaited the nomination of his replacement by Republican president George H. W. Bush.

On July 1, Bush announced that he had selected Clarence Thomas, an African American federal judge, to fill Marshall's seat. Many saw Bush's choice of Thomas as cynical: Bush had replaced Marshall with an African American judge who had spent his career opposing the liberal policies advanced by Marshall, including affirmative action and abortion rights. Civil rights, feminist, and other progressive groups spent the rest of the summer protesting the nomination.

But nobody anticipated the spectacle of Thomas's confirmation hearings before the Senate Judiciary Committee in September and October of 1991, and few who watched these nationally televised hearings will forget their inherent drama. Anita Hill, an African American lawyer who had worked with Thomas at both the Department of Education and the EEOC, came forward to provide an account of Thomas's sexually harassing behavior in the early 1980s. Hill reported that Thomas had routinely used sexually offensive language at work, including discussing the size of his penis, joking about pubic hair on a Coke can, and pressuring Hill to go out with him.

At the time of Thomas's confirmation hearings, the Senate was still nearly all white and all male, with only two Asian American male senators and two white women senators.[2] The Senate

Judiciary Committee that oversaw the proceedings—discussing sexual harassment, racism, and gender equality and openly challenging Anita Hill's testimony–was composed entirely of white men. These senators had little grasp of the impact that their own proceedings would have on the audience who sat transfixed in front of their televisions to watch them. The sight of these fourteen men debating the veracity of Hill's claims and trying to understand the concepts of sexual harassment and intraracial gender politics "seemed to shake latent feminists out of their slumber," wrote feminist commentator Deborah Siegel. "Because of Anita Hill, scads of younger women realized that some of the rights they had taken for granted were tentative at best and that accused sexual harassers could get promoted to Supreme Court Justice, while the women who accused them got discredited and disgraced."[3] The Senate ultimately voted to confirm Thomas to the Court; the vote of 52–48 marked the narrowest Supreme Court confirmation vote in over a century.

The Clarence Thomas confirmation hearings were a wake-up call for why feminism was still urgently needed. The Senate Judiciary Committee that oversaw it was a clear sign that the Senate itself was in need of a feminist revolution. Patty Murray, then a state senator in Washington State, thought while watching the hearings, "Who [on the Judiciary Committee] is saying what I would say if I was there?" After talking to other women who were similarly frustrated by the lack of women in Congress, Murray decided to run for the U.S. Senate in the 1992 elections. So did Carol Moseley Braun, a former representative to the Illinois State House. Murray and Moseley Braun were joined by Dianne Feinstein and Barbara Boxer, who, because of a special election coinciding with a regular election, both ran for separate U.S. Senate seats in California. All four women won their elections, increasing the number of women in the Senate from two to six (or 6 percent), and making Moseley

Braun the first—and so far the only—African American woman elected to the U.S. Senate. In elections for the U.S. House in 1992, women also increased their ranks, with nineteen new female representatives, for a total of forty-seven women, or 11 percent of the House. The media called 1992 "the Year of the Woman," and the congressional elections (to say nothing of President Bush's defeat that same year) were seen as a direct by-product of the Thomas hearings and Anita Hill's treatment by the male senators. As Eleanor Holmes Norton, congressional delegate for Washington, D.C., noted: "It is very hard to think of any legal proceedings that had the effect of the Anita Hill hearings in the sense that women clearly went to the polls with the notion in mind that you have to have more women in Congress."[4]

The Clarence Thomas hearings also had a major impact on feminists at the grassroots level. A month after Thomas's appointment to the Court, a group of women published a nearly full-page statement in the *New York Times*. Signed by 1,603 women, "African American Women in Defense of Ourselves" emphasized the necessity of taking an intersectional feminist approach to understanding how gender, race, sexuality, and power all converged in the hearings, noting that "many have erroneously portrayed the allegations against Clarence Thomas as an issue of either gender or race. As women of African descent, we understand sexual harassment as both."[5] African American women also responded to the Thomas hearings in a special January 1992 issue of *Ms.* magazine whose cover read "Rage + Women = Power." Among the contributors to the issue were noted second-wave African American feminists such as Eleanor Holmes Norton and Barbara Smith, as well as Anita Hill herself. Also included was twenty-two-year-old Rebecca Walker. Outraged by the Thomas hearings, Walker spoke directly to her peers, urging them to take up the feminist mantle for a new generation: "So I write this as a plea to all women, especially the women of my generation. Let Thomas' confirmation hearings serve to remind you, as it did me, that the fight is far from over. Let this dismissal of a woman's experience move you to anger. Turn that outrage into political power." Walker closed the essay with a line that deliberately used feminism's wave metaphor to situate herself in feminist history and to galvanize younger feminists into action, encouraging them to see themselves as the next generation, or wave, of the women's movement. She wrote: "I am not a postfeminism feminist. I am the Third Wave." As she would later reflect, "Hill's courage made me write those words."[6]

This chapter focuses on feminists who, like Rebecca Walker, came of age in a United States profoundly shaped by the movements for women's rights described in this book's earlier chapters, describing the feminism they articulated and advocated in the 1990s and the early twenty-first century. Born during and after the social upheavals of the 1960s and 1970s—and part of the two demographic cohorts known as Generation X (born 1964–82) and the Millennial Generation (born 1982–2000)—this group of activists grew up taking for granted many of the social, political, and economic gains achieved in the decades prior to and surrounding their births. Born into a world in which at least a basic level of gender equality had been achieved, raised to believe they could do anything boys could do, educated by women's studies programs, and offered opportunities never before available, women in this period absorbed feminism all around them—in their homes, in their classrooms, in the media, and in the political landscape they entered into as adults. For this group of women, feminism initially was more a mindset than a movement. By the twenty-first century, however, as we shall see, a feminist movement was resurfacing, albeit relying on new kinds of collective action and solidarity particular to its historical moment.

While acknowledging their debt to the feminists who came

before them, these feminist writers and activists initially defined their feminism around generational difference and even hostility, stressing their critiques of the earlier movement rather than their continuity with it. This generational focus was, in part, a result of the fact that many of the most visible spokeswomen of this new feminism were the daughters of 1970s feminists—people like Rebecca Walker—and thus they often spoke of feminism as familial, writing as daughters rejecting their mothers' feminism. Their critiques of 1970s feminism rightly homed in on its weakest points, such as its overwhelming whiteness and inability to create an interracial movement, as well as its hostility to popular commercial culture. Yet other criticisms were only partially correct, such as their view of the women's liberation movement as predominantly anti-sexual and humorless.

In the twenty-first century, feminism in the United States shifted form. As it developed as both a set of activist practices and a body of thought, it focused less on generational conflict and more on how to address the political and social inequalities that remained even after a century of feminist activism. In the aftermath of September 11, 2001, feminism became even more global, connecting feminists around the world with the Internet technologies that emerged during this period, like blogs and social networks. It focused its energies on issues such as sexuality, media representation, work-life balance, and violence against women, as well as growing economic disparities. These issues are not new, of course, but both the larger changes in our culture and the successes of the earlier feminist movements have shifted their meaning. While connected to earlier movements to advance gender equality and social justice, this new feminism was not a mass-based movement for social change like its 1970s predecessor discussed in chapter 2; nor was it tied to concrete political and policy goals like the social justice feminisms described in chapter 1.

Rebecca Walker as Emblem of the New Feminism

Rebecca Walker was an emblematic spokeswoman for her generation—the post-baby-boomer, Generation X feminists who began calling themselves feminism's "third wave"—inasmuch as she expressed the ideas and perspectives found in much contemporary feminism. Born in 1969, daughter of African American writer Alice Walker and goddaughter of white feminist icon Gloria Steinem, Rebecca Walker was raised with feminism all around her; in her writing, she regularly described feminism as being like a kind of "home." It is worth noting that when she was eighteen she legally changed her last name from Leventhal—from her father, white civil rights lawyer Mel Leventhal—to Walker, in order to connect more to her mother and her mother's side of the family. Alice Walker's prominence as a second-wave feminist, Pulitzer Price–winning novelist, and occasional writer for *Ms.* magazine helped Rebecca to publish her essay "Becoming the Third Wave." The essay can be read as a sign of her entitlement and her sense of responsibility: the daughter of feminism, both literally and figuratively, she saw feminism as her own, yet as its inheritor she felt compelled to continue it by launching another wave. While Anita Hill was a reluctant activist—coming forward to testify at the Senate hearings only after being strongly coaxed to do so—Walker used the opening provided by Hill's testimony to claim a central spot on the feminist stage. "I am ready to decide, as my mother decided before me, to devote much of my energy to the history, health, and healing of women," she wrote, describing feminism as something that can be passed down from mother to daughter but also something that must be claimed anew by each generation.[7]

In her 1992 essay's final declaration—"I am not a postfeminism feminist. I am the Third Wave"—Walker made three rhetorical moves that would reverberate throughout the 1990s and be repeated by other "next generation" feminists. First, in calling herself and, by extension, her generation the "third wave," she used feminism's wave metaphor in order both to highlight the connections between the "second" and "third" waves of the women's movement and to distance herself from "postfeminism feminists." The term "third wave" thus signaled a shared feminist lineage and a rejection of postfeminism, or the idea that feminism is no longer needed. Second, in calling herself "third wave" rather than merely "feminist," Walker stressed generational differences within feminism, arguing that the time had come for a new movement led by young women. "From my experience talking with young women and being one myself, it has become clear to me that young women are struggling with the feminist label," she would later write. "Young women coming of age today wrestle with the term because we have a very different vantage point on the world than that of our foremothers."[8] Finally, by naming herself—and, by extension, her generation—as "third wave" from its very inception, Walker used feminism's wave metaphor to brand the new movement, a move that helped its launch into the public sphere but also demonstrated that this younger group of activists did not necessarily share their predecessors' antipathy to feminism being marketing like a commodity.

Rebecca Walker's writing therefore symbolized in a vivid way the daughter's struggle with her mother's feminism. When her essay was published in *Ms.* in 1992, she described herself as following in her mother's footsteps in carrying the feminist movement forward; three years later, when she edited a collection of essays entitled *To Be Real: Telling the Truth and Changing the Face of Feminism*, she directly challenged the feminism of her mother's generation, arguing that the new generation was impatient with inherited feminist orthodoxies. As she writes in *To Be Real*: "For many of us it seems that to be a feminist in the way that we have seen or understood feminism is to conform to an identity and way of living that doesn't allow for individuality, complexity, or less than perfect personal histories."[9] Walker's development as a writer and spokeswoman for feminists in Generation X exhibited an increasing emphasis on intergenerational difference and conflict, focusing on the third wave's rejection of many of the tenets of the second-wave movement. She argued for a feminism committed to "being real," encouraging feminists of her generation to acknowledge the full complexity and contradictions of people's lives and to discard any form of feminist dogma. Finally, writing as a biracial and bisexual woman who did not neatly fit into prescriptive categories—including feminism's own categories—she challenged feminism to broaden its focus to include a wide range of social justice issues beyond "just" women's rights.

Walker's activism in the early 1990s also demonstrated her complex relationship with the prior generation's feminism. In the summer of 1992, a few months after the publication of her *Ms.* article, Walker graduated from Yale. After "trying to figure out how to organize the two hundred or so young women from around the country who have written me passionate letters echoing my sentiments that 'I am not a post-feminist feminist, I am the third wave,'" she cofounded Third Wave Direct Action Corporation with white 1990 Harvard graduate Shannon Liss.[10] The group's first project, Freedom Summer '92, drew on "the tactics and ideals of the civil rights movement," sending an interracial group of 120 young women and men on a cross-country bus ride to register voters for the upcoming election; this action led to twenty thousand new registered voters, "most of them low-income, young women of color."[11] As Liss told a reporter in 1992, "I grew up thinking that women's problems had been solved," but "I'm starting to see now that women are actually moving backwards, particularly on the issue of abortion."[12] The group was committed to continuing the feminist fight of the past and bringing younger women into the process, "cultivating young women's leadership and activism in order to bring the power of young women to bear on politics as usual," said Walker.[13] Yet the group's founders also saw themselves as doing something different than had the feminists of the previous generation. Like its name, Third Wave Direct Action Corporation was "a response to critiques of the Second Wave. It was important to us (the founders) that Third Wave be, at its very core, multi-racial, multi-ethnic, multi-issue, pan-sexual orientation, with people and issues from all socio-economic backgrounds represented."[14] The group's mission statement articulated a broad vision of feminism and an inclusive call for participants, framing this expanded vision of feminism as a critique of where the second wave had fallen short.

After the 1992 elections, Third Wave Direct Action Corporation continued to work on young feminist issues with the alumni of the Freedom Summer action—the word "corporation" in the group's name yet another sign that this generation's approach to collective action was different than that of their feminist predecessors'. Walker was recognized for her work with Third Wave when she was named Feminist of the Year by the Fund for the Feminist Majority in 1992 and, later, as one of the fifty most influential American leaders under the age of forty by *Time* magazine in 1994. In 1995, the group originally envisioned by Walker and Liss refocused its energies on creating a foundation that could financially support young women's activism. In 1997, as the Third Wave Foundation, it became a grant-giving organization led by a "multi-class, multi-gendered, multi-racial board comprised of 25 young people," that focused its financial support on "emergency funding for abortions, scholarships, building young-women-led reproductive rights organizations, and providing general operating support for young-women-led groups and projects."[15]

Walker's actions paralleled other signs of a new feminist movement. In the aftermath of the Clarence Thomas hearings, existing feminist organizations like the National Organization for Women saw a rise in their membership rolls, and new organizations such as the Women's Action Coalition (WAC) emerged. As the *New York Times* reported in its 1992 coverage of these new groups: "In a surge of feminism not seen since the late 1970's, thousands of women in New York City have started to embrace the radical tactics of groups like ACT-UP . . . to press for undiminished abortion rights, improved women's health care, pay equity, artistic freedom and an end to violence against women."[16] When in April 1992, six months after the Thomas hearings, NOW held its March for Women's Lives in Washington, D.C., 750,000 people from across the country participated, many wearing I BELIEVE ANITA T-shirts and buttons. The hearings also had a major impact on the reporting of sexual harassment cases: the number of sexual harassment complaints filed with the EEOC more than doubled after the hearings, from 6,127 in 1991 to 15,342 in 1996.[17]

The Thomas hearings occurred at the end of more than a decade of anti-feminist rollbacks that began in the late 1970s. The election of President Ronald Reagan in 1980 signaled that the liberalism of the 1960s and '70s was officially under attack, as progressive issues such as abortion rights, affirmative action, and the gay and lesbian movement were all targeted by the Right. In an uncanny repetition of past history, the so-called postfeminist generation of the 1980s made many of the same arguments put forward by young women in the 1920s after women won the vote: arguing that women and men were now equal and any obstacles in a woman's path could be solved by individual, rather than political, solutions. The 1980s ushered in "a powerful counterassault on women's rights, a backlash, an attempt to retract the handful of small and hard-won victories that the feminist movement did manage to win for women," as Susan Faludi described this period in her bestselling book *Back-*

lash: *The Undeclared War Against American Women.*[18] When Walker and others called for a new wave of feminism in the early 1990s, they were thus challenging this backlash against feminism and the postfeminist belief that feminism was obsolete because gender equality had been achieved.

Articulation of a New Feminist Sensibility

In their book *Manifesta: Young Women, Feminism, and the Future,* white activists Jennifer Baumgardner and Amy Richards, both born in 1970, write: "For anyone born after the early 1960s, the presence of feminism in our lives is taken for granted. For our generation, feminism is like fluoride. We scarcely notice that we have it—it's simply in the water."[19] For members of the post-baby-boomer generation, this "fluoride feminism" was present both in the private sphere of their homes, families, and relationships and in the public sphere of education, work, politics, and the media. Baumgardner and Richards represented the experience of many in their generation, those raised by self-identified feminist mothers—and sometimes fathers—who instilled in their daughters a "girls can do anything boys can do" attitude. As children, they sang along to the title track of *Free to Be . . . You and Me,* the bestselling record of feminist children's stories and songs released in 1972, and they absorbed egalitarian principles—with mothers working alongside fathers for income outside the home and fathers cooking dinner alongside mothers inside the home. As one such feminist would write, "We are the first generation for whom feminism has been entwined in the fabric of our lives."[20] In other words, what made this generation unique was that it had grown up *after* the feminist movement had already made significant gains, changing the way that girls and women saw themselves and their place in the world. As one commentator noted, all women born after 1960, "whether they embrace or reject feminism, are the daughters of feminism, heir to its struggles, failures, and successes."[21]

Yet, unlike Rebecca Walker, many other women of this generation did not grow up with self-identified feminist mothers; instead they were raised in families where the feminist revolution had not made an impact, families where sexism and patriarchal values still dominated and where gender roles remained relatively unchanged after decades of feminist activism. As white feminist scholar Amber Kinser, born in 1963, describes her journey to feminism, even though it was present in the world, it still had to be worked for: "There may have been a second-wave revolution happening out there when I was growing up in the '60s and '70s, but there was little that was revolutionary happening in my house. Any feminism I learned was by working relentlessly to move away from my conservative upbringing and find some other mode of living."[22] This point is echoed by Shelby Knox, a white feminist activist and blogger born two decades after Kinser, in 1986, and the focus of the 2005 documentary *The Education of Shelby Knox* about her fight for comprehensive sex education in her conservative Lubbock, Texas, high school. Describing how she came to identify with the experience of second-wave feminists, Knox says that Gloria Steinem "had experiences that mirrored mine. She found feminism and felt like she saved herself—it was something new to her. I felt that way. I had never heard the word 'feminism' growing up—not in a bad way, not in a good way; it just didn't exist. So when I discovered it, it validated my humanity and experiences and I understood it was the 'world split open,' which is the Second Wave phrase."[23] Knox was born two decades after the National Organization for Women was founded, yet in many ways her experience was more similar to that of second-wave feminists like Steinem than it was to that of her generational peers, those who grew up with feminism "in the water" all around them.

For many younger feminists of color the pathway to feminist identity involved both finding feminism outside the home and then retroactively realizing that it was always present within the home in the examples of strong women role models. Kristina Gray is an African American feminist activist who was born in 1979. As the senior program coordinator at the Young Women's Project, she worked with teen girls lacking economic and family resources, training them to become women leaders. She described her own path to feminism this way: "Growing up in a black household, I never heard the F-word [feminism] used too much . . . most black women in my life saw feminism as a white thing. It wasn't meant for us and it didn't include us." Yet she also argued that women in her family offered her a kind of "proto-feminism" as they "led by example, showing me how to defiantly make my way in a world that told black women we didn't matter."[24] Rather than writing off feminism as "a white thing," Gray, like many other young women of color in the post-1990 period, instead challenged the idea that feminism is the exclusive property of white women by both claiming the feminism she learned outside the home and reclaiming the feminism that she had been taught within it.

A new generation of men also began to call themselves feminists during this period. Many of these men had—like their sisters and female cousins—grown up in families in which feminism was all around them: they lived with moms who worked outside the home and had dads who played an active role in their upbringing. Some of them were raised by single mothers who provided a clear example of strength and determination; they grew up knowing how difficult it was to make ends meet and how much sexist discrimination there still was in the workplace. Others became radicalized when they saw their sisters or female friends being harassed or assaulted. Many men could relate to the experience of Jason Schultz, a founder of Men Acting for Change at Duke

University, who strongly identified with the women in his life: "I grew up with female friends who were as ambitious, smart, achieving, and confident as I thought I was—on a good day. . . . When I got to college, these same women began calling themselves feminists. When I heard men call women 'dumb chicks' I knew something was wrong."[25] From that moment on, Schultz identified as a feminist.

These different examples reveal multiple pathways into feminist identification. For some, feminism was always a part of how they saw themselves; for others, it was something they had to seek out and fight for. While feminism may have been "in the water," feminist identity—like any political identity—still had to be claimed. In contrast to their second-wave predecessors, this group did not experience a feminist "click" where a new perspective suddenly opened up, like a camera shutter; rather, they more often experienced a "surfacing" in which they began to "identify how feminist ideas have shaped an individual's life course, and then through a process of gradual, and sometimes unconscious, transformation, adopt[ed] a feminist identity."[26] Yet even those Generation Xers and Millennials who did not imbibe feminism at home—and who, like Kinser and Knox, had to work to find it—had been raised in a culture profoundly shaped by the women's movement of the 1960s and 1970s. The passage of Title IX in 1972 expanded the educational opportunities they received in school and the athletic experiences they pursued after classes were over. They went into careers previously closed to women by sexist attitudes and overt (and often legal) discrimination. Abortion was legal during their entire reproductive lives, and effective forms of birth control widely available.

An important factor in the adoption of a feminist identity for this group of feminists has been the academic field of women's studies, which until the early 1970s essentially did not exist. In the late 1960s and early 1970s, as noted in chapter 2, feminist scholars working in a variety of academic disciplines—especially in English, history, psychology, and sociology—began to construct an interdisciplinary field of study around the new knowledge they were producing; they initially called this field women's studies in order to mark its focus on women, whose lives, creative talents, and histories had been virtually absent from the curriculum of most academic fields up until that point. The number of undergraduate programs in women's studies more than tripled between 1970 and 2010, and universities throughout the United States began offering both master's and doctoral programs in the field; many of these programs would eventually be renamed to indicate an expanded focus on gender and sexuality. By the time the generation examined here went to college, they were likely to encounter courses that introduced them to the history of the women's movement and to the development of feminist thought. Because of the dramatic changes in U.S. higher education made by the women's movement, this generation was also provided with both female and feminist professional role models. As AnnJanette Rosga, born in 1966, described her experience as an undergraduate student: "I went to college from 1986 to 1990, during which time I believe I had a total of *three* male professors. During both college and graduate school, my mentors and advisers were among the leading feminist scholars in this country."[27] Rosga's experience provides a sharp contrast to that of women pursuing higher education in earlier decades, for whom having a female, let alone a feminist, professor was a rare occurrence.

Women's studies courses and programs strengthened this generation's feminist identity. Unlike the earlier women's rights activists described in chapters 1 and 2, many in the post-baby-boomer generation initially learned about feminist activism from studying it in college rather than from participating in such activism themselves. They learned about the history of the women's movement as something that had *already taken place*—and had been taking place for a long time—rather than as something they were inventing anew. What they might have lacked in firsthand experience as activists was replaced by their in-depth education of the history and theory of the earlier movements. But this history was not taught as hagiography. Quite the opposite: this generation learned the history of feminism through a critique of its past. Works like *This Bridge Called My Back: Writings by Radical Women of Color* and *All the Women Are White, All the Blacks Are Men, but Some of Us Are Brave: Black Women's Studies* introduced younger feminists to feminism through a critical assessment of white feminists' singular focus on gender and the use of middle-class white experience as the foundation of feminist analysis and action. This generation developed their own feminist theory and activist strategies in the 1990s and 2000s, building on these critiques and attempting to put forward a feminism grounded in intersectional analysis, in which feminism has a broad social justice agenda. Such an agenda could be seen in anthologies like *Colonize This! Young Women of Color on Today's Feminism* (2002), which articulated "a feminist way of looking at la vida that linked the shit we got as women to the color of our skin, the languages we spoke and the zip codes we knew as home."[28] As *Colonize This!* coeditor Daisy Hernández said, "I wouldn't have come to call myself a feminist if racial justice wasn't a key part of it."[29]

As feminist theory and feminist activism incorporated the insights of feminists of color that gender justice is necessarily linked to the struggles for racial and class justice—an insight that can be traced back to nineteenth-century African American feminists—feminists of all generations increasingly came to expand the contemporary movement's vision of gender equality. Younger feminists saw themselves as reaping, in the words of one, "the benefits of *all* the social justice movements that have come before us; we have come of age in a world that has been shaped by feminism, queer

Queerly beloved wedding
ceremony in Kaua'i, April 2013.

Photograph by Zshots.

liberation movements, antiracist movements, labor movements,
and others."[30] The expansion of feminist ideology is particularly
notable in the women's movement's relationship to the modern lesbian, gay, bisexual, and transgender (LGBT) movement. Whereas
in the late 1960s and early 1970s lesbians often felt unwelcome in
straight feminist spaces and the feminist movement was openly
hostile to the burgeoning transgender movement, in the post-1990
period younger feminists, of all sexual orientations and genders,
saw themselves as inextricably tied to the LGBT movement. Like
the feminist movement, the LGBT movement weathered a great
deal of conservative backlash and hostility during this period while
also achieving historically unprecedented gains, including: the
2003 overturning of sodomy laws that made same-sex sexuality
illegal in thirteen states; the 2011 repeal of "Don't Ask, Don't Tell,"
which barred the military service of openly gay and lesbian people;
the legalization of same-sex marriage in nineteen U.S. states and
the District of Columbia, so that by mid-2014 nearly 44 percent of

the U.S. population now lives in a state where same-sex couples can legally wed; and the Supreme Court's 2013 ruling that the Defense of Marriage Act (which prohibited the recognition of such marriages) was unconstitutional. Equally as important as these legal and legislative rulings was the ever greater visibility, acceptance, and support of lesbian, gay, bisexual, and transgender people in the United States.

After September 11, 2001, feminists increasingly focused their attention on how to work toward a transnational and global movement for gender justice that did not place U.S. women at the center of analysis or posit them as the embodiment of gender equality—in other words, an anti-imperialist feminism that does not assume that " 'We' the liberated Americans must save 'them' the oppressed women," as Pakistani-American feminist Bushra Rehman argued.[31] The shift to a global vision of feminism began in the 1970s, as American feminists increasingly made political, activist, and scholarly connections with their feminist colleagues around the world. Some women of color in the United States identified themselves as "third world women" in order to highlight the experience and perspective they shared with women in the global south. Other women, of all races and ethnicities, worked with global partners in shared feminist projects, such as the education of girls and women or the use of microlending to help female entrepreneurs begin businesses. Others participated in United Nations–sponsored conferences that brought together women leaders and activists from around the world, including the 1995 Fourth World Conference on Women held in Beijing, at which then–First Lady Hillary Rodham Clinton famously proclaimed, "If there is one message that echoes forth from this conference, let it be that human rights are women's rights and women's rights are human rights once and for all." The introduction of new Internet technologies—such as e-mail and various forms of social media—made it increasingly possible for activists to work together online, just as the greater availability and cheaper cost of international travel made it easier for them to work together in person. An ongoing area of debate—and, at times, even tension—within this global movement was how to work toward shared political goals that would help to advance gender justice and sexual equality while also retaining a respect for differences, whether of religion, culture, or even definitions of feminism.

Demographic shifts within the United States have also made their mark on contemporary feminism. Generation Xers and Millennials experienced a United States with more racial, ethnic, and national diversity than did previous generations of feminists. In 1970, white, non-Hispanic Americans accounted for approximately 83 percent of the total U.S. population; by 2010, that number had decreased almost 25 percent, with whites accounting for 64 percent of the U.S. population. While the number of African Americans in the United States stayed relatively consistent during that forty-year period, constituting roughly 12 percent of the total population, there was a dramatic increase in the number of Asians and Latinos, because of immigration and changes in the birthrates of various populations: in 1970 Asian Americans accounted for just under 1 percent of the total U.S. population, whereas in 2010 they accounted for 5 percent, and between 1970 and 2010 the number of Latino Americans increased from 4.5 percent of the population to just over 16 percent. In addition, the number of people who identify as biracial or multiracial—people like Rebecca Walker, for example—also increased. This was formally recognized in 2000 when the U.S. Census for the first time allowed respondents to identify as "two or more races," a group that accounted for roughly 3 percent of the total population in 2010. For many younger Americans of all races and ethnicities, these demographic shifts, along with the political and societal changes brought by the civil rights movement, have profoundly influenced their attitudes about race, racism, and white privilege in the United States—as well as their attitudes about interracial friendships and romantic relationships.

The effect of these changes can also been seen within the contemporary feminist movement, which has itself become much more racially and ethnically diverse and has seemingly not been divided along racial lines in the same ways that feminists were in the late 1960s and 1970s. This is not to say that the feminist movement has fully addressed its own racism, white privilege, or economic elitism. However, the activists and writers discussed here have grown up in a multiracial, multiethnic United States in which discussions of race—as well as whiteness and white privilege—have often been a part of their everyday lives, including in their women's and gender studies classes.

Living in a Half-Changed World

Perhaps the most important defining feature of the post-1990 period is that feminism is both "everywhere and nowhere."[32] That is, feminism has become ubiquitous—everywhere—as its ideals and goals have been woven into every aspect of contemporary life, yet feminism can seem hard to locate—nowhere—in its diffuse and fragmented focus. We are also living in a time of intense contradictions: while women have made tremendous gains since the 1960s, we still live in a "half-changed world," to quote Generation X journalist Peggy Orenstein. For those who had "been girls during the heyday of the women's movement," the expectations of what it means to be female—in careers, in relationships, in families—had undergone a radical transformation. Yet the well-intentioned message that "we could 'be whatever we wanted to be'" ignored the many structural barriers and sexist attitudes that were still firmly in place.[33] The women's movements described in chapters 1 and 2 achieved many legal, economic, and social gains, to be sure, yet

sexism and gender discrimination have continued, albeit sometimes in new forms that make them difficult to address. As Columbia Law School professor Susan Sturm has described it, the earlier
women's movements confronted "first generation" patterns of gender bias, such as overt legal discrimination and exclusion; such
bias could be addressed by changing the law, for example, by formally including women where they had previously been excluded.
According to Sturm, since 1990 we are more likely to confront
"second generation" gender bias, which takes the form of informal
policies, practices, attitudes, and patterns of interaction; this form
of gender bias tends to appear natural and neutral but is, in fact,
grounded in beliefs about women's inferiority to men. For example, there is no law prohibiting women from pursuing careers in
STEM (science, technology, engineering, and mathematics) fields,
yet girls and women are frequently discouraged from pursuing
an education in STEM fields by subtle and omnipresent cultural
messages—including those sent by women themselves—that such
fields are the domain of men. (Sometimes such messages are not
so subtle, as when Mattel issued a Teen Talk Barbie that said "Math
class is tough" in 1992.)

Living in a "half-changed world" has left women in a sort of
limbo, not sure how to navigate the new realities that exist alongside traditional demands. More careers are open to women than
ever before, but women are still paid far less than their male
counterparts—averaging seventy-seven cents to a man's dollar—
and are still disproportionally segregated in low-wage, "feminized"
jobs like clerical and service work. Even when they make it into
elite professional jobs, women are still vastly underrepresented in
positions of power, such as law partners, tenured professors, and
corporate officers. Women's participation in the workforce is almost
equal to men's, yet women are still overwhelmingly responsible for
cleaning, cooking, and taking care of children when they get home

from work. Abortion has been legal since 1973, but if a woman lives in one of the many counties that have no abortion provider—which 87 percent of U.S. counties do not—she will likely have to drive hundreds of miles to get to a clinic and will face many state restrictions for this supposedly legal procedure, one which 30 percent of women will have in their lifetime.[34] Women are told that they are empowered and that no obstacles remain in their path, yet each day they face covert and overt sexist attitudes—as well as epidemic rates of gendered violence—that confirm that this is still very much a man's world. Girls grow up believing that one day they can be president of the United States, but we have yet to elect a woman president (or vice president), women remain a disproportional minority in the U.S. Congress, and those who run for office often face virulent misogyny that sends the message that politics is still an old boy's club.

The unfinished business of the earlier feminist revolution led some younger feminists to initially focus their energies on where the earlier movement had gone wrong—what it failed to accomplish, what it had left undone—rather than on the formidable obstacles they faced in their own lives. In the first decade of this new activism and writing, younger feminists stressed generational differences, and even conflict, in order to articulate how they would improve on feminism. The wave metaphor used to chronicle feminism's history undoubtedly exacerbated generational tensions among feminists in the United States. The term "third wave" seemed to stress that this new "wave"—or political generation—was an improvement on the earlier, "second" wave. While indicating some continuity of feminism across the waves, the numerical delineation of a new, "third" wave also relied on a notion of teleological progress, in which each successive wave—because of its newness, because of its youth, because of its difference—improves upon the last. In asserting themselves as the "third wave," this next generation of activists had to describe the previous generation in monolithic and even caricatured ways in order to present themselves as the improved version of feminism. Younger feminists argued that the second wave was almost exclusively white (ignoring second-wave feminists of color), overly puritanical when it came to sexuality (ignoring diverse second-wave perspectives on sexuality), and prescriptive and overly dogmatic (ignoring the multiplicity of second-wave feminisms, plural). In order to describe their own feminism as focused on the intersections between gender, race, class, and sexuality, they ignored the century-long history of intersectional, social justice feminism in the United States.

Misrepresentation of one feminist generation by another occurred in both directions. Older feminists were quick to respond to how they were being characterized—and equally quick to critique the feminist ideas advanced by this new generation. Some criticized the younger feminists for being nothing but "sex-obsessed young thangs with a penchant for lip gloss and a disregard for recent history."[35] When intergenerational groups of feminists gathered at conferences and political meetings throughout the 1990s and early 2000s, conversation often turned into debate. For example, at an April 2002 Veteran Feminists of America conference held at Barnard College, a panel of well-known second-wave feminists began to lament the lack of feminist consciousness among younger women, many of whom were in the audience, arguing that younger feminists' "individualist attitude" couldn't change the world the way the "collectivist drive" of their generation had. "We were action-oriented in a public, political context. We had to challenge laws, change patterns, alter behavior. Being able to bare your midriff is fine as an expression," said second-wave writer Letty Cottin Pogrebin at the conference, "but it doesn't mean things are going to change."[36] For Pogrebin, younger feminists were all style, no substance; all they had to offer was an aesthetic sensibility rather than a political perspective. Throughout the 1990s and early 2000s, this generational debate among feminists was frequently reported by the mainstream media, which seemed to relish portraying feminism as a "cat fight" rather than as a political movement.

As the 2000s progressed, the wave metaphor increasingly came under attack by younger feminists—members of the so-called third wave—who urged their contemporaries to move beyond its simplistic division of feminists into generational, or age-based, groups. Lisa Jervis, the founding editor and publisher of the third-wave magazine *Bitch*, argued in 2004: "We've reached the end of the wave terminology's usefulness. What was at first a handy-dandy way to refer to feminism's history and its present and future potential with a single metaphor has become a shorthand that invites intellectual laziness, an escape hatch from the hard work of distinguishing between core beliefs and a cultural moment."[37] And yet, while the assertion of a new wave is inevitably fraught with problems—stressing difference over continuity, creating a monolithic portrait of a generational cohort, conflating ideology with age—something like the wave metaphor may be necessary in order for each successive generation to claim feminism for itself and to enter the public stage. "Because feminism is not, and cannot be, some form of received wisdom handed down across generations but is an active interpretation of the realities of women's own lives and struggles, the feminism of the future will continue to be reborn different in every generation."[38] Announcing the arrival of one's political generation—as Walker did in her 1992 declaration "I am the Third Wave"—may have been required to energize the next generation into action.

Since the mid 2000s, the intense focus on feminist generational conflict and rebellion that characterized much of the 1990s and early 2000s has been replaced by an increasing concern for how to continue the fight, how to finish the unfinished business of the

women's movement. In part, this shift occurred because the original spokespeople for this new "wave" were getting older, and many
of them began to focus their energies on new goals. A number of
the key figures of the initial "third wave" period stopped writing in
the voice of "feminism's daughters" and began writing about their
own experiences as mothers—including Walker, Baumgardner,
and Richards, among others. New voices began to emerge, including those who used the terrorist attacks of September 11, 2001, to
argue for an anti-imperialist, transnational feminist movement
built by creating coalitions among progressive groups. And a new
generation of feminist scholars began writing about the Millennial
period. As Rory Dicker and Alison Piepmeier, the editors of one
such study of this new feminism, wrote: "We need a feminism that
is dedicated to a radical, transformative political vision, a feminism
that does not shy away from hard work but recognizes that changing the world is a difficult and necessary task, a feminism that
utilizes the new technologies of the Internet, the playful world of
fashion, and the more clear-cut activism of protest marches, a feminism that can engage with issues as diverse as women's sweatshop
labor in global factories and violence against women as expressed
in popular music."[39]

New Feminist Writing: In Print and Online

Texts have helped to spread feminist ideas since the beginning of
the U.S. women's movement—from suffragist newspapers in the
nineteenth century to mimeographed manifestos of the late 1960s
to bestselling feminist books in all eras. As discussed in chapter
2, in the late 1960s, it was not uncommon for feminist groups to
write political statements, or manifestos, outlining their beliefs and
goals. Such documents tended to come out of consciousness-raising
and political groups, produced by a collective of women rather than

just one author. Documents of this type, such as the "Redstockings Manifesto" (1969), were widely circulated in pamphlet form and often republished in feminist journals and anthologies, some of which became bestsellers, such as the collection *Sisterhood Is Powerful* (1970). Likewise, the emergence of a new feminist sensibility in the post-1990 era can be connected to texts, whether Rebecca Walker's 1992 *Ms.* essay or feminist books preceding it, such as Susan Faludi's *Backlash: The Undeclared War Against American Women* (1991) and Naomi Wolf's *The Beauty Myth: How Images of Beauty Are Used Against Women* (1991). Texts were especially important in giving a presence to this new feminism, since it did not rely on the gathering of women in activist groups, as discussed in the previous chapter. If the women's liberation movement of the late 1960s and 1970s was characterized by the rapid formation of groups and publication of their manifestos, the feminism that emerged in the mid-1990s developed primarily through the publication of individually authored texts. Texts named the generation, texts energized it, and reading texts became a way of participating in the contemporary movement.

The boom in new feminist writing in the 1990s and 2000s, much of which used the terms "third wave" or "next generation," often took the form of anthologies of individual essays, almost exclusively written in a first-person voice, which provided concrete examples of how young women (and some men) were living feminism in a supposedly "postfeminist" era. These collections were joined by monographs which also described feminism through an autobiographical voice, as well as books that sought to give young people concrete examples of how to engage in everyday activism. More recent books have attempted to reach even younger women—and girls—to encourage them to see why feminism is still vitally important. Two new feminist magazines also began publishing in the 1990s—*Bust* (created in 1993) and

Bitch (created in 1996)—both of which took a decidedly "third wave" approach in their look and their content. "Just as *Ms.* harnessed the vibrant pamphlet culture of women's liberation, *Bust* and *Bitch* founders tapped into the rich feminist 'zine culture associated with the Riot Grrrls movement," which had combined radical feminist politics with a punk rock, do-it-yourself aesthetic.[40] At the same time, a new crop of feminists began publishing books that discussed the wide range of activist projects that younger feminists were working on, including issues as varied as the environment, the prison industrial complex, and media representations of women. As the 1990s progressed, young feminist scholars—many of whom had been trained in women's and gender studies and were now professors themselves—began publishing books that took a more scholarly approach to this new feminism, tracing its history and its theories and critically analyzing what exactly this new feminism was all about.

What these books all had in common was a central thesis: feminism is still relevant and vitally needed. Whether they presented this point through autobiographical testimony, appeals to younger women to recognize their innate feminism, or blueprints for how to do activism in the twenty-first century, these books reached a broad audience and helped to bring about a renewed interest in feminism in the United States. This writing did not come out of group meetings or collective visions of a feminist movement, but it helped create and foster a feminist mindset among a wide range of younger women and men in the United States, leading them to go out into the world and continue the feminist fight.

The development of the Internet, whose history parallels that of post-1980s feminism, created a new form of collectivity and textual practices that would have been unheard of by prior generations. If women's liberation was "the last American movement to spread the word via mimeo machine," then this new group of feminists would be the first to spread the word via e-mail, text messages, and social media like Facebook, YouTube, and Twitter.[41] (Facebook started in 2004, YouTube in 2005, and Twitter in 2006.) This new technology allowed for previously unimagined speed and reach in disseminating feminist ideas. The emergence of a vibrant feminist online culture—including widely read feminist blogs, a term that emerged in the 1990s to mean a "Web log"—enabled feminists around the globe to respond immediately to each other's ideas and to create virtual communities that provided friendship and political allies.

The events of September 11, 2001, were "a turning point in the blogging boom," as blogs became a way to quickly relay information and communicate with others during a time of national crisis.[42] According to recent studies, women are active members of the blogosphere, online at the same rate as, if not slightly higher than, their male counterparts—leading to what some have described as the rise of the "lady blogger" movement. Blogs and other forms of Internet publishing have thus helped to get women's voices heard in a way that more traditional forms of media have, so far, failed to do. For example, according to the feminist OpEd Project, in 2012 women constituted only 20 percent of the authors featured on the opinion pages of major newspapers, all of which are now also online. While some well-known opinion writers of both sexes focus on feminist issues—for example, both Gail Collins and Nicholas Kristof from the *New York Times* regularly write about gender inequality—in general, such concerns do not make it into the front section of the paper. Feminist blogs have thus provided a much-needed service in keeping feminist issues at the forefront of the national—and international—discussion. And such blogs have become a major part of the blogosphere: a 2006 British study found that feminist blogs made up 6 percent of active blogs, or 240,000 of four million active blogs.[43] Feminists also used Twitter, Tumblr, and other Web applications to analyze pop culture and share feminist ideas, such as in Feminist Disney Tumblr, which deconstructs Disney movies. While the Web is not a utopian space in which sexism has been eliminated—indeed, evidence suggests that the anonymity of the Internet makes hate speech and misogynist attacks more common than in face-to-face encounters—the Web has made it possible for feminists to respond to sexism in new ways, both individually and collectively. The lively presence of feminism in the blogosphere has made feminism more accessible than it has ever been, and it has also ensured that feminist ideas can reach audiences that previously would not have encountered them. In short, a fourteen-year-old girl today is much more likely to discover feminism online than at her local library or bookstore. That means she is much more likely to discover feminism in the first place.

Since the mid-1990s, the Internet has proven to be the primary means by which feminist ideas have circulated and feminist actions have been organized. "Our activism is inseparable from technology," said Shelby Knox. "We began our activism online. Blogs are our consciousness-raising groups. . . . Blogs serve the purpose of helping us figure out our ideology, have disagreements with each other, and figure out what actions might work best without having to all be in the same place. They have equalized feminism, because you don't have to have the money to be in a women's studies class or be able-bodied enough to attend a consciousness-raising group every week or to stand on a picket line."[44] Requiring only that someone have Internet access, blogs have helped to democratize contemporary feminism and have enabled a wide variety of people to make their voices heard—not just a small group of anointed feminist leaders. The blogosphere has been compared to an earlier form of feminist action: consciousness raising. "From our homes, offices, or schools, the Internet permits us to do what feminist

Feminist Disney Tumblr.

consciousness-raising groups did in the 1960s and 1970s—cross boundaries and make connections among and between diverse feminists, diverse women."[45]

Jessica Valenti's popular blog is one example of how feminism has become "wired" in the Internet era. Valenti was born in 1978 and grew up in an Italian American household with a feminist mother who brought her along to reproductive rights marches. After getting a master's degree in women's and gender studies from Rutgers, she became part of the blogging boom when she founded the blog *Feministing* in 2004. As she reflected, she wanted "to provide a space for younger feminists who didn't have a platform. I was a 25 year-old who found it profoundly unfair that an elite few in the feminist movement had their voices listened to, and that the work of so many younger women went misrepresented or ignored altogether."[46] In its first decade, *Feministing* became a global phenomenon, attracting over a hundred thousand readers from around the world. The blog built a consciousness-raising-type community through its "Comments" section, which allowed readers to respond in real time to what they were reading; young women, including teenagers, got involved by posting their own writing. *Feministing* also started a campus program to provide resources and support to feminist groups and bloggers on college campuses.

Valenti would go on to write a number of popular feminist books aimed at younger women, including *Full Frontal Feminism* and *The Purity Myth: How America's Obsession with Virginity Is Hurting Young Women*, publish op-eds in majors newspapers, and become a contributing writer at the *Nation* magazine—so she has not entirely neglected traditional print media. The blog that she started would win numerous awards, including the 2011 Sidney Hillman Prize for social and economic justice in blog journalism. That same year, Valenti retired from the blog, stating that she wanted *Feministing* to provide "a space for new and young voices" and "remain a place for younger feminists to build their careers and platforms."[47]

Moya Bailey is another example of how the feminist blogosphere has produced a new generation of writers and activists. After graduating from Spelman College in Atlanta in 2005, Bailey began a PhD program in women's, gender, and sexuality studies at Emory University, where she met other young women of color who were interested in how to use new Web-based technologies to build feminist community. This led her to cofound a social network called Quirky Black Girls (QBG), which allowed, in her view, "a diverse group of self-identified QBGs to post our own videos, music and imagery, all the while building bravery and challenging each other's thinking."[48] From there she joined the Crunk Feminist Collective, a self-described "hip hop generation feminist blogging crew," which launched a popular blog, Twitter feed, and Facebook page. According to their mission statement, the collective use "crunk"— a southern black term for "crazy drunk," or out of one's mind— "because we are drunk off the heady theory of feminism that proclaims that another world is possible."[49] "The internet allows for people who do not have immediate community to build communities online," said Bailey. "For people with disabilities, the internet has allowed for community in ways that our inaccessible world [hasn't]. It's made feminist language more accessible. Feminists have used digital media to spread feminism and affect real change." Online feminism also provides a space to address white privilege, racism, and other forms of division that have historically divided feminists. "The divisions remain," said Bailey, but she thought that because of the active presence of women of color on social media and blogs, there was "more of an opportunity for folks to be told when they make mistakes."[50]

As Valenti and fellow feminist blogger Courtney Martin described it in a 2012 essay: "Contrary to media depictions of online activity as largely narcissistic and/or 'slactivism,' young women across the country—and all over the world, in fact—are discovering new ways to leverage the Internet to make fundamental progress in the unfinished revolution of feminism."[51] A protest that same year at *Seventeen* magazine illustrates their point. Activists, many of whom were teenage girls, demanded that *Seventeen* stop using Photoshopped images of girls, arguing that such images led to unrealistic body ideals, eating disorders, depression, and low self-esteem. An online petition to *Seventeen*, on Change. org, gathered eighty-six thousand signatures, and an online video documentary on the subject, made by two teens, was viewed by over thirteen thousand people. Protesters also demonstrated outside of *Seventeen*'s New York offices, holding a mock photo shoot to honor what real girls look like. These actions worked: *Seventeen* editor in chief Ann Shoket publicly committed to ending the magazine's practice of Photoshopping girls' bodies in a special "Body Peace Treaty" in the August 2012 issue. In many ways, this protest echoed the one held forty years earlier at the offices of the *Ladies' Home Journal*. As discussed in chapter 2, in 1970 one hundred feminists held an eleven-hour takeover of the magazine, demanding that the *Journal* hire a female editor in chief, end its discriminatory hiring and promotion practices, and devote more of its pages to serious issues. Both protests were successful; both led to changes at the magazines being targeted. The *Seventeen* protest, however, reached a far greater number of people through the power of the Internet, undoubtedly raising the consciousness of thousands, most of whom never set foot in New York.

Pop Culture and Feminist Style

Popular culture in all its various forms—music, television, film—has been an integral part of the assertion of this post-1990 feminism and its particular aesthetic sensibility. The riot grrrl movement—a feminist offshoot of the do-it-yourself punk music scene—that emerged in the late 1980s and early 1990s has been credited as an early example of this new feminist style. Bands like Bikini Kill and Bratmobile played songs that addressed rape, sexual harassment, and eating disorders with lyrics that mixed raw anger with emotional vulnerability. Riot grrrl performances also captured attention. In what became one of her signature moves onstage, Bikini Kill lead singer Kathleen Hanna would take off her shirt to reveal the word "slut" written on her stomach, "confronting audiences with what they might want to see (a topless woman) and what they might think of such a woman, all in one fell semiotic swoop."[52] Other genres of music also began to produce self-identified feminist performers, with rap and hip-hop leading the way; artists like Queen Latifah, Salt-n-Pepa, and TLC used their lyrics and performances to assert agency and claim a voice within a male-dominated genre. These performers and many others—including mainstream pop musicians of the 2000s like Beyoncé and Lady Gaga—sang songs of female empowerment that reached a mass audience. Unlike the women's rock bands of the late 1960s and early 1970s, discussed in chapter 2, this new generation of musical artists often presented their feminist messages while wearing hyperfeminine clothing, rejecting the earlier era's androgyny in favor of the sexually provocative feminist style pioneered by Madonna in the mid-1980s.

Feminist characters became slightly more common on the small and large screen during the 1990s and 2000s, although both television and film continued to focus on male-driven narratives aimed at male viewers, in which female characters were frequently sidelined. On daytime television Oprah Winfrey was queen, becoming one of the most recognized women in the United States and an outspoken advocate for feminist issues—although Oprah seemed to deliberately avoid using the word "feminist" so as not to alienate her audience. During the prime-time slot, women characters took on new jobs as cops and judges, but they still seemed stuck in the same roles that they had been in since television was invented: as wives and mothers. Even the highly successful ABC television series *Modern Family* (2009–)—touted for its progressive portrayal of a gay male couple raising a child—was hardly modern when it came to its women characters, none of whom had jobs outside the home. Behind the scenes, women fared far worse: a 2012 study found that although women account for half of all moviegoers in the United States, they represent only 7 percent of film directors, 13 percent of writers, and 20 percent of producers.[53] And while girls and women were involved in athletics more than ever before—thanks in great part to the changes brought by Title IX in 1972—women's sports could barely be found on television, particularly during the all-male, prime-time evening slot reserved for football.

The HBO series *Sex and the City* (1998–2004) thus provided a unique female-centered universe in its portrayal of four strong working–women characters who defined themselves as each other's family and who regularly discussed topics such as sexual agency and female orgasms, abortion, how to balance motherhood with a career, whether to get married, and economic success. The characters also discussed feminism itself and the choices it had made possible for women, reflecting the values of the many women who worked on the series as writers and directors. The series came to define a new generation of women, just as *The Mary Tyler Moore Show* (1970–77) had three decades earlier. Yet *Sex and the City*— along with its next-generation successor, the HBO series *Girls* (2012–)—focused almost exclusively on white, economically privileged women, and thus did little to dismantle stereotypes about who the beneficiaries of feminism were. In order to find a more diverse representation of women and of feminist issues, viewers often had to turn to smaller, independent films, like *Real Women Have Curves* (2002), a film about one young working-class Latina's journey to self-acceptance, directed by Colombian American filmmaker Patricia Cardoso.

Perhaps one of the biggest changes in popular culture over the last two decades has been the emergence of women (and often feminist) comedians into the previously all-male world of stand-up comedy and comedy writing. Women like writer-actress-producer Tina Fey used humor to challenge sexism and misogyny and to astutely reflect on what passed for gender equality in the twenty-first century. On the inaugural episode of Fey's critically acclaimed series *30 Rock* (2006–13), which she wrote, her alter ego, Liz Lemon, is described as "a third-wave feminist," and over the course of the series Fey humorously poked fun at modern womanhood and the media-hyped crisis over "having it all." Other feminist comedians during this period included Mindy Kaling, Sarah Silverman, Wanda Sykes, and Margaret Cho, who famously summed up her generation's entitlement: "If you say you're not a feminist you're almost denying your own existence. To be a feminist is to be alive."

The rise of what was dubbed "girlie feminism" during this period provides an interesting lens through which to examine what had changed in feminists' relationship to femininity since the 1960s

Tina Fey. *Bust* magazine, Spring 2004.

and '70s. "Girlie feminism" embraced many aspects of traditional femininity on an aesthetic level—wearing dresses, makeup, and high heels, for example—while insisting that the conscious wearing of such feminine garb did not signal that a woman was brainwashed by the patriarchy. Many younger feminists argued that they no longer felt constrained by gender, which they viewed as a social construction rather than a biological fact, and they were thus free to enjoy the pleasures of "girlie" femininity without feeling oppressed. Some went as far as to argue that adopting a feminine style was a way of rebelling against the androgynous uniform mandated by an earlier era of feminists. As one young feminist argued, "Unlike my first- and second-wave predecessors, no one force-fed me femininity. Quite the contrary: I had to fight for it tooth and nail."[54] This "girlie" aesthetic—often performed with a knowing wink—can be seen in much of the iconography and language used by this generation. For example, the blog *Feministing* chose as its logo an ironic appropriation of the traditional "mudflap girl," reworking this sexist image (commonly found on the mudflaps of trucks) by having its "girl" give the viewer the middle finger. Likewise, *Bust* magazine routinely featured cover models in traditionally feminine sexualized poses, such as the pin up girl, while advocating feminist, progressive points of view. The reclaiming of the word "girl"—sometimes as a growling "grrrl"—and the use of terms like "lady blogger" also were signs that this generation had an ironic detachment from the linguistic markers that had defined earlier generations, when feminists fought for female adults to be recognized as mature and capable women not child-like girls.

All of these different examples of "girlie" culture point to one of the ongoing challenges of post-1990 feminism: namely, how to (re) claim aspects of traditional female sexuality and femininity in a culture in which the sexual objectification of women is omnipresent and in which any expression of female sexual agency becomes co-opted by the dominant culture. The riot grrrl movement's political, feminist assertion of "grrrl power," for example, was easily transformed into the Spice Girls' watered-down "girl power," used to sell bland Top 40 songs and T-shirts rather than incite a revolution. Embracing high heels, lipstick, and the term "girl" as markers of a new feminist style may have made sense at feminist gatherings where these signifiers were used to indicate a generational shift within feminism, yet within the larger culture high heels and lipstick still signified a commitment to traditional femininity that no ironic wink could undermine. Some argued that what matters is a woman's agency; as long as it is the woman herself who is choosing to present herself in a hyperfeminine or sexualized manner, then what's the problem? Others disagreed, saying that women's reclamation of traditional feminine culture under the banner of feminism is a sign of how far we still have to go to truly escape from the rigid confines of gender and to move beyond a limited view of empowerment.

Ideology

The most defining feature of this generation of feminists is its inability to be defined by any single political goal, ideological perspective, or way of being feminist. Some have criticized post-1990 feminism for its resistance to identifying a shared set of political goals, yet others have argued that this very lack of cohesion is a sign of its strength—the fact that it is now truly "everywhere," engaged with a wide spectrum of political projects and theories. While the forms of feminist activism after 1990 dispersed across a wide range of projects, the feminist ideologies that emerged were grounded in three core principles: 1) that feminism must be polyvocal and acknowledge multiple perspectives; 2) that feminism must be intersectional and acknowledge that gender justice is inextricably tied to other social justice movements; and 3) that feminism must be nondogmatic and acknowledge the complexities and contradictions of lived experience.

The first principle—that feminism must be polyvocal and acknowledge multiple perspectives—developed out of a critique of second-wave feminism and the perception that it minimized differences among women in order to assert a monolithic "sisterhood." This "sisterhood" was meant to include all women but in actuality most often represented only white, middle-class, heterosexual women and their concerns. Developing this critique through their study of the earlier women's movement and through insights from feminist and queer theory regarding the instability of identity categories—including gender—younger feminists were skeptical of any claims to a universal "woman" around which feminism should organize. In order to avoid the presumption of speaking on behalf of all women, post-1990 feminists tended to describe feminism in individual terms—each person defining feminism for herself, in a first-person singular voice. This has led to a polyvocal form of feminism, made up of many feminisms, plural, rather than any singular definition. Most feminists today, of all ages and generations, now recognize that the category "women" is a diverse group and that no one woman can represent her entire gender.

Although this first principle is grounded in a belief in the value of diversity and multiplicity—that feminism is strongest when it combines the voices of many rather than just a few—the expression of individualized forms of feminism has led to a concern that feminism as a concept is now so watered down as to be meaningless. If feminism is merely whatever one defines it to be—merely the assertion of a woman's autonomy and choice—what differentiates it from the ideology of individualism that shapes so much of the United States? If we are all doing feminism in our own individual ways, how can we work collectively to effect structural change? What does feminism have to offer as a political stance on the world? These are questions that post-1990 feminists continue to debate and work out through their engagement with various political issues, but they have also led to the charge that this generation of feminists are nothing but navel-gazing narcissists, as famously depicted in a 1998 *Time* cover story on the new generation of activists entitled "Feminism: It's All About Me!"

The second principle—that feminism must be intersectional and acknowledge that gender justice is inextricably tied to other social justice movements—also reflects younger feminists' study of the earlier women's movement. As discussed in chapter 1, feminism's history of understanding the links between gender, race, and class oppression goes back at least a century. Since the 1970s, U.S. feminists of color have developed a large body of work on the concept of intersectionality, or the idea that identity categories intersect and mutually shape each other: in other words, gender, race, ethnicity, sexuality, socioeconomic class, and nationality, among other identity categories, never function in isolation but always work as interconnected categories of oppression and privilege. Feminism, therefore, must be a broad-based social justice movement concerned with a range of issues that affect women's (and men's) opportunities and rights. In this way, younger feminists try to practice a "feminism without borders," to use theorist Chandra Talpade Mohanty's phrase; they attempt to see feminism as being intertwined with a broad agenda of political issues, since true gender justice can only be achieved through addressing racism, economic injustice, xenophobia, and homophobia.

Although this second principle has broadened the scope of contemporary feminism in exciting and much-needed ways, some have wondered whether this broadening—like the individualization of definitions of feminism—has led to a dilution of feminism as gender shifts from being its sole focus to being merely one part of its agenda. Others, including young feminists of color, have questioned whether their white generational peers have really expanded their vision of feminism to include a commitment to combating racism and white supremacy. As African American feminist Veronica Chambers writes of her Generation X college classmates, "The young women I went to school with, for all their notions of feminism, still basked in the glory and privilege of their whiteness."[55] Chambers's experience suggests that while younger white feminists may wish to see themselves as more enlightened about race than were their white second-wave predecessors, white privilege and racism within feminism have by no means been eliminated. Ensuring that feminism truly represents women of all races, ethnicities, and socioeconomic classes is an ongoing project, one that must continue with each generation.

The third principle—that feminism must be nondogmatic and acknowledge the complexities and contradictions of lived experience—is a response to the perceived prescriptive agenda of second-wave feminism, in which there was one right way to do feminism and one right way to be a feminist. Rebecca Walker and her co-writers wanted to "embrac[e] their contradictions and complexities" by "being real" and "telling the truth" about their lives, the implication being that this truth telling could pull back the curtain on what an earlier generation of feminists had kept hidden so as to avoid uncomfortable truths.[56] As self-described hip-hop feminist Joan Morgan writes, "Only when we've told the truth about ourselves—when we've faced the fact that we are often complicit in our oppression—will we be able to take full responsibility for our lives."[57] For Morgan and other writers, one truth that needed to be faced head-on was that some feminists have no problem supporting traditional gender roles. In Morgan's case, for example, this involved recounting her love of strong, even domineering men and her wearing of high heels—a way of loving and a way of dressing that she described as part of her attachment to traditional femininity.

Although this third principle has ensured that contemporary feminists have not been torn apart by the factionalism and self-policing that accompanied earlier forms of feminism, some have wondered whether this embrace of contradictions and complexity is merely an excuse to avoid taking a critical look at personal behavior. If so-called second-wave feminists may have made the personal too political—where every aspect of one's life was open to scrutiny—has this generation of feminists depoliticized the personal so that all individual choices are to be accepted as long as a feminist is the one making those choices? In the spirit of being nonjudgmental and open to all ways of living, this feminism runs the risk of being merely an identity to claim without any political content.

These three core ideological principles developed as a response to—and in some cases a critique of—earlier feminist ideas, but they also reflected the increased acceptance of human diversity and difference that characterizes twenty-first-century life. While arguing that feminism must be welcoming and open to all, this new movement has sometimes been criticized for advocating a feminism without much content, a feminism so inclusive that it stands for everything—and therefore, perhaps, for nothing. While younger feminists express their feminism in different ways than did feminists in the past, they share with their predecessors "a belief in the full personhood of women and an agenda of eradicating all forms of oppression that keep people from achieving their full humanity."[58] By turning to the activist work being pursued by members of this generation, we can see how their feminism is given content and put into practice.

Activism

The political and activist work of this generation has taken many forms, focusing on traditional women's rights issues, such as reproductive rights and ending rape, to new issues that have emerged in the last few decades, such as transgender rights and immigration reform. "Young feminists in large numbers—both women and men—are doing social justice work all over the country. They are moved to action by social and economic injustice, the growing divide between rich and poor, contemporary manifestations of colonialism, the rapid growth of the prison industrial complex, and the deterioration of democracy."[59] Feminists are also developing new ways of doing social justice work that can respond to how power and politics operate in the twenty-first century. Rather than coalescing into a unified movement with a singular goal, this new feminism is present in a diverse array of local movements, as well as in global networks made possible by the Internet and social media— what has been described as "a million little grass-roots movements" rather than one singular vision for social change.[60]

A review of some of the various activist groups that have emerged since 1990 helps to illustrate the diversity of contemporary feminism. Groups like Third Wave Foundation and the Young Women's Project focus on youth issues and provide support and training for future feminist leaders. Other groups like Men Against Rape organize young men to end violence against women and challenge misogyny and rape culture on college campuses. Incite! Women of Color Against Violence, formed in 2000 by radical feminists of color, advances an intersectional approach to ending violence that addresses race, class, immigration status, and gender and that seeks alternatives to the criminal justice system. Numerous groups concerned with LGBT issues—including those focused on queer youth of color, like the Audre Lorde Project—seek to broaden the focus of the historically white and middle-class gay and lesbian movement. Transgender and genderqueer activists protest campus policies that continue to segregate students along gender lines in housing and athletics. Groups like About-Face target the media and its perpetuation of unrealistic and sexist body image ideals. The Radical Cheerleaders can be found on college campuses using humor and cheerleader chants to advance feminist, queer, and anti-racist politics. Numerous groups are working together to ensure that the Equal Rights Amendment finally gets put into law almost a century after it was first introduced into Congress in 1923. CodePink: Women for Peace has led intergenerational protests against U.S. military policies and the wars in Iraq and Afghanistan, often by picketing the White House and disrupting congressional hearings. Hollaback! uses social media and new technology, like cell phone cameras, to document and fight back against sexist and homophobic street harassment. Feminists have also been active members of other contemporary activist movements not explicitly focused on gender, such as the environmental movement, the Occupy movement for economic equality that emerged after the global economic

crisis of 2008, and the Dreamers, the immigration rights movement led by Latino young people who were brought to the United
States as children and who are fighting for the right to live and
work in this country legally.

Rachel Lloyd and Girls Educational and Mentoring Services, or
GEMS, provide an illustrative example of feminist activism after
1990. GEMS was founded by the twenty-third year old Lloyd in
1998 to serve girls and young women who had experienced commercial sexual exploitation and domestic trafficking. "As a survivor
of the commercial sex industry myself," said Lloyd, "I felt deeply
connected to the girls I was meeting and felt compelled to do something. I had no idea what starting a non-profit would entail—which
was probably a good thing! So I founded GEMS on my kitchen table
in 1998."[61] In the decade and a half that it has been in operation,
GEMS has helped hundreds of young women and girls, ages twelve
to twenty-four, to get out of the commercial sex industry; GEMS is
now the largest service provider to sexually exploited young women
and girls in the United States, assisting survivors of the sex industry with getting housing, education, and therapy. It is notable that
when Lloyd "felt compelled to do something," she decided to start a
nonprofit organization, which is run by a small group of paid staff
and unpaid volunteers. The feminist activists discussed in chapter 1 often did their political work through large, national social
reform organizations and unions; the activists profiled in chapter
2 often worked in small, local consciousness-raising and direct
action groups. For post-1990 activists, however, midsize, national
and sometimes international nonprofit organizations—including
nongovernmental organizations (NGOs) and grant-giving foun-
dations, like Third Wave—have been a primary vehicle for social
change work.

While new activist groups and organizations—with diverse areas
of focus—emerged after 1990, many of their goals remain similar

to those from the 1970s. Motherhood, valuing women's work, and fighting sexual assault, for example, remain long-standing concerns for feminist activists.

Motherhood, Employment, and the Labor of Care

In two memoirs published in the years after the 1992 *Ms.* essay that catapulted her onto the public stage, Rebecca Walker publicly criticized her feminist mother, Alice Walker, for regularly abandoning her during her childhood. According to Rebecca, Alice was off doing her feminist work, leaving Rebecca at home to fend for herself. Seeing her mother as representative of second-wave feminism, Walker took feminism to task for discouraging women from having children and for not valuing the mother-child relationship and the responsibilities of mothering. "Feminism," she would argue, "has betrayed an entire generation of women into childlessness."[62] While Walker's high-profile celebrity feminist relationship with her mother is admittedly unique, her story is again illustrative of at least one aspect of the contemporary movement: namely, its interest in reexamining women's relationship to motherhood in light of the societal and cultural changes brought by the earlier women's movements.

As they aged, many feminist activists and writers in the post-1990 generation focused their attention on motherhood, both as a personal experience and as a political institution. Like their feminist predecessors, they fought for the work of motherhood to be recognized—as labor, as care work, and as a contribution to the gross domestic product of the United States. Yet many also struggled with a new set of issues that an earlier generation rarely had to face. Previously women were given just one socially approved option: get married and have children. Women in the early twenty-first century face many more choices—such as if, when, and how to mother—and they often feel deeply ambivalent about whatever decision they ultimately make. Although women's movements have expanded the opportunities and options available to women and men, these possibilities remain deeply embedded in inherited political, cultural, and economic structures that have remained largely unchanged. In short, policies in the workplace and gender expectations in the home have not caught up to the changes in women's lives. The American workplace is still designed around the mythical male worker who can devote long hours to his job because he has no obligations in the home. Women are still expected to do the vast majority of housework and childcare within the home, even as they work outside the home at nearly the same rates as men do. Whereas for a brief period in the 1980s this "having it all" image of the modern superwoman was celebrated, women of all generations today are more likely to be critical of this ideal, recognizing that in practice "having it all" means "having to do it all alone" with very little support. (And we still don't ask men how they manage to "have it all.")

The group MomsRising formed in 2006 to address the issues confronted by mothers in the twenty-first century. In the group's "Motherhood Manifesto," they lay out a progressive agenda to improve the lives, work, and economic conditions of mothers in the United States. Their manifesto argues for paid parental leave, expanded coverage for the Family and Medical Leave Act, flexible work hours and work locations, quality after-school educational programs, universal healthcare for kids, excellent and affordable childcare, living wages and equal pay for equal work, and an end to workplace discrimination against mothers. It is important to remember that today the overwhelming majority of mothers of small children work outside the home, and most have no choice about whether or not to do so: they have to work to make ends meet.

Why would a group like MomsRising emerge during this

period? Over the last few decades there has been a growing aware-ness of the fact that the United States is one of the only nations in the world that does not provide paid family leave for new moth-ers and fathers. "When the United States' work-family policies are compared with those of countries at similar levels of economic and political development, the United States comes in dead last."[63] The majority of the United States' peer nations have adopted humane and family-friendly policies that help mothers (and fathers) to combine paid labor with the work of raising children, such as state-subsidized childcare, shorter workweeks, universal healthcare policies, and, most obviously, mandatory paid parental leave. The United States, however, has never put into law the kinds of social welfare policies that are now commonplace in developed nations across the globe. It has been difficult to implement such policies in a country where "socialism" is treated as a dirty word, where there is a deeply rooted suspicion of "big government," where there is resistance to the wealthy paying higher taxes to ensure a bet-ter quality of life for all citizens, and where social conservatism receives strong political allegiance and expresses itself daily in pop-ular media outlets like talk radio and Fox News. The consequence is that while some workplaces in the United States provide parental leave as part of their benefits package, most do not. This means that a majority of American parents can only take time off after the birth of a child under the Family and Medical Leave Act of 1993; however, this act is only applicable to those who work at compa-nies with fifty or more employees, and it provides twelve weeks of *unpaid* job-guaranteed leave, which makes it an untenable solution for most families, since most families rely on the income of work-ing mothers to survive.

In contrast, let's look at Sweden. In this northern European country, mothers get fourteen weeks of leave at full pay—seven weeks prior to and seven weeks after the birth of a child. Further-

Moms Rising.

more, the parents of each new child are given a total of 480 days of paid leave to use as they see fit: each parent is given 40 days (or two months of work days) of this total, and the remaining 400 days (or year and a half of work days) is assigned as a family benefit that the parents can divide between themselves.[64] In Sweden, the state also provides affordable, accessible, and educational childcare, making it easier for mothers to go back to work without worrying about their children's well-being or their family's economic situation. In the United States, most childcare is privatized, and the quality varies greatly depending on where one lives and where one works; even when good childcare is accessible, its cost often puts women in a difficult situation. Should they go back to work, just to turn over most of their income to the childcare provider who makes it possible for them to go to work? Or should they save the cost of childcare but lose their income—and their retirement contributions, health insurance, and job advancement—by leaving their jobs to take care of their children? "We need to stop sentimentalizing mothers and other caregivers," argues feminist writer Ann Crittenden, "and start according their work the respect and material recognition that it deserves—and earns. I believe that this is the big unfinished business of the women's movement."[65]

Connected to this twenty-first-century motherhood movement is the multi-issue, intergenerational reproductive rights movement, which has increasingly focused on the right *to* parent as well as the right *not* to. Feminist leaders like Loretta Ross, of the group SisterSong Women of Color Reproductive Justice Collective, which formed in 1997, have critiqued the rhetoric of choice that has been so central to feminist arguments for abortion rights. Focusing on choice alone, according to Ross, ignores the ways in which the choices of women of color have been limited by economic constraints and a history of regulating brown and black women's bodies in the United States. "We wish all women had choices," said Ross. "But not all women do because of healthcare disparities, immigration policies, racism, homophobia, etc."[66] Building on the work done by feminists of color in the 1970s and '80s, discussed in chapter 2, SisterSong argues that reproductive rights must include not just the right to safe and legal abortions but also the right to parent, an end to enforced sterilization, and access to comprehensive sex education and free birth control, as well as prenatal care and other forms of healthcare. This movement has broadened the reproductive rights movement using an intersectional approach that places race and class at the center of analysis.

Groups like SisterSong argue that women should be able to parent (or not parent) without being coerced by economic pressure, racism, and other concerns. Groups like MomsRising argue that the United States should support those who raise children by becoming more like Europe and increase state funding for social services and early childhood education. Expanding the social safety net would provide crucial support to mothers—and fathers—and make it possible for them to both raise healthy children and engage in meaningful work outside the home. SisterSong, MomsRising, and other feminist groups working to change the way society supports women in their ability and choice to mother (or not), understand that the work of parenting will not be solved on an individual level; rather, this problem will only be solved with government intervention and employer compliance to ensure that all mothers, regardless of their education or their occupation, are able to truly balance the work of parenting with paid work outside the home.

Other contemporary feminists take a different approach to solving women's inequality. They argue that it is not laws or employment policies that should be changed; rather, capitalism and the free market will ultimately help to liberate women and bring about the gender equality they've been seeking—as long as women are willing to pursue careers in traditionally male-dominated spheres. According to this approach, as women rise to the top of the corporate workforce and break through its glass ceiling, they will have access to the leadership roles, the power, and the wealth that have historically been the exclusive province of men. A example of this approach can be seen in the 2013 bestselling book *Lean In: Women, Work, and the Will to Lead,* by Facebook chief operating officer Sheryl Sandberg. A member of Generation X, Sandberg was born in 1969 and, like many others of her generational cohort, she describes being "raised to believe that girls could do anything boys could do and *all* career paths were open to me."[67] Yet after achieving great success in her own field—first at Google, later at Facebook— she was surprised to see how few women there were with her "at the top." For example, in 2013 just twenty-one of the Fortune 500 CEOs were women. Sandberg wanted to understand why women raised to believe that they were just as smart and competent as men were not achieving the same level of professional success as their male peers. (It is worth noting that Facebook's board of directors was all male until 2012.)

What Sandberg ultimately decided is that women are often their own worst enemy—choosing to decline greater professional opportunities because of their own timidity, their desire to have children, or their lack of supportive partners. Rather than "lean out" by choosing to step back when faced with risk and challenge, she argues, women must "lean in" to the leadership opportunities of the corporate world, just as men have historically done. They should be present "at the table" when big decisions are made, put themselves forward for advanced job opportunities, and demand the salaries that they deserve. For Sandberg, "leaning is" is decidedly a feminist project. "I believe that if more women lean in," she writes, "we can change the power structure of our world and expand opportunities for all."[68] The high-paying jobs are there for women, according to Sandberg; women just need to lean in and grab them. She believes that as women gain access to the highest levels of power in the corporate world—and with it "the power structure of our world" generally—this world will inevitably be transformed by the increased presence of women within it.

Sandberg's argument isn't new; indeed, some of *Lean In*'s ideas about how women's entry into male-dominated spheres of employment will liberate them can be traced back to Betty Friedan's 1963 *The Feminine Mystique,* in which Friedan described the world of work as women's escape route from a life of gendered oppression. What is new is the extreme economic disparity between the world that Sheryl Sandberg lives in and the one inhabited by the average woman in the United States. As one commentator noted, "while we all worry about the glass ceiling," the invisible barrier that prevents women from rising to the top, "there are millions of women standing in the basement—and the basement is flooding."[69] Sandberg encourages women to lean in to the jobs that await them at the very, very top of the corporate structure, but the reality is that 62 percent of working women in the United States make an hourly wage of less than fifteen dollars an hour, and most work in female-dominated sectors, like service and clerical work, which offer few opportunities to "lean in."[70] The majority of women in the United States do not have the college and graduate degrees needed to enter into the high-powered corporate world described by Sandberg. And even when women work in high-wage professions, they still get paid less than their male colleagues doing the same work. In short, it is highly unlikely that the lives of most women in the United States will be changed as more women make it into the ranks of the elite group of Fortune 500 CEOs. The economic successes of women like Sheryl Sandberg and Oprah Winfrey are symbolically important of women's increasing power in the twenty-first century, but they do little to change the day-to-day realities of most women's lives in a country in which one in seven people lives in poverty.

Sandberg's "trickle-down feminist" approach assumes that as the lives of elite, educated (usually white) women in high-paying jobs get better, their increased economic prosperity and power in the male-dominated workplaces of high finance, government, and Silicon Valley will eventually lead to gains for the average working women in the United States.[71] Yet history suggests that this is not the case. Income equality is unlikely to trickle down to those at every level of the economic structure without substantial changes to that structure. While progressive groups like MomsRising understand that it is the workplace—and governmental policies that govern the workplace—that needs to change, people like Sandberg seem to suggest that it is women who should change to conform to the capitalist workplace. "By arguing that women should express their feminism by remaining in the workplace at all costs," writes one critic, "Sandberg encourages women to maintain a commitment to the workplace without encouraging the workplace to maintain a commitment to them."[72] In her belief that individual women should worker harder, should "lean in" to the competitive world of the corporate workforce, Sandberg's presents a neo-liberal view of feminism, in which the "free" markets will produce a fair economy that will enable those who try hard enough to succeed.

Wealthy moms like Sandberg will be able to hire help to achieve their life-work balance, but her proposals will do little to help the majority of mothers in the United States who struggle to pay their bills, take care of their children, and engage in meaningful work in which opportunities to lean in are even available.

We should definitely applaud that a few women have risen to power within the previously all-male ranks of the corporate workplace; yet we should not forget that the work of childcare, housecleaning, and other care work is still overwhelmingly a female-dominated sphere—and as such remains underpaid and undervalued within our economic system. For many professional women, the ability to pursue careers is dependent upon being able to hire other women to do this work in the home. As economist Alison Wolf argues in *The XX Factor: How the Rise of Working Women Has Created a Far Less Equal World*, "Without the new servant classes, elite women's employment would splutter and stall."[73] While the women's movement brought massive changes to every aspect of women's lives, for the women who work as nannies, childcare providers, and housecleaners, in many ways their work experience remains the same as it was in the early twentieth century. The progressive New Deal labor policies that brought much-needed regulation and protection to workers in a variety of employment sectors explicitly excluded domestic work, leaving it unregulated and subject to great abuse— including long hours with undefined workdays, little time off, discrimination, and the expectation that one worker can provide a wide range of services, involving both taxing physical work and empathetic emotional care work. In the twenty-first century, the overwhelming majority of those doing this work, particularly in major U.S. cities, are immigrant women of color. Indeed, a 2013 ACLU study of domestic workers in New York City found that 93 percent are women, 95 percent are people of color, and 99 percent are immigrants.[74]

It is precisely these women that Ai-Jen Poo wanted to work with when she founded the National Domestic Workers Alliance in 2010, another example of contemporary feminist activism. The daughter of Chinese immigrants, Poo is a first-generation American who was born in 1974 in Pittsburgh. As someone who had been "really passionate about women's issues since high school," it was in the Women's Studies Department at Columbia University that she got "the opportunity to explore the intellectual work that had been done around women's rights and how gender has shaped our world and our history."[75] After graduating with a major in women's studies in 1996, she worked for a domestic violence shelter that served immigrant women from Asian countries. In 2000, she cofounded Domestic Workers United, a membership-based advocacy organization dedicated to establishing fair labor standards for domestic workers, such as nannies and housekeepers, in the state of New York. The group successfully lobbied for legislation recognizing the labor rights of domestic workers in the state, work that had previously been excluded by other labor bills since the New Deal, and in September 2010 New York became the first state to pass a Domestic Workers' Bill of Rights. In a job in which workers are often on call twenty-four hours a day and expected to work around the clock, the bill ensures that domestic workers get at least one day off per week and at least three paid days off per year, as well as receive overtime when they work for more than forty hours per week. The bill also provides legal protection for sexual and racial harassment encountered on the job. After this legislative success in 2010, Poo went on to found the National Domestic Workers Alliance, which has taken this movement for workers' rights to a national level by creating a coalition of forty affiliate domestic workers' organizations across twenty-nine states. The group is working to replicate the New York Domestic Workers' Bill of Rights in other states, such as California, Illinois, and Massachusetts.

Ai-Jen Poo. Reprinted by permission of Gillian Laub, © 2012.

Poo often cites her mother and grandmother as important influences on her work, describing them as role models who recognized the value of all kinds of labor, including the care work traditionally assigned to women. "They were both really strong women with a lot of wisdom," she said. "I always knew that if we could just see the world through the eyes of women we'd have a much clearer picture of both what the problems are and what the solutions are."[76] Poo pursued this goal by encouraging policy makers to listen to the voices of the 2.5 million housekeepers, nannies, and elder caregivers in the United States. For her work toward what she has described as "peace and justice in the home," she achieved international recognition and numerous awards, including being named as one of *Newsweek*'s "150 Fearless Women" and one of *Time*'s "100 most influential people in the world."[77] "So much of the unfinished business of the women's movement," she said, "is really about bringing respect and dignity to this work," work that has remained feminized—and thus marginalized—throughout the world, even after decades of feminist change.[78] The National Domestic Workers Alliance is part of a growing transnational movement for domestic workers' rights, which includes organizations and trade unions from around the world. At the same time that women like Poo are working to build a broad, multifocused feminist movement organized around social justice for all, another contemporary movement has also proven that feminism is indeed global.

Challenging Rape Culture and Violence Against Women

In late January 2011 in Toronto, Canada, York University students Sonya Barnett and Heather Jarvis attended a forum on crime prevention and safety on campus. Little did they know that what they were about to hear would lead them to launch a global protest movement. After hearing a local police constable tell the audience, "I've been told I'm not supposed to say this—however, women should avoid dressing like sluts in order not to be victimized," Barnett and Jarvis decided to take action. Describing themselves as "fed up and pissed off" that anyone could blame girls and women for the sexual assaults committed against them, they "wanted to do something other than just be angry." So they began the work of organizing a protest demonstration, using Facebook, Twitter, and other forms of social media to spread the word. In early April 2011, over three thousand people gathered in downtown Toronto to take part in the action planned by Barnett and Jarvis—a protest they called SlutWalk.[79]

Barnett and Jarvis's reclamation of the sexist slur "slut" was intended to shock and to mobilize. "We called ourselves something controversial," said Jarvis. "Did we do it to get attention? Damn right we did!"[80] They designed the SlutWalk protest to stress one main point: no matter what they wear, no matter what their sexual histories have been, all women should be free from sexual assault. As they stressed, "We are tired of being oppressed by slut-shaming; of being judged by our sexuality and feeling unsafe as a result. Being in charge of our sexual lives should not mean that we are opening ourselves to an expectation of violence, regardless if we participate in sex for pleasure or work. No one should equate enjoying sex with attracting sexual assault."[81] Although the most widely distributed photos of the event depicted women wearing what could be described as "slutty" clothing—worn by participants in order to directly counter the suggestion that "women should avoid dressing like sluts in order not to be victimized"— in fact attendees at the Toronto SlutWalk dressed in a wide range of styles; many wore everyday clothes that covered most of the wearer's body.

Like earlier feminist protests, SlutWalk was deliberately designed to gain media attention—and it did. The SlutWalk movement quickly became a global phenomenon as information about the event and photos of the protest went viral. In the months that followed the Toronto march, feminist activists all around the world were inspired to organize SlutWalks in their own communities, including cities in Australia, Brazil, India, Israel, and Poland, as well as many cities in the United States. The ability of this movement to resonate with women around the world—even as sexual mores and definitions of female sexual autonomy varied greatly in the countries that had SlutWalk protests—was a sign of how violence against women is a global human rights problem that affects all women's lives. No matter where or how they live, all women face

SlutWalk, Auckland, New Zealand, June 2011. Hannah Johnston, Getty Images.

the risk of sexual assault and rape. Yet all women, the protesters argued, have a right to control their own sexual agency. All women have a right to pursue sexual pleasure without shame.

As *Feministing* founder Jessica Valenti noted in the summer of 2011, "In just a few months, SlutWalks have become the most successful feminist action of the past 20 years." What made this action so successful, said Valenti, is that it "translated online enthusiasm into in-person action in a way that hasn't been done before in feminism on this scale."[82] The SlutWalk movement proved that traditional forms of protest, such as marching in the streets en masse, are still vitally useful, while also demonstrating how twenty-first-century technology, like Facebook and Twitter, can be used to mobilize people into action. It built on earlier feminist activism against violence, most notably the Take Back the Night movement that has brought women into the streets to march against sexual assault since the 1970s, proving that sexual freedom and an end to rape are feminist issues that transcend time and generations. The movement was also quintessentially grassroots, organized in individual communities by local activists.

The SlutWalks have not been without criticism, however. A group of black feminists in the United States publicly criticized the movement for its attempt to reclaim the word "slut," noting that the organizers' desire to redeem this word ignored the long history of how race has shaped sexual stereotypes about women. As the signers of the 2011 "An Open Letter from Black Women to the SlutWalk" argued: "As Black women, we do not have the privilege or the space to call ourselves 'slut' without validating the already historically entrenched ideology and recurring messages about what and who the Black woman is."[83] This document echoed many of the points made twenty years earlier in the 1991 statement "African American Women in Defense of Ourselves" in response to the Clarence Thomas hearings, and it served as an important reminder of how gender, race, class, and sexuality are intertwined such that the discussion of one concept is inextricably bound with the discussion of another.

Other feminists have been critical of how the SlutWalk movement relied on a very narrow view of female liberation—put bluntly, the right to be a slut—that does little to challenge patriarchal norms around female sexuality. This critique stressed that the term "slut" comes from a misogynist view of female sexuality and "is so deeply rooted in the patriarchal 'madonna/whore' view of women's sexuality that it is beyond redemption."[84] Yet this view was challenged by still other feminists, including Alice Walker, who argued that "I've always understood the word 'slut' to mean a woman who freely enjoys her own sexuality in any way she wants to; undisturbed by other people's wishes for her behavior. Sexual desire originates in her and is directed by her. In that sense it is a word well worth retaining."[85]

The feminist debates over the SlutWalks are just the latest episode in the ongoing discussion within feminism about the role of sexuality in women's liberation. For earlier generations of feminists, the key issue at hand was to get the larger society to acknowledge that women are sexual beings with desires of their own. For example, as discussed in chapter 2, when "The Myth of the Vaginal Orgasm" was first distributed in 1968, many of its female (and feminist) readers were shocked to learn about the role of the clitoris in female sexuality. Up until this point in history, women's bodies and women's desires were defined almost exclusively in male terms. One of the most important gains of the women's liberation movement of the 1960s and '70s was its challenge to cultural norms around women's sexuality: women were encouraged to pursue their own pleasures and desires, including with other women, and to see themselves as sexual agents as much as men are. Although feminists of that period disagreed mightily about what sexual liberation meant for women—intensely debating such issues as pornography, sex work, censorship, sadomasochism, and other sexual practices, as well as what constituted "good" feminist sex—they passed on a legacy of speaking frankly about female sexuality and female pleasure that carried into the next generation. This legacy can be seen in everything from the career of pop icon Madonna—who famously sang that she felt *"like* a virgin," suggesting she was clearly not one—to the success of the television series *Sex and the City* to the fact that over half of women today own a vibrator and female masturbation is no longer the taboo subject it once was.

Since the early 1990s, feminists have become increasingly concerned with how women can pursue their own desires and assert their own agency within a highly sexualized culture where women's bodies continue to be commodified and exploited. As pornography has become widely accessible and acceptable within U.S. culture—what's been termed the "pornification" of sexuality—the representation of women as sex objects is ubiquitous. At the very historical moment when women have more economic, social, and political power than ever before, they are still overly represented as sexualized and subservient beings—and nowhere is this more evident than in pornography, the vast majority of which is still made for and consumed by heterosexual men. When the second-wave anti-pornography movement began in the 1970s, pornography was itself quite different. In order to see a pornographic film, one needed to go to a movie theater where such films were shown. Pornographic images were primarily distributed through magazines sold behind the counter. As in so many other areas of life, technological changes since 1990 have dramatically changed the pornography industry. The digitalization of images moved pornography from the seedy porn theater of the 1970s to the privacy of one's home and laptop, as most consumers of pornography now access porn through the Internet.

Those who have come of age after the Internet revolution have lived their entire lives in a media-saturated society, where sexualized images of women are everywhere. Porn has had a dramatic impact on how boys and girls, men and women, learn about human sexuality and human desire. Porn's representation of gender relations and sexuality is now everywhere, including advertising. Women are all too often depicted as nothing more than sex objects for male viewers, just as they were in the mid-twentieth century, and some argue that the situation has only gotten worse. As one commentator noted: "Despite the massive gains we've made, thanks to our feminist foremothers, we've barely dented the veneer of sexism in our culture. . . . Some forms of sexism have actually *worsened* since the second wave. There is more pressure than ever on women to starve and despise their bodies in mimicry of a false, fantasized ideal."[86] In short, women still face the same pressure to conform to a male fantasy of womanhood, only the fantasy has shifted: it is no longer the virginal "good girl" who is the ideal, but rather the porn-star-like "bad girl" who is. At the same time that this hypersexualized image of "female liberation" is being touted as the new goal, young women in the United States receive little in the way of comprehensive sex education, they have the highest rate of teen pregnancy in the developed world, and they risk being called "sluts" when they demand that birth control be affordable and accessible.

While feminist critics of the SlutWalks may take issue with various aspects of this movement, they have all agreed with its basic premise: namely, that women are not responsible for sexual assault, no matter what they wear or what they do. The ability of this message to resonate globally was reaffirmed two years after the first SlutWalk protest when, in February 2013, another anti-gendered-violence protest took place—although this time it occurred on the same day in cities, towns, and villages all around the world. Planned to occur on Valentine's Day 2013, One Billion Rising was organized by Eve Ensler, author of *The Vagina Monologues* and founder of the V-Day movement to end violence, along with her V-Day colleagues around the globe. The name of the action highlighted the fact that one in three women around the world—or 1 billion women—will "suffer some form of violence at the hands of men in the course of her lifetime," according to a report by the United Nations.[87] Using creativity and performance to garner attention, the One Billion Rising protests involved large groups of activists dancing, singing, and giving speeches to challenge the cultural norms that perpetuate violence against women. Activists in cities such as Buenos Aires, Helsinki, Johannesburg, Kabul, London, New Delhi, and Washington, D.C., representing over thirteen thousand organizations and 203 countries, participated in the event.[88] According to Kamla Bhasin, the coordinator for One Billion Rising in Southeast Asia, the date of the event was strategic:

"On this St. Valentine's Day, we are saying we don't want violence. We want love. What kind of love? Just love. Loved based on justice, love based on equality, love based on mutual respect."[89] Many of the One Billion Rising protests took the form of flash mobs, where large groups of seemingly unconnected people suddenly gathered together and began choreographed dance movements, moving en masse to the song "Break the Chain" by Tena Clark (the official One Billion Rising anthem). Throughout the globe, the protests also received recognition and support from elected officials, ranging from the first lady of Somalia to the mayor of San Francisco.

Like the SlutWalks, One Billion Rising was propelled by social media: word of the Valentine's Day protest spread via a short film posted to YouTube five months in advance of the event; organizers used Facebook, Twitter, and Instagram to rally participants; actions were streamed live on the Internet; and after the demonstration was over, photos and videos from the highly visual event were distributed using social media. This day of simultaneous protest once again proved that new forms of technology could be used to advance feminist causes—this time on a truly global scale—in a way previously unheard of or seen. As the South Africa coordinator for One Billion Rising, Gillian Schutte, said, "When a billion voices make that call on the same day—something is bound to change."[90]

These recent movements bring much-needed focus to violence against women at the hands of men, which the World Health Organization has described as "a global health problem of epidemic proportions."[91] A 2010 study by the Centers for Disease Control (CDC) found that "intimate partner violence, sexual violence, and stalking are important and widespread public health problems in the United States." According to the CDC, one in five women (and one in seventy-one men) has been raped; one in six women (and one in nineteen men) has been stalked; and one in four women (and one in seven men) has been the victim of severe physical violence by an intimate partner.[92] While decades of feminist activism, survivors' testimonies, and changes in the law—such as the Violence Against Women Act passed by Congress in 1994—have increased awareness of this global health problem, the rates of violence against women at the hands of men remains extremely high and little changed around the globe.

Global Feminism in the Twenty-First Century

The One Billion Rising movement provides a clear example of how feminist activists from different parts of the world can become a truly global force, fighting a transnational problem like gender-based violence—including rape, intimate partner violence, child marriage, female genital mutilation, and sex trafficking—that affects all women and girls. Such activism is greatly advanced by the new, Web-based technologies that permit immediate communication between individuals and groups, coordination of efforts, and broadcasting of outcomes. But these new technologies also help to facilitate and publicize many local efforts—by both community organizations and transnational NGOs—to change the practices in a particular country or region. Some examples of the diverse range of activist projects in the early twenty-first century include: women in Saudia Arabia driving cars to protest their country's de facto ban against female drivers; Pussy Riot, the punk rock, guerrilla-style activist group, using music to fight sexism and homophobia in Russia; feminist bloggers in Egypt using self-made videos to challenge sexism and to place women's rights at the center of the "Arab Spring" movement for democracy; members of the European group Femen protesting topless at the Spanish Parliament to challenge restrictions on abortion rights; Young Feminists Movement Namibia, or Y-Fem, working for comprehensive sex education through its Facebook group; and activists in Ciu-

dad Juárez raising international awareness of the record number
of rapes, murders, and disappearances of young women in their
Mexican border city. Feminism in the twenty-first century, aided
by technology, has become more *global*, in the sense that activists
can work toward a shared goal that crosses borders, and more *international*, in the sense that activists can gain knowledge of the feminist issues that define specific nations.

Perhaps no one better symbolizes the future of feminism than
Malala Yousafzai, the young feminist activist from Pakistan.
Yousafzai was an eleven-year-old Muslim schoolgirl when she first
came to public attention in early 2009 for her blog, written under
a pseudonym for the BBC's Web site, which detailed her life under
Taliban rule and her opposition to the Taliban's closing of schools
for girls. Although she was just a young girl, her intelligence, charisma, and public speaking skills quickly identified her as a natural
leader, and she soon gained international attention as an inspiring activist in a country where only 40 percent of women over
the age of fifteen can read and write.[93] Encouraged and inspired
by her father, who had long championed the rights of girls to an
education, Yousafzai was profiled in a 2009 *New York Times*–produced documentary entitled *Class Dismissed* about the closing of
girls' schools in Pakistan's Swat Valley, and in 2011 she was nominated by the KidsRights Foundation for its International Children's
Peace Prize. It was only a short time before Yousafazi's public stand
against the Taliban made her a target. In October 2012, a Taliban
assassin jumped onto her school bus, demanding to know "Which
one is Malala?" He then shot Yousafzai in the head. Gravely injured
and in a coma, Yousafzai was transported to the United Kingdom,
where she received medical care and months of rehabilitation, ultimately surviving the assassination attempt without any permanent
brain damage. Unable to return to Pakistan because of threats
against her life, Yousafzai has continued her fight for girls' rights

and has become internationally known for her human rights work, becoming the youngest person in history to be nominated for a Nobel Peace Prize. In her 2013 speech before the United Nations Youth Delegation, upon being awarded the UN's Children's Peace Prize, she spoke of receiving her inspiration from the nonviolent movements led by Mahatma Gandhi, Martin Luther King Jr., and Nelson Mandela. As she said at the UN, "Today I am focusing on women's rights and girls' education because they are suffering the most. There was a time when women social activists asked men to stand up for their rights. But, this time, we will do it by ourselves. I am not telling men to step away from speaking for women's rights[,] rather I am focusing on women to be independent to fight for themselves."[94] Yousafzai's eloquence and passion captured the world's attention, and she brought much-needed focus to the issue of gender discrimination in education, which according to the UN is a widespread problem leading to epidemic rates of female illiteracy throughout the world.

While American feminists will undoubtedly continue to play an important role in the global movement for gender justice and equality, there are many signs that the United States has been decentered from the world stage and that it is neither the preeminent model for women's equality nor the site of women's most urgent struggles. It has become increasingly clear that the United States has fallen behind its international peers and no longer serves as a world leader when it comes to gender equality. The United States is one of only five countries—along with Lesotho, Liberia, Papua New Guinea, and Swaziland—that does not mandate paid parental leave. Most countries require at least three months of paid leave, and many of the United States' peer countries offer far more than that. (Recall Sweden's policy of almost two years of paid leave per child.) When it comes to the number of women in elected office, the United States is also lagging. According to a 2013 study, the United

States ranks eightieth out of 142 countries based on the percentage of elected federal positions held by women.[95] While women now make up 20 percent of such positions in the United States, the top ten countries in this study have at least 40 percent of comparable positions held by women. Many countries—including Chile, Germany, Indonesia, Liberia, and South Korea—have elected women to their highest political office, but so far the United States has yet to have a female president or even vice president. The United States also lags behind in changing cultural norms and attitudes about gender, which too often seem stuck in retrograde ideas about dominant masculinity and subservient femininity that only exacerbate the structural conditions that keep women and girls from achieving full equality. Even when we examine the elite class of women who rise to the top of the corporate workplace—the Sheryl Sandbergs of the world—one sees how behind the United States is: according to a 2013 report, only 20 percent of senior corporate leaders in the United States are women.[96]

But the challenges facing U.S. feminists, struggling to equal the gains made by women elsewhere, nonetheless pale in comparison to the obstacles confronting women in many other parts of the world. Women who live in nations lacking basic human rights, where human needs are unfulfilled, and where the oppression of women and girls is a daily reality are a reminder of how privileged and comfortable most U.S. women are. In their urgent fight for women's rights—including access to education, economic opportunities, sexual freedom, reproductive healthcare, political participation, and an end to violence—activists in Southeast Asia, Africa, and Latin America have inspired and reenergized U.S. feminists. As women's rights activists around the world focus on both local and global issues, it is important to remember the conclusion reached by a 2012 report by the U.K.-based organization Womankind: "In no country in the world do women enjoy the same rights, access to resources or opportunities as men. Everywhere women and girls face discrimination, poverty and violence just because they are female."[97]

Feminism Unfinished, Feminism Ongoing

Sandra Fluke was a third-year law student at Georgetown University when she was invited by Democrats in the House of Representatives to speak on a congressional panel discussing contraception insurance in President Barack Obama's healthcare bill and how the bill would affect the health insurance provided by nonprofit religious organizations, such as Catholic universities like Georgetown. House Republicans successfully blocked Fluke from addressing the panel, one with not a single woman on it. Born in 1981, Fluke graduated with a major in feminist, gender, and sexuality studies from Cornell University; a lifelong feminist activist, she was president of the group Georgetown Law Students for Reproductive Justice when she was called to speak before Congress. When Democrats eventually convened another meeting on the birth control provision, Fluke was finally heard, and the thirty-year-old spoke passionately about the importance of contraception coverage for low-income female students who relied upon their student health insurance to cover the high cost of birth control pills; as she noted during her testimony, the pill is often prescribed for medical reasons other than preventing pregnancy, including for menstrual irregularities, acne, and endometriosis.

It was February 2012 when Fluke spoke before Congress, but it might as well have been fifty years earlier: there were no women on the House panel (all the more startling given that the topic was contraception), and Fluke was derided for raising the issue of birth control in public. Popular conservative radio host Rush Limbaugh viciously attacked Fluke, equating the demand to have birth

control pills covered by health insurance with prostitution. Limbaugh asked his listeners about Fluke: "What does that make her?
It makes her a slut, right? It makes her a prostitute. She wants to
be paid to have sex. She's having so much sex she can't afford the
contraception. She wants you and me and the taxpayers to pay her
to have sex."[98] Putting aside Limbaugh's lack of understanding of
how birth control pills work—the cost of a month's prescription
remains the same no matter how much (or how little) sex one is
having—his comments were a reminder of how deeply entrenched
sexism remained in the United States, even after decades of wom-
en's movements.

Limbaugh's crude attack on Fluke—which played out over several days and ultimately led to many of his advertisers withdrawing
their support for his radio program—was only one of a series of
sexist, misogynist, and just plain nutty comments that filled the
airwaves during the 2012 election season. A Missouri congressman insisted that if a woman was "legitimately raped" she couldn't
get pregnant because "the female body has ways to shut that whole
thing down." Later, a candidate for the U.S. Senate from Indiana
claimed that "even if life begins in that horrible situation of rape, that
it is something that God intended to happen."[99] As they attempted
to justify their anti-abortion—as well as anti-birth-control—views,
a number of Republican candidates for office seemed to condone
rape, if it led to conception. The feminist blogosphere immediately
responded, using humorous images (spread via Twitter, Facebook,
and other social media) and more serious journalism to fight back.
In a *Feministing* article entitled "Republican Men Need to Shut Up
About Rape Forever," a rape survivor named Zerlina argued: "I
don't even know why these anti-choice Republicans think they are
entitled to speak about the topic. This is about the power of women
as independent actors to make choices about their own bodies. A
rape survivor has already lost power and control over her bodily

autonomy and now Republican men want to let us know what they think we should be allowed to do after the rape?"[100] When Election Day came in November 2012, all of the "Republican rape apologists" lost their bids for office.[101]

In a repetition of the so-called Year of the Woman from twenty years earlier, the 2012 elections saw a record number of women elected to Congress. This brought the total number of women senators to twenty, ten times as many as the two who had been in the Senate when Anita Hill testified before Congress in 1991. (It also led to a renovation of the women's restroom in the Senate, which until 2013 had only two stalls.) The increase in women senators was something to celebrate, as was the election of the nation's first openly gay U.S. senator, Tammy Baldwin, a Democrat from Wisconsin, and the first Asian American woman U.S. senator, Mazie Hirono, a Democrat from Hawaii. Women also increased their ranks in the House after the 2012 elections, filling ninety-eight seats, or 18.3 percent of the total. This critical mass of women in Congress made its importance known in its response to the epidemic of sexual assaults in the military, an ongoing problem that gained more political attention after women were allowed to serve in combat positions. More women also filled seats on the Supreme Court. When Clarence Thomas joined the Court in 1991, he sat next to only one woman, Sandra Day O'Connor, the first woman justice, who was appointed in 1981 by President Ronald Reagan. By 2012, Thomas was still on the Court, but now he sat next to three women justices, all appointed by Democratic presidents: Justices Ruth Bader Ginsburg (in 1993), Sonia Sotomayor (in 2009), and Elena Kagan (in 2010).

President Barack Obama—the nation's first African American president—was reelected in 2012, and this was also a sign of victory for those fighting for progressive social change. Obama's first act as president was to sign the Lilly Ledbetter Fair Pay Act in 2009, which expanded workers' rights to sue for pay discrimination based on gender. His egalitarian partnership with his wife, First Lady Michelle Obama, the feminist values he absorbed from his single-parent mother, Ann Dunham, and, most importantly, his strong political support for women's and LGBT rights all suggested that he was the nation's first feminist president—as *Ms.* magazine famously depicted on its Winter 2009 cover, which featured Obama wearing a THIS IS WHAT A FEMINIST LOOKS LIKE T-shirt.

This snapshot of the 2012 elections suggests both the successes and the ongoing challenges for feminism in the twenty-first century. Women hold more positions of power than ever before, yet when it comes to elected office they still are woefully underrepresented given that they account for half of the population. Conservative women, such as 2008 Republican vice presidential nominee Sarah Palin, are cheered for their public proclamations against feminism, while outspoken feminists, like former presidential candidate and secretary of state Hillary Clinton, are virulently attacked in hateful and misogynistic terms. Seemingly even President Obama's feminist rhetoric and policies are more palatable to the general public because he is a man—and a man whose wife, Michelle, now prefers the title "mom in chief" to her previous one of "Barack's boss." All this suggests that feminism when espoused by a powerful woman is still deeply threatening.

At the grassroots level, feminist activists in the United States continue to fight for gender equality and social justice, particularly in areas where there has been no progress or where things have gotten worse, such as ensuring reproductive rights and access to abortion services, ending violence against women, challenging racism and white supremacy, and addressing the widening economic inequalities that characterize twenty-first-century life in the United States. Feminists are using the new technologies of the Internet age to bring together progressive activists and

Reprinted by permission of *Ms.* magazine, © 2009.

to respond in real time to threats against women's rights. Feminism is becoming more global, as activists around the world share knowledge, organizing strategies, and political support in ways previously unimagined. Yet even as feminism becomes more democratic and diverse—more accessible to all and more representative of all—its gains are still most strongly felt by those at the top. It is not surprising that many of the feminist activists featured in this chapter—including Rebecca Walker, Ai-Jan Poo, and Sandra Fluke—went to elite, Ivy League schools and benefited from the open doors and expanded opportunities that such an education makes possible.

When they first emerged on the scene in the 1990s, many of the "new wave" of feminists conceived of feminism in very individualistic terms. For these younger women, feminism represented greater personal choice—in their career opportunities, decisions about motherhood, and expressions of sexuality. For them, feminism was a way of life, a way of seeing the world, a mindset as much as a movement. This gave them the freedom to create lives that were much different than those of their mothers or grandmothers. Yet as they developed their own activist agendas and participated in ongoing feminist projects, they began to recognize that individual empowerment, while important, is not enough. In its current manifestations—whether we look at the One Billion Rising global movement to end rape, the feminist blogosphere, or groups fighting for the rights of mothers and other caregivers—feminism demonstrates the continued importance of collective action. Looking forward, the unfinished work of feminism will require a diversity of voices, willing to come together to secure freedom and justice for all.

1. Rebecca Walker, "How Anita Hill Woke a Generation of Feminists," *The Root*, October 15, 2011, http://www.theroot.com/views/how-anita-hill-woke-generation-feminists.

2. In 1991, there were two Asian American senators, both Democrats from Hawaii: Daniel Inouye and Daniel Akaka. There were also two white women senators: Nancy Kassebaum, Republican from Kansas, and Barbara Mikulski, Democrat from Maryland.

3. Deborah Siegel, *Sisterhood Interrupted: From Radical Women to Grrls Gone Wild* (New York: Palgrave Macmillan, 2007), 112.

4. Eleanor Holmes Norton quoted in Krissah Thompson, "For Anita Hill, the Clarence Thomas Hearings Haven't Really Ended," *Washington Post*, October 6, 2011, http://articles.washingtonpost.com/2011-10-06/politics/35280664_1_thomas-hearings-anita-hill-sexual-harassment.

5. "African American Women in Defense of Ourselves," *New York Times*, November 17, 1991, A-53.

6. Rebecca Walker, "Becoming the Third Wave," *Ms.*, January/February 1992, 41; Walker, "How Anita Hill."

7. Walker, "Becoming the Third Wave," 41.

8. Rebecca Walker, "Being Real: An Introduction," in *To Be Real: Telling the Truth and Changing the Face of Feminism*, ed. Rebecca Walker (New York: Anchor Books, 1995), xxxii–xxxiii.

9. Walker, "Being Real," xxxiii.

10. Rebecca Walker, "Foreword: We Are Using This Power to Resist," in *The Fire This Time: Young Activists and the New Feminism*, ed. Vivien Labaton and Dawn Lundy Martin (New York: Anchor Books, 2004), xv.

11. Catherine S. Manegold, "No More Nice Girls: In Angry Droves, Radical Feminists Just Want to Have Impact," *New York Times*, July 12, 1992, http://www.nytimes.com/1992/07/12/nyregion/no-more-nice-girls-in-angry-droves-radical-feminists-just-want-to-have-impact.html; "Rebecca Walker," *Time*, December 5, 1994, 94.

12. Manegold, "No More Nice Girls."

13. Walker, "Foreword," xvi.

14. "Riding the Third Wave," the *Satya* interview with Rebecca Walker, *Satya*, January 2005, http://www.satyamag.com/jan05/walker.html.

15. Third Wave Foundation, www.thirdwavefoundation.org.

16. Manegold, "No More Nice Girls."

17. Rory Dicker, *A History of U.S. Feminisms* (Berkeley, CA: Seal Press, 2009), 117.

18. Susan Faludi, *Backlash: The Undeclared War Against American Women* (New York: Crown Publishers, 1991), xviii.

19. Jennifer Baumgardner and Amy Richards, *Manifesta: Young Women, Feminism, and the Future* (New York: Farrar, Straus & Giroux, 2000), 17.

20. Barbara Findlen, "Introduction," *Listen Up: Voices from the Next Feminist Generation*, ed. Barbara Findlen (Seattle: Seal Press, 1995), xii.

21. Rose L. Glickman, *Daughters of Feminists* (New York: St. Martin's Press, 1993), xiii.

22. Amber E. Kinser, "Negotiating Spaces For/Through Third-Wave Feminism," *NWSA Journal* 16, no. 3 (2004): 124–25.

23. Shelby Knox interviewed in Jennifer Baumgardner, *F'em: Goo Goo, Gaga, and Some Thoughts on Balls* (Berkeley, CA: Seal Press, 2011), 108.

24. Kristina Gray, "I Sold My Soul to Rock and Roll," in *Colonize This! Young Women of Color on Today's Feminism*, ed. Daisy Hernández and Bushra Rehman (New York: Seal Press, 2002), 261.

25. Michael Kimmel, "Real Men Join the Movement," in *Women's Voices, Feminist Visions: Classic and Contemporary Readings*, ed. Susan Shaw and Janet Lee (New York: McGraw-Hill, 2011), 663.

26. Jo Reger, *Everywhere and Nowhere: Contemporary Feminism in the United States* (New York: Oxford University Press, 2012), 56.

27. AnnJanette Rosga and Meg Satterthwaite, "Notes from the Aftermath," in *The Feminist Memoir Project: Voices from Women's Liberation*, ed. Rachel Blau DuPlessis and Ann Snitow (New York: Three Rivers Press, 1998), 473, emphasis in original.

28. Bushra Rehman and Daisy Hernández, "Introduction," in Hernández and Rehman, *Colonize This!*, xxiii.

29. "An Interview with Daisy Hernández," *Feminist Studies* 34, nos. 1–2 (2008): 325.

30. Vivien Labaton and Dawn Lundy Martin, "Introduction: Making What Will Become," in Labaton and Martin, *The Fire This Time*, xxv–xxvi, emphasis added.

31. Rehman and Hernández, "Introduction," xvii.

32. Reger, *Everywhere and Nowhere*.

33. Peggy Orenstein, *Flux: Women on Sex, Work, Love, Kids, and Life in a Half-Changed World* (New York: Doubleday, 2000), 2.

34. Alan Guttmacher Institute, "Induced Abortion: Facts in Brief," 2013, http://www.guttmacher.org/pubs/fb_induced_abortion.pdf.

35. Lisa Jervis, "The End of Feminism's Third Wave: The Cofounder of *Bitch* Magazine Says Goodbye to the Generational Divide," *Ms.*, Winter 2004, http://www.msmagazine.com/winter2004/thirdwave.asp.

36. Jennifer Friedlin, "A Clash of Waves: Second and Third Wave Feminists Clash over the Future," *Women's ENews*, May 26, 2002, www.vfa.us/Clash.htm.

37. Jervis, "The End of Feminism's Third Wave."

38. Myra Marx Ferree and Beth B. Hess, *Controversy and Coalition: The New Feminist Movement Across Four Decades of Change*, 3rd ed. (New York: Routledge, 2000), 219.

39. Rory Dicker and Alison Piepmeier, "Introduction," in *Catching a Wave: Reclaiming Feminism for the 21st Century*, ed. R. Dicker and A. Piepmeier (Boston: Northeastern University Press, 2003), 5.

40. Leandra Zarnow, "From Sisterhood to Girlie Culture: Closing the Great Divide between Second and Third Wave Cultural Agendas," in *No Permanent Waves: Recasting Histories of U.S. Feminism* (New Brunswick: Rutgers University Press, 2010), 279.

41. Susan Brownmiller quoted in Gail Collins, *When Everything Changed: The Amazing Journey of American Women, from 1960 to the Present* (New York: Little, Brown, 2009), 195.

42. Tracy L. M. Kennedy, "The Personal Is Political: Feminist Blogging and Virtual Consciousness-Raising," *Scholar and Feminist Online* 5, no. 2 (Spring 2007): http://sfonline.barnard.edu/blogs/kennedy_01.htm.

43. Kira Cochrane, "The Third Wave—at a Computer Near You," *Guardian*, March 30, 2006, http://www.theguardian.com/world/2006/mar/31/gender.uk.

44. Knox interviewed in Baumgardner, *F'em*, 110.

45. Kennedy, "The Personal Is Political."

46. Jessica Valenti, "Farewell, Feministing!" *Feministing*, February 2, 2011, http://feministing.com/2011/02/02/farewell-feministing/.

47. Valenti, "Farewell, Feministing!"

48. Moya Bailey and Alexis Pauline Gumbs, "We Are the Ones We've Been Waiting For," *Ms.*, Winter 2010, 42.

49. Crunk Feminist Collective, "Mission Statement," http://www.crunkfeminist collective.com/about/.

50. Moya Bailey, interview with author via e-mail, October 29, 2013.

51. Jessica Valenti and Courney Martin, "#FemFuture: Online Revolution, Executive Summary," 2012, Barnard Center for Research on Women, http://bcrw .barnard.edu/wp-content/nfs/reports/NFS8-FemFuture-Executive-Summary .pdf.

52. Sara Marcus, *Girls to the Front: The True Story of the Riot Grrrl Revolution* (New York: Harper Perennial, 2010), 75.

53. "Casting Call: Hollywood Needs More Women," NPR, June 20, 2013, http:// www.npr.org/2013/06/30/197390707/casting-call-hollywood-needs-more- women.

54. Jeannine DeLombard, "Femmenism," in Walker, *To Be Real*, 33.

55. Veronica Chambers, "Betrayal Feminism," in Findlen, *Listen Up!*, 24.

56. Walker, "Being Real," xxxv, xxxiv.

57. Joan Morgan, *When Chickenheads Come Home to Roost: My Life as a Hip-Hop Feminist* (New York: Simon & Schuster, 1999), 23.

58. Alison Piepmeier, *Girl Zines: Making Media, Doing Feminism* (New York: New York University Press, 2009), 28.

59. Labaton and Martin, "Introduction," in Labaton and Martin, *The Fire This Time*, xxi.

60. Courtney Martin, "The End of the Women's Movement," *American Prospect*, March 27, 2009, http://prospect.org/article/end-womens-movement.

61. "Interview with Rachel Lloyd," *ClaudiaChan.com*, February 15, 2012, http:// www.claudiachan.com/interviews/rachel-lloyd/.

62. Rebecca Walker, "How My Mother's Fanatical Views Tore Us Apart," *Daily Mail*, May 23, 2008, http://www.dailymail.co.uk/femail/article-1021293/How -mothers-fanatical-feminist-views-tore-apart-daughter-The-Color-Purple-auth or.html. See also Rebecca Walker, *Baby Love: Choosing Motherhood After a Life- time of Ambivalence* (New York: Riverhead Books, 2008).

63. Stephanie Coontz, "Why Gender Equality Stalled," *New York Times*, February 16, 2013, http://www.nytimes.com/2013/02/17/opinion/sunday/why-gender- equality-stalled.html.

64. Catalyst, *"Catalyst Quick Take: Family Leave—U.S., Canada, and Global,"* 2013, http://www.catalyst.org/knowledge/family-leave-us-canada-and-global.

65. Ann Crittenden cited in Joan Blades and Kristin Rowe-Finkbeiner, *The Moth- erhood Manifesto: What America's Moms Want and What To Do About It,* (New York: Nation Books, 2006), 5.

66. Loretta Ross interviewed in Baumgardner, *F'em*, 175.

67. Sheryl Sandberg, *Lean In: Women, Work, and the Will to Lead* (New York: Knopf, 2013), 14, emphasis in original.

68. Sandberg, *Lean In*, 171.

69. Laurie Penny quoted in Sarah Jaffe, "Trickle-Down Feminism," *Dissent*, Winter 2013, http://www.dissentmagazine.org/article/trickle-down-feminism.

70. Bureau of Labor Statistics, "Highlights of Women's Earnings 2012," October 2013, http://www.bls.gov/cps/cpswom2012.pdf.

71. See Jaffe, "Trickle-Down Feminism."

72. Kate Losse, "Feminism's Tipping Point: Who Wins from Leaning In?" *Dissent*, March 26, 2013, http://www.dissentmagazine.org/online_articles/feminisms-tipping-point-who-wins-from-leaning-in.

73. Alison Wolf, *The XX Factor: How the Rise of Working Women Has Created a Far Less Equal World* (New York: Crown, 2013), 59.

74. Christine Kim, "The Caregivers Coalition," interview with Ai-Jen Poo, *Guernica*, January 15, 2013, http://www.guernicamag.com/interviews/the-caregivers-coalition/.

75. Nathalie Alonso, "The Home Front," *Columbia College Today*, Fall 2012, 42.

76. Mark Engler, "Ai-Jen Poo: Organizing Labor—with Love," *Yes! Magazine*, November 29, 2011, http://www.yesmagazine.org/issues/the-yes-breakthrough-15/ai-jen-poo-organizing-labor-with-love.

77. Gloria Steinem, "Ai-jen Poo," *Time*, April 18, 2012, http://www.time.com/time/specials/packages/article/0,28804,2111975_2111976_2112169,00.html.

78. "*Time* 100: Ai-Jen Poo," 2012, http://www.time.com/time/video/player/0,32068,1567605638001_2112245,00.html.

79. Jessica Valenti, "SlutWalks and the Future of Feminism," *Washington Post*, June 3, 2011, http://articles.washingtonpost.com/2011-06-03/opinions/35235904_1_successful-feminist-action-slutwalks-young-women.

80. Valenti, "SlutWalks."

81. SlutWalk Toronto, http://www.SlutWalktoronto.com.

82. Valenti, "SlutWalks."

83. "An Open Letter from Black Women to the SlutWalk," September 23, 2011, http://www.blackwomensblueprint.org/2011/09/23/an-open-letter-from-black-women-to-the-slutwalk/.

84. Gail Dines and Wendy J. Murphy, "SlutWalk Is Not Sexual Liberation," *Guardian*, May 8, 2011, http://www.theguardian.com/commentisfree/2011/may/08/slutwalk-not-sexual-liberation.

85. "Michael Archer: Q&A with Alice Walker," *Guernica*, June 15, 2011, http://www.guernicamag.com/daily/michael_archer_qa_with_alice_w.

86. Abigail Rine, "The Pros and Cons of Abandoning the Word 'Feminist,'" *Atlantic*, May 2, 2013, http://www.theatlantic.com/sexes/archive/2013/05/the-pros-and-cons-of-abandoning-the-word-feminist/275511/, emphasis in original.

87. Julie McCarthy, "'One Billion Rising' Campaigns to End Violence Against Women," NPR, February 15, 2013, story www.npr.org/2013/02/15/172078654/indias-one-billion-rising-campaign.

88. Gillian Schutte, "One Billion Bodies Reclaimed!" *Huffington Post*, February 19, 2013, http://www.huffingtonpost.com/gillian-schutte/violence-against-women_b_2718813.html.

89. McCarthy, "'One Billion Rising.'"

90. Schutte, "One Billion Bodies Reclaimed!"

91. World Health Organization, "WHO Report Highlights Violence Against Women as a 'Global Health Problem of Epidemic Proportions'" June 20, 2013, http://www.who.int/mediacentre/news/releases/2013/violence_against_women_20130620/en.

92. Centers for Disease Control and Prevention and the National Center for Injury Prevention and Control, "The National Intimate Partner and Sexual Violence Survey: 2010 Summary Report," November 2011, http://www.cdc.gov/violenceprevention/pdf/nisvs_executive_summary-a.pdf.

93. UNESCO, "Key Messages and Data on Girls' and Women's Education and Literacy," April 2012, 1, http://www.unesco.org/new/fileadmin/MULTIMEDIA/HQ/ED/pdf/globalpartners-key-messages.pdf.

94. "Malala Yousafzai Speech in Full," BBC News, July 16, 2013, http://www.bbc.co.uk/news/world-asia-23291897.

95. Inter-Parliamentary Union, "Women in National Parliaments," September 1, 2013, http://www.ipu.org/wmn-e/classif.htm.

96. Shelley DuBois, "Women Leaders in Business: Why Is the U.S. a Laggard?" CNNMoney March 22, 2013, http://management.fortune.cnn.com/2013/03/22/women-business-leaders-us/.

97. Womankind, "Impact Through Partnership: Annual Report for 2011–12," http://www.womankind.org.uk/wp-content/uploads/downloads/2012/09/Womankind-Annual-Report-2011-12.pdf.

98. "Limbaugh Slut Slur Student Sandra Fluke Gets Obama Call," BBC News, March 2, 2012, http://www.bbc.co.uk/news/world-us-canada-17241803.

99. "Rep. Todd Akin's Rape Remark at Odds with Science of Pregnancy," *Huffington Post*, August 20, 2012, http://www.huffingtonpost.com/2012/08/20/akin-rape-remark-science-pregnancy_n_1811642.html; Annie Groer, "Indiana GOP Senate Hopeful Richard Mourdock Says God 'Intended' Rape Pregnancies," *Washington Post*, October 24, 2012, http://www.washingtonpost.com/blogs/she-the-people/wp/2012/10/24/indiana-gop-senate-hopeful-richard-mourdock-says-god-intended-rape-pregnancies/.

100. Zerlina, "Republican Men Need to Shut Up About Rape Forever," *Feministing* November 1, 2012, http://feministing.com/2012/11/01/republican-men-need-to-shut-up-about-rape-forever/.

101. Zerlina, "Republican Men Need to Shut Up about Rape Forever."

Afterword

We chose to name our book *Feminism Unfinished* because the movement has not ended. Women's subordination is an ancient human practice, integrated into nearly every major religion and nearly every economic system. Women's subordination has been so deeply embedded—socially, economically, culturally, politically—that it will take many more generations to overcome it.

Our book has shown that American feminism over the last hundred years took many forms and that feminists had varied priorities and strategies. Some feminists worked in woman-only groups, some in organizations with men. (And many feminists *were* men.) Some focused on the workplace, others on healthcare, others on the law, others on personal life. Some organized demonstrations; others fought battles in court, helped pass new laws, wrote articles, went on strike, or circulated petitions. For some feminists, being a woman was a primary identity; for others it never was. So it is not surprising that there have been many women's movements and they haven't all agreed. At times, this lack of unity has held back social change, but at other moments the multiplicity of feminisms has been a strength: diverse movements of women have influenced each other toward a fuller concept of what women's equality and freedom might mean.

Since the women's suffrage amendment was adopted in 1920, most legal restrictions on women have been abolished: women now serve on juries, fight in the armed forces, and can apply for any job or to attend any educational institution, for example. Women can wear what they want and love whom they desire.

Perhaps the biggest gains have been in women's transformed expectations. Fewer women in heterosexual couples expect to do all the housework; fewer women expect to stay in abusive relationships; fewer women want to swear to obey their husbands; more women expect sexual pleasure; more expect to plan their pregnancies and childbirths; and more women have grown up believing that they can and are entitled to do anything a man can do.

Of all these gains, it is important to ask, who benefits? The answer is, by no means only feminists. The majority of employed women have gained greater opportunities and higher wages because of the sustained efforts of feminist activists. Nonemployed women have become fewer, not only because of feminism but also because fewer men are able to support families single-handedly; those women who do not work outside the home benefit from greater recognition of domestic labor as work. Most children have gained a freer childhood, with somewhat less pressure to conform to gender ideals. More men now experience the pleasures of fatherhood and find they enjoy the more egalitarian partnerships and intimacy that women want. Lesbians have benefited greatly from the fact that heterosexual marriage is now a choice, not an economic and social necessity as it once was. All lesbian, gay, bisexual, and transgender people have benefited from the feminist rejection of gender and sexual conformity and the feminist insistence that sexual pleasure is a human right, not a source of shame.

Even people who consider themselves anti-feminist today have gained enormously from feminism. Few gender-conservative women would want to be barred from driving, excluded from schools and professions, required to give birth to more children than they can care for, or see their daughters prevented from achieving their full potential. Many people who do not consider themselves feminists actually agree with much of the feminist agenda.

Yet despite the gains made by feminist movements over the last century, inequality between men and women persists. Women are far from equal when it comes to their representation in the media, the government, or the economy. Violence against women is commonplace. Economic and other inequalities between men and women remain deeply entrenched as well. Some professions have opened to women while others remain male dominated, and the gender pay gap stubbornly persists. Women still do the vast majority of childcare and housework, even as they work outside the home at the same rate as men.

Moreover, the benefits of feminism have not been equally distributed among all women and men. The major lines of inequality stem from class, race, motherhood, and nation, or geographical position in the global balance of power. For example, feminists brought rape out of hiding and extended our understanding of it to include date and marital rape, but poor women, young women, and women of color are still more likely to suffer sexual assaults. Reproductive rights, good healthcare, and education are much harder to access for the increasing number of Americans in poverty, while most of the income progress among women has gone to childless women and the top 20 percent of earners. In short, few feminist gains are equally distributed; the struggle for sex equality cannot be separated from other dimensions of inequality. The fact that inequality is growing is a direct threat to the goals of feminism.

Meanwhile, the pushback against women's gains has been powerful. Anti-feminism is a fundamental part of the rise of right-wing conservatism since the late 1970s. Many Americans, like others throughout the world, are anxious about what feminism means. Accustomed to a culture in which motherhood and domesticity define women's role in society, those who have benefited from that role may feel threatened by feminism; similarly, those who chose to make motherhood and domesticity central have often felt disrespected by feminism. Some fear that as women become more ambitious, the whole society will become a masculinist, competitive free-for-all, with no one left to defend the values of nurturance and family solidarity.

In contrast to that caricature, feminism has, in the main, valued caregiving and cooperation. It has asserted the dignity and value of all labor and has joined with those seeking more leisure time for the pleasures of family, friends, and community. U.S feminism was never just a celebration of individualism or of individual achievement. It was always a broad stream with many currents. And some of the most powerful of those currents understood that the fortunes of each are intertwined with the fortunes of all. As with all progressive social movements, solidarity and a sense of responsibility toward others have been fundamental to feminism.

One of the biggest mistakes in looking back at women's history would be to conclude that progress is inevitable. It is not. Women's rights require continuous defense and expansion to meet new needs. We hope that reclaiming the multiple and unfinished feminisms of the twentieth century can inspire the movements of the future. The women and men who sought gender justice and equality in our past believed progress was possible. They did not accomplish all they hoped for. They could not control or predict the future.

Feminism is far from over. We don't know what it will look like, because each generation will reinvent it. Just as the feminism of the past has always been influenced by changes in society as a whole, so too will the feminism of the future be. It may well be more global and may well be led by women from the poorer countries of the world. They in turn will also invent feminisms that meet their needs and aspirations. It is impossible to understand the world's problems and hopes without taking into account the growing global movements for women's health, education, bodily integrity, sexual freedom, political participation, and economic equality. Just as American feminism transformed American society, so global feminism is likely to transform the world.

SELECTED SOURCES

CHAPTER I
MORE THAN SEX EQUALITY: FEMINISM AFTER SUFFRAGE
by Dorothy Sue Cobble

Rosalyn Baxandall and Linda Gordon, *America's Working Women: A Documentary History, 1600 to the Present*. New York: Norton, 1995.

Jacqueline Castledine, *Cold War Progressives: Women's Interracial Organizing for Peace and Freedom*. Urbana: University of Illinois Press, 2012.

William H. Chafe, *The American Woman: Her Changing Social, Economic, and Political Roles, 1920–1970*. New York: Oxford University Press, 1972.

Dorothy Sue Cobble, *Dishing It Out: Waitresses and Their Unions in the Twentieth Century*. Urbana: University of Illinois Press, 1991.

Dorothy Sue Cobble, *The Other Women's Movement: Workplace Justice and Social Rights in Modern America*. Princeton: Princeton University Press, 2004.

Robert Cohen, *When The Old Left Was Young: Student Radicals and America's First Mass Student Movement, 1929–1941*. New York: Oxford University Press, 1993.

Nancy Cott, *The Grounding of Modern Feminism*. New Haven: Yale University Press, 1987.

Kirsten Marie Delegard, *Battling Miss Bolsheviki: The Origins of Female Conservatism in the United States*. Philadelphia: University of Pennsylvania Press, 2012.

John D'Emilio and Estelle B. Freedman, *Intimate Matters: A History of Sexuality in America*, 3rd ed. Chicago: University of Chicago Press, 2012.

Glenda Gilmore, *Defying Dixie: The Radical Roots of Civil Rights, 1919–1950*. New York: Norton, 2008.

Stephanie Gilmore, *Groundswell: Grassroots Feminist Activism in Postwar America*. New York: Routledge, 2013.

Nancy Hewitt, ed., *No Permanent Waves: Recasting Histories of U.S. Feminism*. New Brunswick: Rutgers University Press, 2010.

Nancy MacLean, *Freedom Is Not Enough: The Opening of the American Workplace*. Cambridge: Harvard University Press, 2006.

Gordon K. Mantler, *Power to the Poor: Black-Brown Coalition and the Fight for Economic Justice, 1960–1974*. Chapel Hill: University of North Carolina Press, 2013.

Serena Mayeri, *Reasoning from Race: Feminism, Law, and the Civil Rights Revolution*. Cambridge: Harvard University Press, 2011.

Danielle L. McGuire, *At the Dark End of the Street: Black Women, Rape, and Resistance—A New History of the Civil Rights Movement from Rosa Parks to the Rise of Black Power*. New York: Vintage, 2011.

Joanne Meyerowitz, ed., *Not June Cleaver: Women and Gender in Postwar America, 1945–1960*. Philadelphia: Temple University Press, 1994.

Robyn Muncy, *Creating a Female Dominion in American Reform, 1890–1935*. New York: Oxford University Press, 1991.

Pauli Murray, *Song in a Weary Throat: An American Pilgrimage*. New York: Harper & Row, 1987.

Premilla Nadasen, *Welfare Warriors: The Welfare Rights Movement in the United States*. New York: Routledge, 2005.

Annelise Orleck, *Common Sense and a Little Fire: Women and Working-Class Politics in the United States, 1900–1965*. Chapel Hill: University of North Carolina Press, 1995.

Rebecca Jo Plant, *Mom: The Transformation of Motherhood in Modern America*. Chicago: University of Chicago Press, 2010.

Barbara Ransby, *Ella Baker and the Black Freedom Movement: A Radical Democratic Vision*. Chapel Hill: University of North Carolina Press, 2003.

Yevette Richards, *Maida Springer: Pan-Africanist and International Labor Leader*. Pittsburgh: University of Pittsburgh Press, 2000.

Benita Roth, *Separate Roads to Feminism: Black, Chicana, and White Feminist Movements in America's Second Wave*. Cambridge: Cambridge University Press, 2004.

Vicki Ruiz and Virginia Sánchez Korrol, eds., *Latina Legacies*. New York: Oxford University Press, 2005.

Leila J. Rupp and Verta Taylor, *Survival in the Doldrums: The American Women's Rights Movement, 1945 to the 1960s*. New York: Oxford University Press, 1990.

Landon R. Y. Storrs, *The Second Red Scare and the Unmaking of the New Deal Left*. Princeton: Princeton University Press, 2013.

Amy Swerdlow, *Women Strike for Peace: Traditional Motherhood and Radical Politics in the 1960s*. Chicago: University of Chicago Press, 1993.

Mary K. Trigg, *Feminism as Life's Work: Four Modern American Women Through Two World Wars*. New Brunswick: Rutgers University Press, 2014.

Susan Ware, *Beyond Suffrage: Women in the New Deal*. Cambridge: Harvard University Press, 1981.

Kate Weigand, *Red Feminism: American Communism and the Making of Women's Liberation*. Baltimore: Johns Hopkins University Press, 2001.

Deborah Gray White, *Too Heavy a Load: Black Women in Defense of Themselves, 1894–1994*. New York: Norton, 1999.

CHAPTER 2
THE WOMEN'S LIBERATION MOVEMENT
by Linda Gordon

Rosalyn Baxandall and Linda Gordon, *Dear Sisters: Dispatches from the Women's Liberation Movement*. New York: Basic Books, 2000.

Leslie Bow, *Asian American Feminisms*. New York: Routledge, 2012.

Patricia Bradley, *Mass Media and the Shaping of American Feminism, 1963–1975*. Jackson: University Press of Mississippi, 2005.

Flora Davis, *Moving the Mountain: The Women's Movement in America Since 1960*. New York: Simon & Schuster, 1991.

Rachel Blau DuPlessis and Ann Snitow, *The Feminist Memoir Project: Voices from Women's Liberation*. New York: Three Rivers Press, 1998.

Alice Echols, *Daring to Be Bad: Radical Feminism in America, 1967–1975*. Minneapolis: University of Minnesota Press, 1989.

Sara M. Evans, *Personal Politics: The Roots of Women's Liberation in the Civil Rights Movement and the New Left*. New York: Knopf, 1979.

Sara M. Evans and Harry C. Boyte, *Free Spaces: The Sources of Democratic Change in America*. New York: Harper & Row, 1986.

Shulamith Firestone, *The Dialectic of Sex: The Case for Feminist Revolution*. New York: Morrow, 1970.

Estelle B. Freedman, *No Turning Back: The History of Feminism and the Future of Women*. New York: Ballantine, 2002.

Estelle B. Freedman, *Redefining Rape: Sexual Violence in the Era of Suffrage and Segregation*. Cambridge: Harvard University Press, 2013.

Alma M. García, ed., *Chicana Feminist Thought: The Basic Historical Writings*. New York: Routledge, 1997.

Paula Giddings, *When and Where I Enter: The Impact of Black Women on Race and Sex in America*. New York: Morrow, 1984.

Linda Gordon, *The Moral Property of Women: A History of Birth Control Politics in America*. Urbana and Chicago: University of Illinois Press, 2007.

Bell Hooks, *Feminist Theory: From Margin to Center*. London: Pluto Press, 2000.

Bell Hooks, *Talking Back: Thinking Feminist, Thinking Black*. Boston: South End Press, 1989.

Gloria T. Hull, Patricial Bell-Scott, and Barbara Smith, eds., *All the Women Are White, All the Blacks Are Men, but Some of Us Are Brave: Black Women's Studies*. New York: Feminist Press, 1982.

Joy James and T. Denean Sharpley-Whiting, eds., *The Black Feminist Reader*. Malden, MA: Blackwell, 2000.

Judith Walzer Leavitt, *Make Room for Daddy: The Journey from Waiting Room to Birthing Room*. Chapel Hill: University of North Carolina Press, 2009.

Cherríe Moraga and Gloria Anzaldúa, eds., *This Bridge Called My Back: Writings By Radical Women of Color*. New York: Kitchen Table Press, 1984.

Robin Morgan, ed., *Sisterhood Is Powerful*. New York: Vintage, 1970.

Jennifer Nelson, *Women of Color and the Reproductive Rights Movement*. New York: NYU Press, 20003.

Ruth Rosen, *The World Split Open: How the Modern Women's Movement Changed America*. New York: Viking, 2000.

CHAPTER 3

FROM A MINDSET TO A MOVEMENT: FEMINISM SINCE 1990
by Astrid Henry

Amrita Basu, ed., *Women's Movements in the Global Era: The Power of Local Feminisms*. Boulder, CO: Westview Press, 2010

Jennifer Baumgardner and Amy Richards, *Manifesta: Young Women, Feminism, and the Future*. New York: Farrar, Straus and Giroux, 2000.

Chris Bobel, *New Blood: Third-Wave Feminism and the Politics of Menstruation*. New Brunswick: Rutgers University Press, 2010.

Marilyn Jacoby Boxer, *When Women Ask the Questions: Creating Women's Studies in America*. Baltimore: Johns Hopkins University Press, 1998.

Rory Dicker, *A History of U.S. Feminisms*. Berkeley, CA: Seal Press, 2008.

Rory Dicker and Alison Piepmeier, eds., *Catching a Wave: Reclaiming Feminism for the 21st Century*. Boston: Northeastern University Press, 2003.

Susan J. Douglas, *The Rise of Enlightened Sexism: How Pop Culture Took Us from Girl Power to Girls Gone Wild*. New York: St. Martin's Griffin, 2010.

Sarah Erdreich, *Generation Roe: Inside the Future of the Pro-Choice Movement*. New York: Seven Stories Press, 2013.

Barbara Findlen, ed., *Listen Up: Voices from the Next Feminist Generation*. Seattle: Seal Press, 1995.

Rosalind Gill and Christina Scharff, eds., *New Femininities: Postfeminism, Neoliberalism and Subjectivity*. London: Palgrave MacMillan, 2011.

Stacy Gillis, Gillian Howe, and Rebecca Munford, eds., *Third Wave Feminism: A Critical Exploration*. New York: Palgrave Macmillan, 2004.

Astrid Henry, *Not My Mother's Sister: Generational Conflict and Third-Wave Feminism*. Bloomington: Indiana University Press, 2004.

Daisy Hernández and Bushra Rehman, eds., *Colonize This! Young Women of Color on Today's Feminism*. New York: Seal Press, 2002.

Leslie Heywood, ed., *The Women's Movement Today: An Encyclopedia of Third-Wave Feminisms*. Westport: Greenwood Press, 2006.

Leslie Heywood and Jennifer Drake, eds. *Third Wave Agenda: Being Feminist, Doing Feminism*. Minneapolis: University of Minnesota Press, 1997.

Paula Kamen, *Feminist Fatale: Voices from the "Twentysomething" Generation Explore the Future of the "Women's Movement."* New York: Donald I. Fine, Inc., 1991.

Vivien Labaton and Dawn Lundy Martin, eds., *The Fire This Time: Young Activists and the New Feminism*. New York: Anchor Books, 2004.

Ariel Levy, *Female Chauvinist Pigs: Women and the Rise of Raunch Culture*. New York: Free Press, 2005.

Gwendolyn Pough, *Check It While I Wreck It: Black Womanhood, Hip-Hop Culture, and the Public Sphere*. Boston: Northeastern University Press, 2004.

Jo Reger, ed., *Different Wavelengths: Studies of the Contemporary Women's Movement*. New York: Routledge, 2005.

Jo Reger, *Everywhere and Nowhere: Contemporary Feminism in the United States*. New York: Oxford University Press, 2012.

Kristen Rowe-Finkbeiner, *The F-Word: Feminism in Jeopardy: Women, Politics, and the Future*. Emeryville, CA: Seal Press, 2004.

Deborah Siegel, *Sisterhood, Interrupted: From Radical Women to Grrls Gone Wild*. New York: Palgrave Macmillan, 2007.

Jessica Valenti, *Full Frontal Feminism: A Young Woman's Guide to Why Feminism Matters*. Emeryville, CA: Seal Press, 2007.

Rebecca Walker, ed., *To Be Real: Telling the Truth and Changing the Face of Feminism*. New York: Anchor Books. 1995.

Acknowledgments

All three of us thank Norton's marvelous editor Robert Weil, a rare treasure. We are grateful for the sage counsel of Charlotte Sheedy and the guidance and hard work of Will Menaker, India Cooper, and the rest of the Norton design and editorial team.

Dorothy Sue Cobble extends gratitude to Linda Gordon, who invented and believed in this joint project. I thank my coauthors, Linda and Astrid, for being the best possible writing "sisters": tolerant of dissent, worthy of emulation. It was the feminist consciousness-raising group I had always wanted. My thanks also to my dear friends Nancy Hewitt and Joanne Meyerowitz, who took time away from their own writing and teaching to read my first unwieldy drafts. Your unflagging optimism and astute interventions made more of a difference than you know. Of course, no one is more familiar with the various drafts of this book and the emotional states that accompanied each one than my husband, Michael Merrill. His patience, wisdom, and love amaze and delight me every day.

Linda Gordon thanks above all Rosalyn Fraad Baxandall, who has taught me about feminism for forty years. Dorothy Sue and Astrid taught me vast amounts in just one year of working together and blessed me with their intelligence, commitment, and patience in undertaking this book, which, as always, I imagined as far less work than it turned out to be—so I am everlastingly grateful not only for their willingness to do it but for their friendship. A big thank-you to the Radcliffe Institute for Advanced Study and the NYU Graduate School, who gave me a year's leave in which I finished my part of this book. Thanks to Karen Nussbaum and Tony Platt for reading and commenting. My beloved students and my daughter, Rosie, try, with mixed success, to keep me aware of current popular culture. My life's pal, Allen, tries, also with mixed success, to complicate my thinking. Generations of women's studies scholars shaped me in every way. It's been a collective trip throughout, and my gratitude to all these people is vast.

ASTRID HENRY is enormously grateful to Linda for the invitation to participate in this project. Writing this book with Linda and Dorothy Sue was everything feminist collaboration should be: invigorating, challenging, intellectually stimulating, and fun. I will never forget our many lively discussions around Linda's dining room table. Many thanks to the Louise R. Noun Program in Women's Studies at Grinnell College for financial support for this project. Anna Banker's assistance with research was invaluable to the completion of my chapter, as were the astute insights of my writing group: David Cook-Martin, Karla Erickson, and Dan Reynolds. I couldn't have completed this book without the love, support, and insightful editing skills of David Harrison. I am indebted to my students for helping me to stay up-to-date on contemporary feminist issues, and I drew much inspiration and guidance from my fellow scholars working on feminism in the early twenty-first century.

INDEX

Page numbers in *italics* refer to illustrations.

248 INDEX

About the Authors

Dorothy Sue Cobble is the author or editor of numerous books and articles, including, most recently, the award-winning *The Other Women's Movement: Workplace Justice and Social Rights in Modern America* (2004) and *Sex of Class: Women Transforming American Labor* (2007). She is Distinguished Professor of History and Labor Studies at Rutgers University, where she specializes in the study of work, social movements, and social policy in the United States and globally.

Linda Gordon teaches U.S. history and comparative courses about gender, social movements, and imperialism at New York University, where she is University Professor of the Humanities and History. Her most recent books are *Dorothea Lange: A Life Beyond Limits* (2009) and *The Great Arizona Orphan Abduction* (2001). She is working on a history of social movements in the twentieth-century United States.

Astrid Henry is the author of *Not My Mother's Sister: Generational Conflict and Third-Wave Feminism* (2004), as well as numerous articles on U.S. feminism since 1990. She is Louise R. Noun Chair in Women's Studies at Grinnell College, where she teaches gender, women's, and sexuality studies. She is working on a study of feminist subjectivity and historiography in memoirs by U.S. feminists since the 1970s.